Conversations with Grace Paley

Literary Conversations Series
Peggy Whitman Prenshaw
General Editor

Conversations with Grace Paley

Edited by
Gerhard Bach and Blaine H. Hall

University Press of Mississippi
Jackson

Books by Grace Paley

Short Stories:
The Little Disturbances of Man. New York: Doubleday, 1959
Enormous Changes at the Last Minute. New York: Farrar, Straus & Giroux, 1974
Later the Same Day. New York: Farrar, Straus & Giroux, 1985
The Collected Stories. New York: Farrar, Straus & Giroux, 1994

Poetry:
Leaning Forward. Penobscot, Me.: Granite Press, 1985
Long Walks and Intimate Talks. With Vera Williams. New York: The Feminist Press, 1991
New and Collected Poems. Gardiner, Me.: Tilbury House, 1992

Copyright © 1997 by the University Press of Mississippi
All rights reserved
Manufactured in the United States of America

The paper in this book meets the guidelines for permanence and durability of the Committee on Production Guidelines for Book Longevity of the Council on Library Resources.

Library of Congress Cataloging-in-Publication Data
Paley, Grace.
    Conversations with Grace Paley / edited by Gerhard Bach and Blaine H. Hall.
    p. cm. — (Literary conversations series)
    Includes index.
    ISBN 978-1-61703-695-8

    1. Paley, Grace—Interviews. 2. Women authors, American—20th century—Interviews. 3. Feminism and literature—United States.
4. Women and literature—United States. I. Bach, Gerhard, 1943-   .
II. Hall, Blaine H.   III. Title.   IV. Series.
PS3556.A46Z82   1997
813'.54—dc21   96-47449
                                                                              CIP

British Library Cataloging-in-Publication data available

Contents

Introduction   vii

Chronology   xvii

Grace Paley Interview   *Celeste Conway and others*   3

Grace Paley   *Alan Burns and Charles Sugnet*   14

Conversation with Grace Paley   *Leonard Michaels*   26

Interview with Grace Paley   *Kathleen Hulley*   36

Grace Paley: Fragments for a Portrait in Collage   *Blanche H. Gelfant*   56

Clearing Her Throat: An Interview with Grace Paley   *Joan Lidoff*   72

Grace Paley   *Ruth Perry*   95

A Conversation with Grace Paley   *Peter Marchant and Mary Elsie Robertson*   117

PW Interviews Grace Paley   *Wendy Smith*   126

Grace Paley, Voice from the Village   *David Remnick*   131

Grace Paley: A Conversation   *Barry Silesky, Robin Hemley, and Sharon Solwitz*   135

Grace Paley Talking with Cora Kaplan   *Cora Kaplan*   146

An Interview with Grace Paley   *Melanie Kaye/Kantrowitz and Irena Klepfisz*   153

Grace Paley on Storytelling and Story Hearing   *Jacqueline Taylor*   163

An Interview with Grace Paley   *Kay Bonetti*   177

Looking at Disparities: An Interview with Grace Paley   *Martha Satz*   192

An Interview with Grace Paley *Eleanor Wachtel* 204

Grace Paley *Shirley M. Jordan* 213

Grace Paley *Mickey Pearlman* 226

Grace Paley: An Interview by Joann Gardner *Joann Gardner* 235

Grace Paley *Birgit Fromkorth and Susanne Opfermann* 249

Index 269

Introduction

Grace Paley's contribution to American Literature, while comparatively small in volume, has been substantial in impact. With a voice very much her own, Paley has been a critical force in post-World War II American culture, particularly at its controversial centers. Reviewers and critics overwhelmingly agree that her short stories are vivid examples of a genre still very much alive in western culture and that one of their distinguishing marks is a language which manages to re-establish the long lost dialogue between writers and their community of readers in America. In this as well as other respects, Paley's writings are judged to be refreshingly, even radically, different from the contemporary American mainstream.

Paley herself acknowledges this difference, attributing it less, as one might expect, to her artistry, her inimitable style and technique, than to the often warring interplay of three social factors which have continually shaped her biography—family, writing, and politics. When asked how she manages these three careers simultaneously, Paley sometimes in joking exasperation responds, "by pure neglect"; more often, however, she admits to the physical and emotional strain involved in such a life: "I can't live without writing, but I couldn't live without my children. And I couldn't bear not to respond to the awful things that are." People close to Paley, such as her biographer Judith Arkana, the critic Jacqueline Taylor, her artist companion Vera Williams, or her neighbor and friend Donald Barthelme bear witness to the fact that Paley's involvement—as a parent or grandparent, as a writer and teacher, as a peace demonstrator and political activist—always has been unconditional and total. "I've always felt that all these things have strong pulls," Paley admits looking back at her career at midpoint: "The politics takes it from the writing, the children take from the politics, and the writing took from the children. . . . But the truth is, all those things pull from each other, and it makes for a very interesting life."

Part of this drive stems from Paley's curiosity and seemingly innocent approach to the pressing issues of her time. She welcomes dialogue, the sharing of experiences, the intensity of verbal exchanges as much as the ability to listen, to search for undercurrents that establish meaning and contact. While undemanding of publicity, she is a public persona embodying the conscience of the American post-war generation. This may also account for the fact that despite her modest literary output and despite the equally modest critical response her fiction and poetry have received, Paley has been a much sought-after interview subject. From 1968 onwards, she has granted more than fifty interviews, most of them printed in newspapers, magazines and professional journals, and a few prepared for radio broadcast.

These interviews move, in varying degrees but consistently so, within a set range of concerns, many of them described by Paley herself as discoveries: family and generational relationships; personal background and educational impact; women, their need for communication and the public's need to redefine women's roles; the process of finding her "voice" and seeing it as representative of women's voices of her generation; her early life as a writer of poetry, the fictional voice not developing until her social identity was more clearly defined; the interrelatedness of politics, environmentalism, feminism, and immensely personal and local issues; the art of teaching; the importance of friendship as well as the importance and moral impact of community. As a collection, the interviews show how Paley, over the course of nearly thirty years, modifies, refines, alters and solidifies her perspectives. They also show what at different times her interviewers and her public at large have considered important.

This chronology should not mislead; it reveals Paley's *inner* biography only, reveals the meaning-making process through diverse reconstructions of reality. In these interviews, then, Paley creates her very personal time-place continuum in much the same way her fictional characters do, trying to make meaning out of momentary conditions, conflicting messages, and often contradicting emotions. In structuring our lives, Paley explains in her conversation with Joan Lidoff, we constantly compress and expand time. A story thus "can curl around on itself, it can just fall down and slip out through one of the spirals and go back again. That's the way I see. I see us all in a great big bathtub of time just swimming around."

Paley's first collection of short stories, *The Little Disturbances of Man* (1959) suffered the fate of many first books. It was sparsely reviewed, made no impact beyond a small group of professional associates and friends, went out of print within five years and was quickly forgotten. After considerable effort it was reissued in paperback in 1968, some of the stories having found their way into anthologies in the meantime. Quite likely, the moderate success the reprint enjoyed resulted from the fact that the social climate of the late sixties seemed better attuned to

Paley's voice than that of the late fifties. Still, Paley remained a "writer's writer," as Beatrice Berg, Paley's first interviewer, says.[1] Berg's interview was strategically placed in the *Washington Post* shortly before *Little Disturbances* was distributed to the booksellers. Interestingly, Paley addresses issues here that will concern her for the next several decades: dividing her time between "lots of pulls" in diverse directions, in particular her active opposition to the Vietnam War and participation in anti-war demonstrations. In this as in so many interviews to follow, Paley stresses how these conflicts keep her alive as an artist: "in a sense, everything I write comes out of the way I live."

Not until the publication of *Enormous Changes at the Last Minute* (1974) was the attention Paley got from critics and interviewers more than ephemeral. Then, however, the picture shifted radically. This new collection was widely reviewed in the mainstream press, and also, more importantly, in the professional journals. Renee Winegarten, writing for *Midstream*, squarely accommodates Paley with the master storytellers Twain and Bellow in stating that the voice of her characters sounds like that of "a young person sorely tried by experience, a wryly sagacious, long-suffering innocent, a sort of remote urban female descendant of Huck Finn, or younger New York sister of Augie March."[2] While Winegarten sees the relationship as one characterized by writing style and technique, Paley herself, in the interviews following the book's publication, stresses the gendered context of her stories and the particularity of female perspectives and women's voices, even though it would take another decade before she would assert that "our voices are, if not getting a lot louder, getting so numerous. We're talking to each other more and more." Besides representing gender concerns these stories as a group represented in Paley's mind a compressed critique of America's social system, the country's "economic arrangements" according to which "people are rich or poor, make a living or don't have to, are useful to systems, or superfluous."

At the same time, Paley's political activism got front-page coverage in the national press, after she was imprisoned on several occasions (even if only for very short periods each time), events Paley herself plays down since she doubts that much was accomplished by them. But she does stress the importance of the experience: "You never really understand what it means to hear those gates clang shut until you really have heard them more than a few times," she says in conversation with Alan Burns and Charles Sugnet. Paley is more adamant about having different movements and interest groups join forces, particularly the merger of the women's movement, the disarmament movement, and diverse environmental movements. In an interview with Judy Slawson, for her home-turf paper *The Villager*, she generalizes: "It's war, whether it's war now or a war being waged against future generations by using up their resources."[3] Later, talking with Barry Silesky she specifies her position: "[Many feminists] don't see the connection between the patriarchy of militarism and the patriarchy of ordinary daily life."

Paley's spectrum of political involvement, ranging from organizing local village activities to assisting in the organization of the 1981 Women's Pentagon Action, is central to several of the interviews of the late seventies, certainly a reflection of Paley's strong personal involvement and not simply a response to media attention. These gradually give way in the early eighties to an emerging public interest in Paley the writer. In 1980, Leonard Michaels interviewed Paley on the occasion of her participation in that year's Berkeley Writers' Conference, a public interview before a large audience. Here, for the first time, Paley addresses at length issues of style and technique. She comments on how her stories germinate in her mind, how she reviews her subject matter, implanting "lines from life" into the stories, explains organic vs. inorganic developments of ideas, and stresses the importance of listening to the stories others have to tell: "A lot of people cannot begin to speak out of their own throats until they have listened enough, and heard enough the stories of others." Multiple perspectives and shifting positions are the secret of storytelling, Paley concludes: "If you speak for others . . . you'll really begin to be able to tell your own story better." Paley further elaborates on technical details, such as time compression and expansion, in her conversation a year later (1981) with Joan Lidoff. Here (as well as in her interview with Ruth Perry of the same year) she defines more expansively her position in the community of contemporary writers, female and male, seeing her own literary output as part of an emerging tradition.

It was not until the early eighties, and particularly the years surrounding the publication of *Later the Same Day* (1985), that Paley and her interviewers moved beyond these topics to address the writer's work in terms of her own biography and background, not so much in the sense of identifying her writing as personal autobiography but rather by investigating biographical and generational links as well as the broader social and cultural atmosphere of her youth and early adulthood from which Paley draws so much "information" for her stories. It seemed as though Paley finally began to feel liberated from the constraints of warring obligations and could pursue her goals with greater ease. This is the tenor of her talk with Ruth Perry, when she says: "I think that in almost any culture the older women really begin to have a certain power. So I'm getting older,

Introduction

so I really feel freer than I ever felt." About half of the interviews Paley has ever granted come from this period, and most of them are occasioned by Paley's public appearances at writers' workshops and conferences, by the filming of three stories from *Enormous Changes*, and by the publication of *Later the Same Day*. Paley's activities in the United States and Europe were further sparked by the publication of the first critical collection of essays on this writer, in a special issue of *Delta*, a scholarly journal published in France by Paul Valéry University's American studies department. The volume, edited by Kathleen Hulley, contains Hulley's essay-length introduction and her interview with Paley, Paley's story "Lavinia," and eight critical essays on Paley's poetry and fiction. Given the fact that there was hardly any critical response to Paley prior to this publication, Hulley's collection paved the way for the attention the author now gains from critics and interviewers alike.

Central among the topics dealt with in the interviews dating to this period is Paley's feminism—her insistence on women's need to establish their voice and to initiate networks of friendship and community. Paley sums up her growing concern in the interview with Kathleen Hulley: "For a long time I thought . . . my life as a woman was shit. Who could be interested in this crap? I was very interested in it, but I didn't have enough social ego to put it down. I had to develop that to a point where I said, 'I don't give a damn.' Women who have thought their lives were boring have found they're interesting to one another." Having secured her own position in the larger spectrum of feminist concerns— motherhood, friendships, sexuality, gender, and self—Paley toward the end of the eighties speaks out more assuredly in generalizing terms: "I see feminism as an analysis that sees the world in terms of domination, by one class, by one sex, by one tree (laughter). No, that's a joke, but if you watch the woods, you get very annoyed at certain trees. I'll tell you that (laughter)." The practical side to this argument is emphasized by Paley and her interviewers as well. Looking back, Paley sees a great advantage in the sometimes enforced companionship of (often single) mothers meeting in the park to "air" their children. She cherishes the "collective existence" they forged, and "raising our kids . . . together" for them at the time was a political act. Her story "Friends" (1979), of which Paley says she "wrote it toward [her friends in the park] and also from them," reflects this position. It is simultaneously a highly personal homage to women's communal capabilities and a political statement, a position best summarized by the story's narrator: fighting "him-itis, the dread disease of females," the women unite in the assurance that "we were, in fact, the soft-speaking tough souls of anarchy."

Feminism is only one prominent theme in the interviews of the eighties. Tied to this by the roots of her personal history, Paley opens up in these interviews about her family background and her Judaism. The author describes how thoroughly a product of the Bronx and of Lower Manhattan she is. Born to Isaac and Mary Goodside, Russian-Jewish immigrants, Paley early experienced the hardship as well as the excitement of New York immigrant life. Paley here corrects the notion that she was raised in a politically active home. Her parents were active while in Russia, she says, but once in America they became, like so many immigrants, "extremely patriotic, very hardworking," even though "they always retained their political interest." So, as Paley remembers, the general ferment of social and intellectual radicalism in America was reflected in the Goodside home as well. "My father's brothers and sisters all belonged to different leftist political parties. My grandmother used to describe how they fought every night at the supper table and how hard it was on her!"

Paley also specifies and corrects public notions about her family's religious attitudes and their importance in her upbringing. When she says that her parents were "anti-religious," that "they laughed at religion," this does not indicate any sentiments of Jewish self-hatred. Her parents, Paley imparts, simply had no desire to pretend to be what they were not, and so rebelled against her grandmother's insistence on observing religious traditions. She goes on to explain that her upbringing as well as her first marriage disconnected her from Jewish traditions and an active religious life, but that her social and political activities have brought back "a real longing to be with your people." She particularly deplores the "terrible split" that mutual hatred has brought between Jews and Blacks. She is also convinced that Jewish women need to establish new traditions for themselves in order to safeguard their identity: "That word identity has been hard for many women who live secular lives and maybe harder for religious women and also feminists. But the women's movement has made a big difference. . . . It's given a lot of Jewish women courage to stay Jewish and fight . . . for those ordinary rights. R-i-t-e-s. Rights to have rites."

A third concern of Paley's, beginning to show in these interviews and continuing well into the nineties, is to pinpoint more definitely aspects of her craft and the purpose of her writing. Asked often who her literary influences and models have been, Paley makes the usual references to the Russian writers of the nineteenth century as well as to the shapers of European and American modernism, but then quickly moves to another aspect apparently more important to her, namely the richness of the

Introduction

spoken word and its diverse regional and ethnic variations—what she calls the "longitude and latitude" of one's childhood. This is an influence at least as important as formal education and reading, Paley insists: "When you're talking about influences, you're talking about who talked to you when you were little. . . . It's an influence that's linguistic and social more than anything else." These "linguistic and social" aspects are truly inseparable. "You have two ears," she points out; "one is for the sound of literature and the other is for your neighborhood, for your mother and father's house." Paley says she begins writing by listening closely for speech authenticity, because other people's voices give her "the strength or the permission" to follow through with a story. This is the source of Paley's conviction that in order to become a storyteller one must first learn to become a "story-hearer." This approach not only invites the reader into the text, it also invites the reader to share the complexity of the truth hidden within the text. She considers it "a bad habit" in our culture to speak of "a work of art" when we should call it "a work of truth." This claim to the moral commitment of the contemporary writer projects Grace Paley as a *conservative* writer in the strict sense of the term—"saving" and "rescuing": "Art," Paley insists, "makes justice in the world," and "to tell . . . stories as simply as possible" means "to save a few lives."

For Paley, the breakthrough to such truths comes when writers are prepared to "look into the darkest corners" of life and illuminate the lives lived there. This is the major achievement of women's literature in the United States. "Women illuminate realities that haven't been looked at for a long time—their own lives," Paley says, and then generalizes: "For me revolutionary art is the way a new group of people becomes finally visible—Blacks, women, Native Americans—it *seems* that they were there all along but they were not in the limelight of their own or others' attention."

A no-nonsense devotion to revealing hidden truths appears to be the fabric that holds together Paley's life as a writer and social communitarian. As the interviews collected here reveal, there always is that unflinching, almost stoic devotion to "ordinary life," the fumbling attempts to find a balance between what appear to be irreconcilable opposites. Paley's own multiple lives as a parent, a writer, and an activist are constantly revealed in these interviews as being exemplary of a citizen responsive to social and political demands. Paley herself, not prone to historical, psychological or sociological theorizing, usually has answers so straightforward as to sound simple. What they reflect is an unusual depth of personal experience turned over many times in the mind, exposed to light from different, often opposite directions. A basic, one might even say "religious," optimism speaks from such experience. "Despair" is not part of her vocabulary, just as it isn't for the two protagonists in "Ruthy and Edie," who, Paley points out, are "ideologically, spiritually and on puritanical principle" opposed to such feelings.

What Paley says about finding the right voice for her characters accounts as well for her own life and how she reflects upon it: "When I was able to get into somebody else's voice, when I was able to speak in other people's voices, I found my own. Until then I did not have a voice that could tell a story." In search of her voice Paley—the true autodidact—has learned her diverse lessons, the most momentous of these being the ability to listen and the significance of silence. In several of her stories, as critic Jacqueline Taylor has pointed out, her characters fall silent, either because they are muted by forces of unkindness and abuse—verbal or physical—or because they know the power of the word not spoken. This is what Paley herself points out in the story "Listening": "Silence—the space that follows unkindness in which little truths growl."

In accordance with the conventions of the Literary Conversations Series the interviews collected here are unabridged and reprinted in their original form. To allow readers to discover developments, coherences, and disparities more clearly, the interviews have been arranged according to the date each was given, not the date of publication. In some cases, the difference is substantial, ranging from one to three years. We have left the interviews unedited except for correcting obvious typographical errors; inserting full titles in italics of works to which Paley or her interviewers make reference; supplying omitted or missing words; and providing needed punctuation marks. We are, of course, aware of repetitions—interviewers tend to ask similar questions relating to the author's life, work, influences, likes and dislikes, convictions, and theories. Such repetition may be considered a valuable resource for closer investigation, particularly with respect to the consistency or inconsistency of the answers given. Even though this collection offers a full-scale, representative cross-section of Paley's ideas, the reader may find it worthwhile to consult other (and look forward to future) interviews for added nuances.

GB
BH
September 1996

Notes

1. Beatrice Berg, "Grace Paley: Writer's Writer," *Washington Post*, 29 Dec. 1968: D2.
2. Renee Winegarten, Untitled Review, *Midstream* 20 (Dec. 1974): 65–67.
3. Judy Slawson, "Grace Paley: Changing Subject Matter with a Changing Passionate and Committed Life," *Literature in Performance* 7.2 (1987): 46–58.

Chronology

1922 Born on 11 December in the Bronx, the third and last child of Manya Ridnyik and Isaac Goodside, who had immigrated from the Ukraine in 1906

1938 Drops out of high school and enters Hunter College, but is expelled for poor attendance; also attends City College, New York University, and Merchants and Bankers Business and Secretarial School.

1940? Takes class from W. H. Auden at the New School for Social Research in Manhattan. He reads some of her poems and encourages her to write her own language, what she actually hears and speaks; publishes some of her poems in the college newspaper.

1942 Marries Jess Paley, a photographer and filmmaker, on 20 June; follows him to several army camps near Chicago and Miami Beach; while in Florida publishes a few poems in a magazine called *Experiment;* returns to Greenwich Village following the war.

1944 Mother dies of breast cancer

1949 Daughter Nora born in September

1951 Son Danny born in May

1956 Publishes her first story, "Goodbye and Good Luck," in *Accent: A Quarterly*

1958 Publishes "The Contest" in *Accent*

1959 Doubleday publishes *The Little Disturbances of Man,* her first collection of stories.

1960 Publishes "Faith in the Afternoon" in *Noble Savage;* founds the Greenwich Village Peace Center with her neighbors, PTA members of PS 41. The group protests civil defense drills in schools, atomic bomb testing, the New York air raid shelter program, and U.S. policy in Vietnam.

1962 Publishes "Gloomy Tune" in *Genesis West*

1965 Begins teaching "general studies" at Columbia University; publishes "Living" in *Genesis West*.

1966 Begins teaching fiction writing at Sarah Lawrence College in Bronxville, New York; she usually taught part-time, but some years taught full-time to make more money. The job was offered to her through recommendations of Harvey Swados and Muriel Rukeyser, with whom she had participated in a series of teachers and writers meetings in 1965. Arrested on Armed Forces Day for sitting on Fifth Avenue under the rockets and missiles.

1967 Leaves Jess Paley and moves out of the Eleventh Street apartment; publishes "Distance" in *Atlantic;* "Faith: In a Tree" in *New American Review;* and "Northeast Playground" in *Ararat*.

1968 Publishes "Two Stories from Five Boroughs: I. 'Samuel,' II. 'The Burdened Man.' " in *Esquire,* "Come On, Ye Sons of Art" in *Sarah Lawrence Journal,* and "Politics" in *Win;* goes to France and Sweden on a fact-finding mission with other writers, clergy, lawyers and professors to visit Vietnam War draft dodgers.

1969 Goes to Vietnam with a small delegation of peace activists to receive three prisoners of war and bring them home; "Distances" chosen for Prize Stories of 1969: O Henry Awards.

1970 Receives award for short story writing from the National Institute for Arts and Letters

1971 Publishes "A Conversation with My Father" in *New American Review* and "Two Stories: I. 'Debts,' II. 'Wants.' " in *Atlantic*

1972 Divorces Jess Paley; marries Bob Nichols on 26 November in Judson Church on Fourth Street in Greenwich Village, where he wrote plays for its poet's theater; publishes "Enormous Changes at the Last Minute" in *Atlantic* and "The Immigrant Story" in *Fiction*.

1973 Father dies; attends World Peace Congress in Moscow in October as a delegate of the War Resisters League.

1974 With Bob Nichols, tours China for three weeks in spring with a group sponsored by *The Guardian,* using the "little bit of money" she had inherited from her father; Doubleday Dell publishes her second short story collection, *Enormous Changes at the Last*

Minute; publishes "The Little Girl" in *Paris Review* and "The Long Distance Runner" in *Esquire*.

1975 Writes a regular column, "Conversations," for *Sevendays;* publishes "Mom" in *Esquire;* goes to Paris to meet with Vietnamese representatives at the international peace negotiations as a representative of War Resisters League.

1976 Publishes "In the Garden" in *Fiction*

1977 Publishes "Dreamer in a Dead Language" in *American Review* and "This Is a Story about My Friend George, the Toy Inventor" in *Transatlantic Review*

1978 Publishes "Somewhere Else" in *New Yorker*. Arrested with "White House Eleven" for placing an anti-nuclear banner on the White House Lawn; fined $100 and given a six-month suspended sentence.

1979 Publishes "Friends" and "Love" in *New Yorker*

1980 Publishes "Mother" (called "My Mother") in *Ms* and "A Man Told Me the Story of His Life" in *Poets and Writers;* elected to American Academy of Arts and Letters.

1981 Publishes "At That Time, or The History of a Joke" in *Iowa Review*

1982 Publishes "Lavinia: An Old Story" (called "Lavinia") in *Delta* and "The Story Hearer" in *Mother Jones;* the May issue of *Delta* is devoted to Grace Paley.

1983 Publishes "Unknown Parts of Far, Imaginable Places" in *Mother Jones* and "Anxiety" in *New England Review/Bread Loaf Quarterly*. Three stories, with adaptations by John Sayles, are filmed under the title *Enormous Changes at the Last Minute;* begins teaching at City College of New York.

1985 Granite Press publishes first poetry collection, *Leaning Forward;* Farrar, Straus & Giroux publishes third story collection, *Later the Same Day;* publishes "Ruthy and Edie" (called "Edie and Ruthy") in *Heresies;* travels to El Salvador and Nicaragua with a group from MADRE, a group of North and Central American women opposed to American policies in Central America.

1986 Receives a $1000 PEN/Faulkner Prize for fiction for *Later the Same Day*

1986 On 10 December receives the Edith Wharton Citation of Merit from the New York State Writers Institute, becoming the first State Author of New York. The position carried a $10,000 stipend and a two-year tenure.

1987 Receives the prestigious Senior Fellowship of the Literature Program of the National Endowment for the Arts given to "support and honor those who have made a major contribution to American literature over a lifetime of creative endeavor." The award included a grant of $40,000. Visits Israel for the first time as a delegate to an International Conference of Women Writers; cofounds the Jewish Women's Committee to End the Occupation of the Left Bank and Gaza; War Resisters League honors her in December on her sixty-fifth birthday at a fifty-dollar-a-plate dinner at the Village Gate in Manhattan.

1988 Retires from Sarah Lawrence College; publishes "The Expensive Moment" in *Short Story International.*

1989 Publishes *365 Reasons Not to Have Another War*, a War Resisters League peace calendar

1991 Feminist Press publishes *Long Walks and Intimate Talks*, a collection of essays and poems with pictures by Vera Williams

1992 Publishes "Injustice" in *Literary Review;* Tilbury House publishes *New and Collected Poems*, second poetry collection; receives $25,000 Rea Award for the Short Story.

1994 Farrar, Straus & Giroux publishes *The Collected Stories*, the 45 stories from her three earlier collections.

1996 Reads her story "Zagrowsky Tells" as part of the Arts and Letters Live Series at Dallas Museum of Art

Conversations with Grace Paley

Grace Paley Interview
Celeste Conway, Elizabeth Innes-Brown, Laura Levine, Keith Monley, and Mark Teich / 1978

From *Columbia: A Magazine of Poetry and Prose* 2 (1978): 29–39. Reprinted by permission.

Columbia: *Are there any questions you don't like to be asked?*
Paley: Well, I'll tell you when we get to them.

C: *How has work been going lately?*
P: That's one of those questions.

C: *Has teaching helped your writing any?*
P: No, it takes away a lot of my time. On the other hand, a relationship with young people is very important to me. It's important to have a sense of what's going on in their world and not just in my own. So the opportunity teaching provides is a gift.

C: *Do you think there is any benefit to being involved in a writing program as opposed to just writing?*
P: The writing program itself is the community of writers. It isn't the teacher unless the teacher is very harmful. The tone the teacher sets, I guess, has a lot to do with it, but I think the important thing is that community of people. I wrote alone so long, and I'm telling you that not having people to share your stuff with is very hard and I think it holds you back. I really felt held back by my aloneness. Not in the poem writing, but even there I was so creepily private about it that I think my poems might have gotten better if I only had four or five people to read to, who would show me their work, so that there'd be some back and forth. What I generally tell a class is that if you're not interested in anybody else's work but your own, take another class. I take a very kind of moral, ethical view of that small community—I mean, that's the way I want the world to go. So wherever I live and wherever I work I try to make it move in that direction.

C: *To some people the writing programs are just keeping up jobs for the writers already out in the world.*
P: Isn't that what's happening with philosophy? Hasn't that always

been true in lots of university disciplines: that's what you're doing is taking courses you finally teach other people? And, if it's knowledge, is that bad?

C: *Do you think writing programs ever tunnel people into certain kinds of writing?*

P: God, yes. Especially with poetry. Poets are very strict about what they like. Much stricter than fiction writers. And they often write each other nasty letters. Poets take themselves very seriously.

C: *Do you feel a different kind of writing comes out of those who write in a more isolated atmosphere?*

P: Well, novelists have to be alone a lot, where poets seem to be able to live in a close situation in the city; but because a novel is such a big load that has to be mined and lived in for deep amounts of time, there's a lot more solitary in that. When I went to Vietnam in 1969 to bring back POW's I spoke to people in the writer's union. I said, "How do you work?" They said, "If the writers want to write about the villages, or about the front (the whole place was the front), or whatever, they go and live in that place for a while if they want to and then we send them someplace quiet to work for a couple of months." This was in the middle of the war! This was a hard line socialist place, but they figured writers needed a place to sit down with that material and really work on it. And so do you.

C: *Beyond teaching are there other factors which have gotten in the way of your writing?*

P: My political life—especially the anti-Vietnam war movement—but I would do all that again. When it wasn't the war it was my kids, and even after the kids grew up I was left with very bad habits but I was a naturally distracted person even before they were born. One of the problems with the women of my generation, who weren't absolutely dedicated, was distractibility.

C: *You don't see yourself, or women in general, as victims?*

P: No, that's a language that's been imposed. I see women as oppressed, but I don't see them as victims; I see them rising all the time. I see them as very strong.

C: *In a lot of your stories it seems they're morally superior to men. They are always carrying responsibility while the men seem more unburdened.*

P: Well, it's true, that's what I thought. A lot of my friends at the daycare center where my kids went had been dumped, just left with the kids. And the responsibilities they had toward their kids formed a kind of ballast which kept them from moving and sometimes made them miserable. But the guys were free to just wander around doing this and that, and I think that in a real sense they were adrift.

C: *Weren't there some lines about men not trusting their feelings of being happy?*

P: I mean, those women believed they could be made happy by their kids, but the men distrusted that happiness. It was related neither to freedom nor to success. Now a lot of women have taken the same view: they don't trust that kind of happiness.

C: *Faith seems to be the most recurrent of your female characters. Is it fair to assume a relationship between the name "Faith" and the name "Grace?"*

P: Well, some of that stuff I did early and it was pretty stupid. I got stuck with it. I thought it was a big joke to have characters named Faith, Hope and Charlie. Now I think it's awful, but there's nothing I can do about it. Can't even kill off Charlie in the war.

C: *Do you identify with Faith?*

P: Not really. I didn't lead that kind of life. She was that woman with two husbands who didn't like eggs ("The Used Boy Raisers"), and that wasn't me. That was a good friend of mine. I identify with some of her attitudes, and the times we spent together in Washington Square Park. She was one of many women who interested me in the mid-fifties. They were already leading a life which is more common now, the life of a woman alone with her kids. But I was leading a nuclear family life: a girl and a boy and a husband.

C: *Which of your stories do you feel is closest to your own voice?*

P: I guess "A Conversation with My Father" is close to being a real me talking to my real father, but about an invented situation.

C: *In that story you're arguing with your father: he wants you to write stories that go from A to B, and you say you don't like those stories anymore. Do you feel that that reflects a change between your two books, a change in the type of narrative?*

P: It wouldn't be up to me to say.

C: *Do you see the A to B way of telling stories as a little obsolete now?*

P: No, I don't. I think there are certain stories one would tell that way, depending on what you were trying to do. If it is obsolete at all, it's because we've gotten hold of other techniques, and we've learned from film how to cut back and forth. Also, because the world is a lot smaller, we don't have to do so much explaining. We can assume certain knowledge.

C: *Do you think there is more exposition in the first book?*

P: Probably. And it goes over into a story like "Faith in the Afternoon," which was one of the first stories written in the second book. It had pages of that flashier writing and I didn't really like it as much.

C: *The second book has a quality of being more natural. It's easier to flow into those stories than it is into the stories of the first book, stories whose early pages tend to be loaded with compact, difficult images and denser construction. Was there a conscious effort to change the form of your beginnings?*

P: Well, I can't say that it was conscious, but maybe I was trying to do different things, trying to begin stories at once, be simpler. But actually—those stories were written over a ten year period. There are '63 stories and '72 stories in it. And they're different. What I'm interested in doing in a story is bringing certain different languages, people, events together and then letting the reader make what he wants of it. For example, "The Immigrant Story," which took me about twenty-five years to write, was a very simple story, but I couldn't think of how to tell it. Then twenty years after I started it, I found this one page and realized it was going to be the story. That's the only way you get it sometimes. The form, the vessel, has to be given to you, and that's by grace.

C: *In other words, you write until the idea has gone where it should go, and don't dwell on form or nomenclature.*

P: I don't worry about it so much; I'm writing stories. Just making things up—is that a story? Or what I'm interested in: involving personal experience—is that a story? Is that fiction? I think so.

C: *Ronald Sukenick said writers should recognize fiction as a lie.*

P: Well, you know you can argue truth, lies. I always make a big deal out of telling the truth. He makes a big deal out of telling lies; and we both do pretty much the same thing. I think that by gathering inventions I have truth. I wouldn't be bothered otherwise. I mean: if you spent a lot of time dwelling on Ronald's idea, insisting on the word lie, you'd take away the seriousness of what you'd undertaken.

C: *Then you like to think of your stories as truth, and yet you sometimes have your narrator make a side remark reminding the reader that he is only reading a story; like Josephine in "A Woman, Young and Old" who relates a line from her sister and then says "it's the only thing she says in this entire story."*

P: That's just play, one of the things I'm close to as a writer. A lot of the stuff in that story has a certain truth to it, and a lot is absolutely invented. It never happened on this earth that I know. But then, it probably *did* happen—you know? What you're doing is offering probabilities. I mean, there's no reason why—knowing a specific park and a particular tree and exactly how you lived among certain people—someone might not have been sitting in that tree.

C: *Did it take a long time in your writing to feel free to play?*

P: Well, I didn't write any fiction until I was past thirty. The first three stories I wrote were "The Contest"; "Goodbye and Good Luck"; and "A Woman, Young and Old." And I think there's a lot of play in them. But I'll tell you: "The Contest" was a little playful as far as language was concerned, but I was scared to death when I wrote that. It was very close to fact, it was happening. Sort of next door. It was a rooming house; we were supers, my husband and I, and it was very close to events that were occurring upstairs with the neighbors. So I stuck to it. I was scared to death to get away from the actuality. I did, finally.

C: *You started by writing poetry; were you as playful with it as you are with prose.*

P: No; less so.

C: *Was poetry more constricting?*

P: Well, I allowed it to be more constricting. Writing poetry, which for me was then saying how I felt about this and that, didn't help me to understand the world I lived in. I developed a definition—which I think becomes less and less accurate as poetry moves into the world—that poetry was a way of speaking to the world, but fiction was a way to get the world to speak to me. But it took me quite a while to begin to write fiction, because I thought that the subject was trivial. Coming out of the Second World War were mostly novels about *that,* and also about psychiatry and psychotherapy, all that stuff, and none of it had anything to do with my own life. I worked, I had a part-time job, I ran the house and I had kids, and it seemed to me that that was what the lives of women were. But it seemed trivial, of no interest to anybody but me, though I was really distressed by it all the time. It was that distress—it's always discomfort which makes you move—which made me finally decide I didn't give a damn, and then I was really writing.

C: *In* Enormous Changes *it sometimes seems that the writing approaches a kind of poetry, that each line is gaining an importance of its own. Do you think that this is something happening to fiction in general, possibly because the plots are being exhausted, or is this simply because poetry has been a heavy influence in your life?*

P: It has been a heavy influence in my life. I began as a poet. I worked hard on it, but it didn't come out so good, even though I stayed with it a long while. It would prevent me from not using language in a loving way. In prose I think you sometimes have to write in very plain language, where every line may not *seem* to be so important, though in all writing every line *is* important. I don't mean heavy or anything like that. But, when people want to tell a story, forget literature for a minute, they almost always use the right language and the right words, especially old people, who don't have a lot of time. Within the styles of a culture there's a natural choice of language, an economy of telling. And nobody, whoever he or she is, lives outside their time and culture. So, inside of a culture of long stories and lengthy details you'll tell those stories. Within the style of *that* culture you'll tell *that* story, the story you *want* to tell, to *somebody,* and you'll tell it right.

C: *Then your stories are written with a sense of the oral tradition.*
P: Yes, I think in terms of *telling.*

C: *Do you have any person in mind to whom you're telling?*
P: No, not really. Probably I have certain *people* in mind, but even if I didn't, I'd still write to speak. I write aloud because I write for sound. I think that one of the problems for people in writing is the separation between the spoken word and the written word. And in the United States there should not be such a separation. In other countries the written language is a class language, extremely formal like in France or Greece; their written languages, the language of their exams, in Greece anyway, is totally different from the spoken language. The people can hardly ask intellectual questions. But for us, without this language barrier, I think writing should move closer and closer to our own voices.

C: *Is it because of that kind of obligation, a need to write from your heritage in your natural voice, that you haven't dealt in your stories with other areas of your experience, such as your university life, travelling in other countries, of your Vermont experiences?*
P: Well, I like Vermont. My husband Bob's hometown is there. But I like New York very much, It's *my* home. One person with one life. It's a common ailment. But I am writing a book—I'm writing a story—by me

it's a book if it's only four pages—called *One Day In China*. It might be as big as ten pages. I do have to deal with those things; they interest me. I have to think about the politics, everything, but on the other hand, I'm not really writing about the heroes and heroines of the time. I'm writing about how people live; if they're political people, then that'll happen, but if they're not, it won't.

C: *One critic has already complained that the second book is too political. Do you see that book as more political than the first?*
P: Well, I hope it's political. I like it if it is; I'm all for it. I would wish it were more so probably. By political I mean anything that speaks of the relations of people inside a state, ordinary life and ordinary constrictions and problems. I think that critic was just complaining, not that the stories were political, but that I had been running around doing too much politicking and therefore hadn't been able to produce such good stories.

C: *Do you think of your stories more as descriptive than as didactic?*
P: I don't think of it.

C: *Would you fear being overtly didactic in a story?*
P: Why? I mean, who's in charge of beauty? Who says what's beautiful at any particular time? Why not write a purely didactic story? It could be done.

C: *Would you ever write a novel? Once you said that life was short so you were going to write short stories.*
P: I'd be interested in writing a novel. I mean, I'm not uninterested in it.

C: *But you're not writing one now.*
P: Well, when I'm writing something, unless it's been in my head for a long time, and I know it's going to be three pages, because I've already sort of done it, then I don't know how long it's going to be. How much I might cut it. One recent story of mine, about thirty pages long, had about thirty earlier pages that I threw out.

C: *The world congealing around Faith and Raftery and Ginny and all those characters seems to be developing along Yoknapatawpha county lines, as if a novelistic concern were already present. There are stories which actually refer back to previous stories. If you did write a novel, would it be about those characters?*
P: I don't know. I think almost anyone who writes creates a world in which the events that interest them occur, in which the history of one's time can happen, and also: lives through which certain ideas can be expressed. And for me, that's fun. You get to feel that the people are

really alive, and you feel an obligation not to let them just disappear. When I read as a kid, I loved that stuff. I loved reading almost anyone who had people disappearing and then suddenly reappearing.

C: *Then, when you started writing about those characters, did you have any overall idea of what was going to happen to them, or did it just grow on you?*

P: Yeah, it grew. I just sort of go back and forth. But when you mention Faulkner, I just don't think people are used to thinking of New York in that way. I have lived in this part of the Village all of my adult life. Before that I lived in the Bronx, in one neighborhood, in one house, the house in which I was born. So I have a very strong sense of center; I have never lived anywhere else other than New York. I've lived in different apartments. I've lived here, I first lived across the street, then I lived on 15th Street and 9th Avenue, where most of the Ginny and Raftery stories come from, an Irish neighborhood. So I see the world very much in a Faulkner kind of way. People keep reappearing for me; all those women I knew in their thirties with small children—when that first book came out in '59—I still know them now. There's still a lot of them around. And so I don't see life in what used to be called an alienated way. I see people going away and coming back. And I think a lot of people live that way; I don't think I'm so alone in that. Lot's of people in the different neighborhoods live that way. And I don't think that that's been dealt with enough. What interests me is that ordinary kind of everyday life of people I know.

C: *Do the events in "The Little Girl" stem from the ordinary lives of people that you know?*

P: Yes, the guy telling it is a good friend of mine. He told me the story, told it to me twice. Pretty much the way it is.

C: *Were you aware that having an older black man narrate Carter's story would act as a buffer? If a white woman or man had told a story about a black man raping a white girl it would have had entirely different implications.*

P: Well, it isn't just that he told it—I did it that way because it was his story as well as Carter's—his sadness about the life that was going, the easy, Washington Square life.

C: *But it was risky.*

P: Whew, was it risky! Nobody would buy it. But then, nobody bought the stories from the first book except "The Contest" and "Goodbye and Good Luck," which were published in *Accent,* the University of Illinois magazine. Nobody was buying the stories of an unknown person. Maybe they didn't even read them.

Then, after the first book was out awhile, the new stories I wrote were bought right away, except "The Little Girl." People were scared to death of it, they would think of any reason not to take it. So I finally read it aloud, in public, just to see if it was really wrong. It read well. I saw that it was right, and that it was a right story.

C: *Do you consider yourself an ethnic writer?*

P: I don't really like the word *ethnic*. People say, "How come you wrote that black story?" or "Why'd you do that Irish story? We happen to know where your folks came from." So? It's a *regional* writing. If I were to think of myself in any way I'd say I'm a regional writer. I'm an urban writer with a New York focus. And that enables me to avoid getting stuck in where my grandmother came from. You want to tell your people's story, but if you've been living in Queens or wherever and you move to some other borough, you're still living among people from your region—15th Street Irish or Puerto Rican, blacks or whomever—they're *your* people; they're from *your* city. And they're not so far off, though they may have slightly different sayings or family proverbs or ways of putting things. They won't be so different except for that.

C: *Your stories are drawn from the city, about people who have for the most part bedded down there. Would you consider "The Floating Truth" and exception?*

P: No, that's really a neighborhood story. It's only told in a different way. It's a story about work; it's a story about me, or any young unmarried woman wanting to do decent work in the world. And it's a typical Village guy, to tell the truth, someone trying to figure out a decent way to live without too much commitment—so he lives in a car.

C: *In that story there are so many strange shifting things going on (for example, the man's name changing a number of times in the course of the story) and maybe more than in other stories you go into symbolism, in the name: The Floating Truth. It seems that it might be suggesting, or might have suggested, a new course for your fiction.*

P: Well, I guess I like more of a middle unreality like the story "Politics," thing like that. I'd be more apt not to do a thing like "The Floating Truth" again. Although I'm not against it.

C: *And yet, in the second book you seem to be trying a lot of forms that aren't so realistic, experiments like in the story "Living," where the metaphors almost take over the story.*

P: Yeah, but I'm not consciously experimenting. I'm not saying, "Oh, I'm going to do an experimental story." Like even in "The Floating Truth"; I wasn't especially aware that I was writing something like that. I'm really not interested in doing it that way. I may be doing different forms; but that's because that's the best way for me to tell the story, not because I want to experiment with forms. I think the great experiments to come are not the experiments with forms, but the experiments with subject matter.

C: *Do you think that fiction, in general, is in a healthy place?*
P: I don't know. I don't think about it.

C: *No special paranoia about the death of the novel?*
P: No! That's a lot of crap. That's critics. They're interested in literature so they think about it a lot.

C: *In "The Immigrant Story" the narrator tells Jack, in effect, that he's warped because his head has "been fermenting with the compost of ten years of gluttonous analysis." Do you see the whole self-analytical side of New York as just being destructive to writing?*
P: Well, it could be. I'm anti too much psychology. I never miss a chance to take a snipe at it. If anything in this world is a narrow and structured way of looking at things, kind of a sheet thrown in front of your eyes that tells you how to look at things, it's psychology. I've had psychology teachers tell students who've written very good stories that their characters would never have behaved as they did in the story. They're practically murderers of history; and besides, literature preceded psychology.

C: *It seems consistent with that point of view that your stories are more about states of living than states of mind. Dialogue and action carry the load and you very rarely dip into a character's mind. Do you purposely avoid, for instance, stream-of-consciousness?*
P: Not necessarily. I haven't done that. And I admit, I don't like stream-of-consciousness, but I can see writing a story in which I say, "He thought," "She thought." I've done "He said/she said," but I've never done "He thought/she thought." I'm not against plumbing the mind, but I wouldn't try to psyche some character out. If I said, "She thought this," I wouldn't then say, "However, what she really thought was, . . ." And as for stream-of-consciousness, I think it's been done as well as it ever can be; people are still trying to do it, but it doesn't interest me.

C: *Are the stories in your books arranged in any order?*
P: No. Though in general they're chronological. The Eddie Teitelbaum

story "In Time Which Made a Monkey of Us All" was a late story, possibly the last one written in the first book. And "The Long Distance Runner" in *Enormous Changes* was a late story, but then, so was "Wants." I don't know. I'd put the stories in order and then I'd spend a lot of time fooling around, I'd change it and I'd change it back.

C: *Like seating people around a table.*
P: Yeah. You hope they get along.

C: *Is there any one which is your favorite?*
P: Well, if somebody says to me, "What's wrong with this story?"—that's my favorite story.

Grace Paley
Alan Burns and Charles Sugnet / 1979

From *The Imagination on Trial: British and American Writers Discuss Their Working Methods* (London/New York: Allison & Busby), 1979, 121-32. Reprinted by permission of the authors.

Grace Paley was born in New York City in 1922 to Mary Ridnyik Goodside and Isaac Goodside, a doctor whom she describes as "M.D., artist, and storyteller". She studied at Hunter College and at New York University. In 1942 she married Jess Paley, a movie cameraman, and they had two children. She is now married to a second husband, Robert Nichols, a poet and playwright. After teaching at Columbia University and Syracuse University in the early 'sixties, she joined the faculty of Sarah Lawrence College, where she teaches in the Department of Literature and Writing.

Although she apparently thought of being a writer from an early age, Grace Paley's first collection of stories, *The Little Disturbances of Man,* did not appear until 1959. In 1961, she was awarded a Guggenheim fellowship in fiction, and throughout the 1960s she published stories in such magazines as *Atlantic, New American Review* and *Esquire*. Her first publisher allowed *The Little Disturbances of Man* to go out of print about 1965, but it was reissued in hardcover by Viking Press in 1968, was well received and appeared in paperback. Her second collection, *Enormous Changes at the Last Minute,* appeared in 1974.

Because her subject-matter could be called "domestic" and her stories often centre on "feisty" women, the feminist movement has brought Grace Paley increased attention. But Tillie Olsen, another superb woman writer, has warned that whenever writers are put in a special category, whether it be "women's writer," "proletarian writer," or "black writer," their work is being subtly devalued, someone is putting them on a reservation. It's important, then, not to overdomesticate Paley's work (not to worry—she'd never let 'em get away with it). She writes often of family life, of children, of "love," of friendship between women. These are tremendously important subjects in themselves, but, as her answers to questions printed here show, she knows that these subjects are related to history, that having a stake in one means having a stake in the other. The European holocaust is still having consequences in hundreds of thousands of families; nuclear power plants are affecting the reproductive tissue that makes families possible. These are some of the reasons why one of Paley's characters refers to the "cruel history of Europe" as "one of my known themes," while another concludes by saying that "directed out of that sexy playground by my children's heartfelt brains, I thought more and more every day about the world."

These are also some of the reasons why Paley, who once said that her politics were "anarchist, if that's politics", has been active with the War Resisters League and other groups. It's why she has been in jail and is willing to go back again, to stop the murdering of the young. She was very involved in the movement to end the Vietnam war, and in 1979 was arrested on the White House lawn in a demonstration against nuclear weapons. Politics in our century has been a grim business, and going to jail sounds grim, but there is nothing grim about Grace Paley. Her talk, like the voices in her stories, is colloquial, quirky, direct, energetic, funny. She has a thick "Noo Yawk" accent, chews gum, is anything but chic. After seeing her in public situations a few times, one gets the sense that she is acting down a little, a very smart, talented woman trying to make the point that this is all within the reach of the ordinary, that plain folks can write a book of fiction, change a diaper, and be arrested on the White House Lawn without having to change clothes or vocabularies. At the least, she is deliberately refusing (like John Hawkes) to play the role of the writer or to parade her learning: "I'm just like anyone my age. I read a lot of Joyce when I was a kid." She refers to the students in her audience not as students, or would-be writers, but as *writers,* and there are legends about how supportive she is of others who want help with their work. Anyone who writes is a writer, no trenchcoats, Ph.D.s or other paraphernalia are required.

In what follows, Ms Paley, taking part in the Women's Studies Program at the University of Minnesota, talks briefly about her work and then responds to questions from a group of writers. She clearly prefers the democratic interchange of questions and answers to a formal lecture.

Paley: I've been in Minneapolis for a couple of days, and people have asked me certain questions. I would like to respond in some way to one or two of them. One question that often comes up is, "You're involved in all this political action and so forth and there really is little about it in your writing. How come?"

When people first asked me about this I'd worry about it a lot. I began to try to remember or think if I'd squeezed it in anywhere . . . what had I done? I began to feel a little bit guilty (not a lot guilty—you have to be born to that or trained to that early) and I'd better—and in my next few shots around—try something. . . . But whenever I would go to work again

I would find myself writing about some situation in ordinary life that really perplexed me, or terrified me, or terrified someone I knew. Finally I came to the conclusion that this really was part of my political life, and that though I didn't know this is what I was doing when I began to write about the everyday life of women around me, it seemed to me that that was one kind of political task, and that that moved in one direction, and the other happened in its own way. It certainly seems to me that both these forms of politics, the politics of the ordinary life of women and men, and the organizational or activist politics, are more and more closely related, especially in the disarmament and anti-nuke movement, which brings together our own personal flesh, our bodies, as women. . . . For a long time I thought about ourselves as women, and what places like Three Mile Island or Love Canal meant to us and to the children we bore and to our own flesh. Then I saw that this also involves men in a way I hadn't thought about before, not just in terms of their being affected but also in a sexual way. This unseeable, unsmellable radiation attacks particularly the foetus, the small growing child, and particularly the egg. I thought of the way in which people have always blamed everything on that poor egg. Anything that happened to that kid: something's wrong with the egg. Either it wasn't there, in that case, there were no children; or it was its fault. I thought that was happening to men when they began to realize that they were really about to suffer something called rape, and that they may not want to think of it that way. But if they would think that what was happening to them was the violent if invisible entrance into their sexual bodies, and the attack upon the innocent sperm, if you want to call it that, as well as the pure egg, that men could begin to understand what rape was about also. They would have to begin to understand and see it that way. These are some of the ways I see the work I'm involved in as being all of a piece, none of it is separate, the literature or the politics, in any way.

Do you write when you have to? Or when do you write?

I write all the time, in a way. I'm not a very disciplined person. I write. I wrote yesterday, a little. Writing is a habit, among other things, and if you're a writer you'd better get into the habit. A lot of people don't realize that. When I'm writing a story then I'm really writing all the time, wholly involved in it. When I'm not writing a story, I'm still thinking. . . . Susan Sontag once said that she can't wait to get to a typewriter so she'll know what she thinks! And that's true for most writers, that you really have gotten this habit of thinking on paper. Until you do that all you have is a lot of junk in your head, a lot of stuff swirling around, and the paper is the place where you really begin to think.

An article on you in the paper the other day quoted you as saying that to do well in any art form one must be willing to look foolish. Does that come naturally? [Laughter]

No! No, nobody likes to look foolish. It can be one of the worst things in this world, the fear of embarrassment. I know people who are perfectly willing to sit down and get arrested, and go to jail. But the idea of knocking at the door of a neighbor's house is enough to kill them. They're so embarrassed. They think, oh, what do I look like . . . whereas they'd do quite dangerous things in another context. So fear of embarrassment, fear of sticking your neck out, fear of looking foolish, fear of writing in a way that nobody else is writing (I'm not talking about trying to be extraordinary or avant-garde) . . . there are people who stick through for twenty years. . . . I'll give you an example: William Carlos Williams. In his autobiography he says (I'll have to paraphrase this, he said it with a New Jersey accent), "Well, it looks like this guy T. S. Eliot has hit it real big with *The Waste Land,* it looks like that is the direction for literature." His next line is: "Now I know I will have to wait twenty years to be heard." So he did, he just kept doing what he thought was right, became a powerful influence, stuck to his ideas of the American language. But lots and lots of other people said, "Well, that looks like the way to go," and trotted off, cutting their roots as they went.

A writer may have to work for a very long time before gaining recognition. Do you have anything to say about that, particularly in terms of being a woman and having a family?

For those people who love the idea of being writers and being artists there's a great temptation . . . a lot of us grow up that way, a lot of little middle-class children, like I was, grew up thinking that was the great thing to be. Until I was fifteen or sixteen it was much admired in me, after which point my family turned against it very strongly. After that you're on your own. It has to stop being a question of being crazy about being an artist or being a writer. It becomes then a matter of subject matter. I'm saying that yet I really think a lot about language, all the time, how I write, it means something to me when I work, what sort of language I'm using. At the same time I think you have to come back to where you really are thinking about something. In this country (and probably in most countries) the word "message" is abhorrent. I don't like it myself, but I don't like it because it doesn't mean anything, but there you are, you're thinking about *something.* In my case it was specifically the life of the women around me, and my own at that time, which was the mid-fifties. Not only my life and the women around me, but also my aunts, you know? One of the first stories I wrote was about the female life of my aunt. I then had, in a sense, something to write about, if you want to call it that. What you find sometimes in class (I'm a teacher too), a kid will come up and say, "I want to write but I haven't got anything to write about." Well, that's true. And they may never. But what you do write about begins early in your life, and you somehow have that theme for a long, long time, and for me the theme has continued. And the reason for sticking with it, for persevering (I'm sticking with your question), is that it's still in your mind. It's not that the questions raised in the work are finally answered; life around you is changing all the time, you're getting older, and you're still thinking about these things, the subject matter, and the subject matter has really got you . . . in many cases, for life! And that's the fidelity to it that you have, and it's one that you can't help. And you have it when the children are small, and you have it when the children are bigger, and you have it when the children leave home, and there you are. Is that any kind of answer?

It certainly answers part of it. The other part was the more practical side. It's difficult for women with children to get time for themselves to do things. What is it like getting that time when, particularly as a beginning writer, it's a matter of taking the time from the children for work that has not yet got a great deal of social recognition?

I'd like to go on with that because that's an important question. A couple of women have asked that while I've been here. In the first place, for those of you who are young and don't know: it's very hard. Those of you who are older, and know: you know. But it's hard when the kids are small (if you have kids) and it's distracting. It's one of the reasons I myself have stuck with the short story. My mind has really gotten into short jumps, so to speak, and I think I was very often distracted in those days. I remember when I was a kid and I'd come home and my father was busy, everybody was told, "Shhhhh, Papa's busy" or "Papa's sleeping," or whatever, and we were quiet, very respectful and quiet, and sometimes angry, sometimes noisy and got put out again. Mostly we didn't turn against him, we didn't hate him. It seemed like a new idea to me, and to women I spoke to, to say, "Shhhhh, Mama's busy." Yet that's a perfectly legitimate way of dealing with it. One of the reasons women can't do it, even if their husbands are very helpful, is that society has told you that your egg is responsible for the child, and that you yourself are responsible for the life of the child, for what happens to the kid. The psychology of our life period has enforced that. In my generation particularly we were really sad a lot because we felt a lot was our fault. If there was trouble with the kids and we went to a psychiatrist we were told, "You're damn right, it's your fault." I don't think the present young women suffer to the degree that women in my time did, who were really in great pain about things like that. Truly parents do have something to do with the child, but all children, all people, you and me, are born in a certain time and in a certain place, and the society which brings you up, in which you are rich or poor, has an awful lot to do with what kind of a child you are. A society in which there is a war or drugs, or one of these things, conditions the life . . . the best care you give your kid will not save his life if he's sent off to war . . . so the idea that the mother can't take a couple of hours a day to work is really shameful and no woman should suffer that pain or that guilt. I'm always surprised because I think that young women are getting over that a lot and it was for us old folks that it was so hard, but I know that's not true. I think you should look to the world around you for who's bringing up your kid, because you're not.

How does it feel to go to jail? And does it accomplish anything?

I'll tell you what I think. I haven't really been in jail, in deep jail, if you want to put it that way. I've never been in longer than a week. I know lots of people who've been in a lot longer. The time I was there a week—I don't want to offend anybody—but I was fortunate I was there without a lot of movement people. The reason I was fortunate was that—if you go to jail that way—and that's the way that most people are afraid of—you should think of it as though you were given the opportunity to visit a foreign country, an oppressed nation, under severe repression, and the gift, the opportunity (if you're not going to be there two years and then go back again and again) the opportunity to not live in the Hilton Hotel of that nation, but to really live on the cell block, on the block, with the other people. If you look at it that way you begin to understand an awful lot that you never understood before. You never really understand what it means to hear those gates clang shut until you really have heard them more than a few times. Then you really know that there is an enormous population, a whole other nation out there, a country, that you have to think about and be concerned for. Whenever you're there to share it with them, it's not a bad thing. As for accomplishing anything: Nobody can really answer that question. I can only say that this last time we did this little action of standing on the White House lawn, really the littlest thing in the world that anybody could do, and unfurling this banner which said, "No Nuclear Weapons and No Nuclear Power US or USSR," and other people in Russia did it, our friends from War Resisters did that also. . . . We just did this little thing, and it could have been a little thing, and the government if it had had any brains could have given us a ten-dollar fine or something, they made a great big thing of it, you know? When we were sentenced, my whole community came down, to see the sentencing. (I teach at Sarah Lawrence.) You could never have gotten three bus loads of people down to Washington on some abstract political issue. They all came down. The other ten people also had constituencies or friends or buddies. They all came down. There was another sit-down in front of the White House in which twenty-five people were arrested and they were released immediately, so our sentence was not repeated, which was pretty nasty. On the day of the sentencing, my Vermont affinity group (it was the middle of February, twenty degrees below) went and stood out on the Hanover Green and vigilled for us. And I had talked in Texas the week before and people did a vigil in Austin, Texas, of the same kind, with the same signs, giving out the same literature. There were many others in other places, those are just two. So I don't know what we accomplished. Had the government not responded in a silly manner we might not have accomplished so much, that's true. But . . . the members of my affinity group who had never been arrested before were among thousands who sat down at the Vermont Yankee nuclear plant, and 167 of them were arrested. I feel that it's all related. On the actions of each one of us, since we have two shoulders, at least two other actions can stand. Now whether we'll survive, whether all that can happen fast enough for us all to get through the next couple of years, we'll see.

You said that happened in the USSR also. What was the result there?
That's sort of funny, because they use their brains there. They tore up the banner, immediately, I mean within seconds, slashed it, took it off. Then pulled them in. Didn't arrest them, but ingathered them. Took them some place and yelled at them and told them not to do it any more, and then told them to go on with their journey. They were Americans, War Resisters League people.

You spoke of your Vermont affinity group. Do you live in New York City or Vermont?
I have to clarify this out of loyalty to my city which is always under such terrible attack from the rest of the country. I live in Vermont about every third year, but I am a New Yorker, and all my sad feelings are for my city. . . . For instance, there's going to be an action on October 29th [1979], it's called the Manhattan Project. People are coming in from New England and New York and . . . anywhere—you're all invited—and going to Wall Street, which is the center of much of the disaster and horror throughout the world as well as here in the United States. . . . I work

with a lot of New Englanders . . . their whole sense is that they're going to this awful place, this terrible evil center. What they don't know is that they're going to a city where the people are as cruelly colonized as people anywhere in the world, and by that same power, and that the city itself has been bombed a hundred times over, if you looked at it, if you walked around and saw it, bombed a hundred times over, by things like . . . the Defense budget. All of the money that has gone into that has really destroyed most cities. I'd say. (I've not been around enough of this city [Minneapolis] to see anything but . . . lawns . . . but that's a typical New Yorker's view of out-of-town; it has a lot of lawns.)

I have a question about a character who goes through many of your stories: Faith. She almost seems detached from the action going on around her. Did you intentionally, consciously write that into her character, and why?

She certainly is like that in the very first story in which she appears, but I don't think she's like that in the later stories. But in that first story, what happened was I was going up to visit a friend of mine, and there she was, sitting there, and there were her two husbands, and they were both complaining about the eggs, just in the way the story began! It was exactly like that. She's one of my best friends and I often look at her and I don't think she realizes that I began "Faith" in her sixth-floor kitchen, but that's true, and she was rather cool about it. I think that that story was one of the first stories in which I saw a detachment from, not the story, but the story is about the fact that these four men, two boys and two husbands, are going to go about their business, and she's at the beginning of saying, "It's not my concern." But I don't think she does that afterwards, not so much, maybe now and then, but not when she's with other women.

In one of your stories, "The Long Distance Runner," you have a woman who leaves home for a while to go on a journey—she's not detached from her surroundings, but she's not playing her typical mother role to the boys, either. . . .

Oh, yes, some guy did a review of that, and he said, "What kind of woman would it be who would go off running like that and leave her kids at home?" [Laughter] Well, the kids are kind of big, I think they're much older by that age, and that story has a kinda surrealistic touch to it. It isn't exactly your true story of running.

What touched that story off?

One of the things that touched it off was my going back to my own old neighborhood, which I've described to you as being absolutely bombed out, and seeing my father and mother's house as it stood there. And through the invention of that "running," and staying with that family that now lived there, I tried to understand the way they were the same. The way they were together, the way they could live together. I tried to understand what happened, what it was like. It's hard for me to say what the story's about, only because I could be wrong. It's about something for you, and the reader is part of every writer's writing.

I sometimes find I write better in a depressed mood, do you find that? Do you write better in certain moods? It's almost like getting it out of your system—cathartic, you know what I'm getting at?

I know what you're getting at. No, I don't think so. I sometimes will have a fight with someone, especially a husband or someone like that, and go off and really *work* [laughs] but usually it doesn't turn out so hot. But I think that's a different way of using the work. I don't think it's wrong, it's just that as time has gone on for me, I don't use it like that. I really use it (work) to think about things . . . that I don't understand. More and more it helps me. It doesn't help me succeed in understanding but it helps me see what the world is really about.

Could you talk a little about what the short story should do, what your definition of it is, and has it changed for you over the years?

That's a hard question. A short story seems to me to be related to a poem more than it is to a novel. In some way it is almost as economical as a poem but has a little more happening inside of it. It works in that way. I teach "short story" but I can no more tell my class what a short story is . . . I know it's not a novel, so if they hand me a novel I can say, "This is a short-story class, I don't have time to read this." [Laughter] But I think the short-story form is marvelous and can do anything. It can be one page long, it can be forty pages. What it has to have in it is what is commonly called conflict in the trade, so to speak, but what I don't think of particularly as conflict, but what I think of really as the meeting of two events or ideas or experiences or sounds, and the story is really that sound. So you can do it very lightly, that can be the sound, or it can be really quite explosive, but without that you'd have what you'd call maybe a prose poem. Prose poems are a form I don't like much because they seem mostly to be written by poets who won't do the work of a story. A lot of poets don't like me to say that and I don't say it often. But they want to try their hand at prose and so they write the prose poem, and that doesn't do enough work for me, it doesn't do enough thinking. The cerebral nature, the real thinking nature of all this work is something that people don't want to . . . think about too much. So there's a lot of that. So the main thing for me is that the story has to have these two, this coming together [claps hands] of two people, two events, two ideas, two sounds, two winds, whatever, and it's that bumping into which makes everything in the world happen, which makes energy, and it's that energy which is the sound, which is the story, and if you don't have it it's kind of weak and sloppy. And it has to have a beginning, a middle and an end, but the middle can be anywhere, it can be in the beginning, it could happen anywhere through the story. It has to have shape, a rising and a falling. But no one is the boss of beauty or form, so what can happen in the future with all of this is . . . wonderful, and there's no law. There's a law for me, this minute. A lot of people say you can't write a really good didactic poem or story. I don't see why not. I haven't done it, I haven't seen it done, but someone will come along whose spirit understands that and it'll happen.

Does your reading influence your writing a lot?

I used to read a lot more than I read. For years I was what was called a big reader. Now I read a lot less. I think everything I ever read is very influential on my writing and by that I mean the stuff you read from a very early age. The poets I read had a strong influence on me. But I think when we talk about influences we omit some of the most important influences on our writing, and they're never discussed really, and they're not literary at all. It may be why I feel close to Russian writers. It's because that's the language of my father and mother. So one of the major influences on my writing, I feel, is the street in which I grew up. I was out in it all the time. And the language of my family which was English and Russian and some Yiddish running back and forth a lot at great speed, and the life they talked about, the life they led. That language that I heard, and the language of the street, of the kids and also of the grown ups, who hung out in the street a lot in those days, that was as great an influence on my writing as anything I've read. As for form, that's another thing. I'm just like anyone my age. I read a lot of Joyce when I was a kid and those stories probably had a lot to do with my first ideas of form. I read a lot of Chekhov. I think those old things have influence. I don't think that anything you read . . . now, can strongly influence you, it can superficially do so but not really deeply.

Can you talk about the writing process in terms of your thinking? Do you "think on the page"? Do you do a lot of thinking about something before you begin to write? Or do you discover it as you write?

Well, I begin by writing something, and I just write it, and I may not even look at it for the next two years. So I have a lot of pages lying around. When I finish a story I start going through all my pages. I have all these pages. Some of them I'm amazed to see, are part of what I'm thinking about. We have this one head, so everything is just in there all the time. You write a few pages and then you . . . go away. . . . Which is, again, the distractable way that I work and it's not to be construed as a decent or honorable way of doing things [laughter] but I do think about things a long long time. When I'm really into a story I work very very hard on it. People ask me, How do you know when it's at an end? I just thought last week what was the answer: I know I'm at the end when I say to myself, How'm I going to end this thing? When I think I've finished it I then begin to go over it and I go over it for falsity mostly, and for lies. I just revise. I just think of it in those terms. I don't want anybody to think I just write when I feel like it, especially who are going to go into that line of work. You write also when you don't feel like it. It really is such hard work that if you are naturally lazy, like I am, you often feel like it, so you have to keep that in mind.

What do you think are the most commonly encountered lies that come up in your work?
Wanting certain characters to be something, or pushing them around. You get stuck with your own examples of things. The example I always use is how I got stuck giving some guy the wrong job. I was working on this story for a very long time and I just couldn't move ahead on it, and the reason was I'd given him the wrong job. He really was a taxi-driver and I think I gave him some sort of administrative responsibility somewhere. [Laughter] It really was bad, but until I realized that . . . I'd call that a lie. I wanted him in an office, you know? But once I'd got him out of the office, because he didn't belong there, then a lot of other things changed. There are other kinds of lies too. There are lies of language where you exaggerate, or put in a lot of adjectives, or you try to be high styled, or you try to be up-to-the-minute with what's being done. Those are lies. You can go through a story again and again and again until you can't change it any more, and then at the end . . . don't think in terms, is this story good or bad, you know? Because you never will know. What you can think about is whether it's true as you can make it. And then even if you think it's bad, you're probably wrong. "Oh, this lousy story I just finished." But it's what I had to say, and it's what I said, and everything in it is truly invented and true . . . then you probably have a good story.

Could you say something about humor in short stories?
The only thing I can say about humor is that if you're not funny you

can't be. [Laughter] But did you want me to say something more serious about it? [Laughter] Humor I think by its very nature is out of place. I mean that. You have humor when you have great disparity.

Do you ever feel like your vision is losing steam? I don't mean in the writing sense, but your personal vision, the way that you live. And if that happens, where do you get support?

[Pause] Huh! [Laughter] That wasn't a joke, that "Huh."

Or do you just wait it out?

Yeah, I think so, I think you wait things out. If you're working hard on something and it doesn't seem like it's working out, you get kinda low. But you can't live in this world without friends. There are a lot of therapeutic devices nowadays to take the place of that, but . . . I don't know how I would live without my friends. I've felt that way from a pretty early age, and they have always been—through hard times—as supporting of me as I have been of them.

Conversation with Grace Paley
Leonard Michaels / 1980

From *Threepenny Review* 3 (1980): 4–6. Reprinted by permission of *Threepenny Review*.

The following conversation took place in the summer of 1980, at the Berkeley Writers' Conference, between Grace Paley and me, before an audience of about a hundred people, mostly participants in the conference who had come from all over the country to join seminars conducted by Grace Paley, Thomas McGuane, Robert Stone, and Elizabeth Hardwick. Instead of giving a talk to the conference, Grace Paley agreed to converse this way in public, and we decided to make the conversation very casual and, if possible, to restrict ourselves to the experience of writing as seen from the inside.

There has been some slight editing for the sake of coherence, not smoothness. After I'd asked what seemed to be enough questions from the inside, the floor was opened to the conference participants. They asked questions about particular stories Grace had published, and other questions that tended to be somewhat irrelevant to the original direction of the conversation; but, where her answers touched on that, they have been interpolated here and there in relevant places.

Obviously, a conversation in front of a hundred people might seem slightly unnatural, especially if one person keeps poking at the other with questions, but at least we have tried to preserve, in its disconnections and vagaries, its hope of revelation in unnatural naturalness. As Grace Paley says in the conversation, writing is very hard. At writing conferences, one always seeks relief in persons, in the sound of their talking. This is never irrelevant to writing.

Leonard Michaels: In your writing—in the act of writing, rather—do you have particular things you might want to tell us about the beginnings of stories, particular experiences and observations you might have for us?

Grace Paley: Well, how do stories begin, for me? In one of about four or five ways. One of the simplest ways is I simply am walking down the street—it never happens, really, when I'm sitting at my desk. Taking a bath is very good too. But I simply—sentences occur to me, and those sentences are sometimes—sometimes I lose them because I'm not near any writing material, and that's the first thing you should all know—you should always be near a pencil and paper, your whole life.

Sometimes what it comes from is just pure language. I can't even tell you that I'm thinking specifically of any event of any kind, and I may simply write two or three sentences that seem to me beautiful or right or true for the day. And then what would happen would be that I might type up a page or so. I tend to work like that in general—I just work in pieces, and I don't always know that I've begun a story. I just add that page to an infinite number of pages in a drawer in my desk. And very often they are beginnings, when I go back over it.

I have lots of pages that I'll never turn into a story. I'm sure all writers do. I have lots of pages that are just a paragraph of nice writing, or something like that, and don't seem to me—It's not that they're not worth working with, but nothing in that paragraph gives me that feeling which is one of the impetuses of all storytelling: "I want to tell you a story—I want to tell you something." So those paragraphs may never enter into my "I want to tell you somethings." I may never want to tell you anything about that story. But actually, some of them become two pages, and what they really are, are simply ways of taking stabs at the mystery, really.

Whenever I finish a story, I go back to that drawer. And as a matter of fact, when I'm in the middle of a story and stuck, I go back and look at these other pieces. There's this book by Joan Miró, the artist, called *I Work Like a Gardener*. It's a very small book, it's very beautiful, and he says, "I work like a gardener. I'm never so happy as when I'm rich in canvases." He says, "Then I get up in the morning and I prune one. I water another . . ." I had been working very much like that. It's such a nice corroboration from another art, that I'm grateful to it, and it's become a way that, with my bad habits and my natural disinclinations, I can work.

Another way I begin, often, is with a person speaking, because I have an awful lot of speaking in my ear, and an awful lot of words, ideas, persons having spoken to me, or persons whom I would like to speak through me, and other voices, and so I will often begin with a sentence, a couple of sentences of people speaking. I never have begun with a story, and that's caused some problems for me, but it's the way I've worked.

Michaels: That's very interesting. I think I had one other question that was related to that, and—well, I'll ask it even though in a way you've already answered it, just because I had prepared it. Have you had any experiences in your life that you find make good telling—You tell people about these experiences. They're really interesting. People laugh, and they say to you "Why don't you write that?" and then you try it and fail. Has that ever happened to you?

Paley: Well, everybody tells stories, and we all tell stories all day long. I've told about seven or eight today myself. And we are storytellers—I mean, we're keeping the record of this life on this place, on earth, you know—all the time. And often you tell a story and somebody says to you. "Gee, that's a good story," and you think to yourself, "Well, it certainly is a good story—it must be good—I've told it about six times." But then you don't write it. And you don't write it because you've told it so many times. And also because in writing there has to be—and I'm sure you all know this—there has to be some of the joy of mystery. And to tell a whole story means it's told—it's done—you did the job. You snap the picture—that's it. People like it—you'll tell it again. But for you to sit down and do the work of exploring or of investigating that mystery . . . There's a way I have of thinking about what you write, really *write*—you write what you don't know about what you know.

Michaels: I have another question about subject matter. There are some writers who are remarkable for the way they can deal with the most ordinary kinds of material—material everyone is familiar with, and which has no ostensible dramatic value at all. Have you ever thought about this? How the ordinary figures in your own work as a subject?

Paley: Well, as far as I'm concerned, that's what interests me. What you would call the ordinary. I mean, ordinary life is sufficiently dramatic—I don't know if I can really go further with that. I think for somebody really raised on dramatic tales, or on the literature of right after the Second World War, a whole period of what I consider mostly masculine concerns, if I may—I was most attracted to the ordinary. That is, it seemed to me ordinary, and it seemed to me trivial, and I felt like a fool being interested in it, and I thought "How could anybody care about all this stuff?" So that I had been sold a bill of goods about its ordinariness, too, in a way. And on the other hand, it was really—it was what interested me. Ordinary, everyday life is what seemed to me almost the most mysterious.

You know in any writing class you have people who really seem very talented—I'm speaking really of my own classes at school, where I know people for a whole year, if not for life, practically—and you have people who are very talented, and you have people less so, and you don't know who's going to do the work. And the person who's going to do the work is the person who needs to do the work—you know, who's got to the work, who really exits under extreme pressure if they don't do the work. Some of the students I've had were really quite wonderful—wrote wonderful little poems and essays and stuff. They're really doing great in biology and in lots of other things, because the world is interesting—not only where we are. So the fact is, I just was bugged by that subject matter. I mean, I was living that life, pretty much, and at a certain point I said, "Well, it's trivial, it's ordinary, it's maybe silly, but it's what I damn well have to do." And I did it, I wrote several stories, and I did get a little—my husband liked them, and one or two friends who I dared show them to thought they were okay, and you really don't need more than that—I mean, to keep going. People live on so little—when they need to live, they really live on a little rice. And if you need to do the work, you really live on very little. If you don't need to, everybody should go do something else, because there's lots to do.

Michaels: I'm jumping around from one subject to another—sometimes it'll be very technical and sometimes it'll not be. Here's a technical kind of question.

Paley: Yes. Sounds serious.

Michaels: Technical, that's all. Do you ever think about the relationship between a descriptive paragraph and dialogue that may follow it immediately? Sometimes that relationship feels disjunctive—you know, there's a gap, an unfortunate gap that shouldn't be there. Somehow or other you have to reconcile the two.

Paley: I do know what you mean. I'm not exactly sure what I can really say about it, without being specific.

Michaels: Well, if you don't have any particular thoughts on this now, maybe something will occur to you later. Have you ever used lines from life in your stories? Things that people have said that struck you as adorable or amazing?

Paley: Well, I have—I've used it. I don't use it a lot, but I have to say that I sure have used it, and as a matter of fact, in one of the first stories I ever wrote, which is in my first book, where this old aunt says, "I was popular in certain circles." I have to tell you the truth: my aunt said that. I was about 25 years younger then, and I looked at her, amazed, you know, that that was true. And then I just invented a circle for her to be popular in. I thought about that a good deal—but really, that is an example of a story which began with an absolute true sentence spoken to me by a person. But mostly I don't remember well enough, really. You have to really understand how people speak, and you have to reconstruct it, but you may not, at the same time, have it right. Most pleasure in writing, you know, is in inventing.

Michaels: Now, another thing that maybe you've reflected on in such a way that you could talk about it is the confrontation of characters in a story. For instance, compared to how much they think, and how much their circumstances determine what they're going to say, very little is actually said when characters meet.
Paley: Right. Exactly.

Michaels: What do you think about this—if you have thought about it in a general way? I'm curious.
Paley: I haven't thought about it so much as I've noticed it. No, I mean I've noticed it in my own work. I will have some event happening, and people just barely speaking to one another about it. You have some large events, and your real job is—because the people involved in it may not notice that it's a large event, you see, they don't really know it. You know it, and you have that task, and it's a technical task, of letting the reader know that an awful lot is happening.

Michaels: How about the use of ideas in your work? By which I mean, formulated thoughts on certain subjects—you have a view or whatever. How about its relation to what you write?
Paley: Well, if I understand you correctly—I'm not exactly—

Michaels: Well, say you have certain very gloomy, pessimistic, etcetera views about the nature of the world, and they're clearly formulated in your own mind, and you're writing a story. What do you do with the idea, if anything at all, in the writing of the story?
Paley: Well, it seems to me so organic, I can't see it separated, really. I mean, what you think about the world—which I happen to think is in incredible hot water right now—what you think about the world, you don't omit it. I mean, that's the politics of writing. Whatever you do, you're talking about what you believe and what you think. Every step of the way, every line you write is a selection from an infinite number of lines you could have written, and every person you write about is a person taken from an infinite number of persons you could have written about. You're making selections all the time, so you really are always practicing your own ideas and theories. You can't avoid it. You may think you have none—you know, you may say, "I'm just telling you the way it is—and that's the way it is!" But how it is is what you've been seeing. Whether it's tragic in the end or humorous really depends entirely on you, and who you are, and what your style is. I have some very dark

views of the world, and I think they've found their way into some funny stories.

Michaels: Let me ask you another question related to this subject. Have you ever discovered in the course of writing a story that the story is revealing to you something you didn't intend? That you mean something you didn't think you meant?

Paley: Yes. Often. That's the whole business of really writing—writing through the mystery of it. Let me put it in a slightly different way—I often use this for an example. I have a story called "The Immigrant Story," and I had that—the specific story of that story, the specific tale of that story—in mind for about twenty-five, thirty years, and I never could figure out how to tell the story, I knew what the story was about, I knew it and I couldn't deal with it. And it wasn't until one day I was simply going through these papers that I described to you earlier—these beginnings of stories—that I found two pages of dialogue, rather abstract dialogue, really ideas mostly—and I understood how to tell that story. It simply began with these two people speaking to each other. I knew the story, but I didn't know what a complicated way I would have to tell it. That was sort of the discovery of form—which the Lord gives you sometimes, and sometimes he don't.

But as for finding out what a story is about, that happens to me all the time. And it happened in a rather long story that I had—I think I read it here last year—called "Friends." Well, I began that story simply writing about the death of my friend, and it went on and on, and it just became more and more clear that it was really a story about all of these women that my children and their children had grown up with—and that I had grown up with, really. So that it was really a much more complicated story than I ever intended telling and other characters took over entirely, and seemed to me more important, finally.

Michaels: Could you say something about the way people respond to your work? I don't mean necessarily reviewers—I mean friends, literary acquaintances, and so on. Have you ever thought about the value of their responses, the different kinds of value they may have?

Paley: Well, to tell you the truth, I try not to. I think if people were mean to me, or cruelly critical, I would have some feelings on that subject. My family, in the beginning, was very important to me. I guess I was in my thirties, and I was considered kind of a dead loss in the family up to that point—so that, in a sense, their attitude was very important to me, because really they had regarded me in that way. And I had a very childish response—that is I was glad that at last they thought I was okay.

And as for my friends—I try not to think about that too much. If they have something to say to me, they say it. I cared about how my friends felt about that "Friends" story—especially the friend with whom I hadn't spoken for several years because of a great quarrel. And when she called me up and said, "That was okay, Grace". . .

Michaels: Have you ever had the experience, while writing, that it's going smoothly but something might be wrong and you don't know what it is?

Paley: Yes.

Michaels: Have you ever thought about why it is?

Paley: Well, I think all of us have that—anybody who works in this business knows that after almost any two pages you know that something is going wrong. Your work is going wrong at all times. I mean, that's why writing is really so hard—it's really, like Yeats said, something like digging a ditch. Except it's worse than digging a ditch, because when you dig it, you dig it and there it is, but with writing, you've dug that ditch and it's in the wrong place. So you really have to go off someplace and have to dig it over there. And it's very hard—it's a hard, hard, hard life. It sounds like a joke when I say about every two pages—Sometimes every page you've just gone wrong, and you just have to stop. So you have to give the work that honor and patience to stop. At least I do. Nowadays I think I've been making a mistake—I think I should have just plowed ahead. But that's another style. And sometimes you find out what it is—sometimes it's really you're using the wrong language, sometimes the form is wrong, and sometimes it's a very small thing. One of the funniest things was a story I had where I just gave this guy the wrong job. And he was working away in this factory for about three pages, which for me is a lot of weeks of work—and I couldn't get past it, I couldn't get beyond it. When I figured out that he was a taxi driver, I could move. But up to that point—That was really a very specific character problem. He was a sort of garrulous person, and part of it was he really—I mean, if I tell it to you it'll seem so simple, you'll think. "Why did she think for three weeks?" I mean, he had to make friends with this woman—that's the direction it was going—and he wasn't making friends with her because he was stuck in that place all day long. The story wouldn't go on, and I might just as well have quit at that point, and said, "Well, I don't know—maybe I don't even know what this story is about." People take taxis more often than they go into strange factories. But you could have a good story about that—I mean, I could think of a great story about a woman who really wants to see how factory workers are, and she goes in there—but I'm not going to continue writing it.

Michaels: Have you ever had the experience in small passages within a story of noticing that something is a little bit abstract and asking yourself to make it concrete?

Paley: Right. In fact, we've been talking about that—the fact that it's so easy, in a sense, to just go on in generalities. But whatever it is you're writing—and we haven't even talked about the varieties of writing—but in any form, in any style that you use, you really do have the opportunities to be very specific—to say "He did this, she did that, certain specific acts were undertaken, were done, certain sentences were said." Not "they talked about this and that for a long time." You can put in two pieces of dialogue in which you can really clarify what everybody talked about, give the substance, give the way in which they spoke to each other. You can be specific in terms of actions and the way people move, the way they walk across the room or whatever it is. You need that specificity at all times. And almost any time you're being general—almost any time—you should look and say, "Wait a minute. What happened?"

Michaels: I was just wondering if you ever reflected on why it is that the general not only creeps into our writing, but has so many ways of creeping in? Sometimes, for example, you write sentences that tend toward lyricism, which seems to me already sort of generalizing.

Paley: Self-love.

Michaels: That's the reason for it? Well, all right . . .

Paley: It's easy, too. You know, if you're really in a hurry . . . I mean you get tired of writing these little things, and there's nothing like getting to the end. You figure, "Well, I'll get through that—I have to get that in, but I'll get through it—fast." And you get through it. That's one way of getting through it. And until you change your mind—until you change your way of thinking—you will do it that way. But also, I was not joking when I said self-love. There's an awful lot of writing beautifully in that way—or feeling "Oh, boy, am I writing beautifully! It's really great." And of course that comes from the times of earlier in life, when you were admired for those little sentences you wrote in school, and stuff like that. You were really wounded by those.

Michaels: Have you ever had the experience of writing a dialogue or a description in one mood, and hearing the response to it and discovering— say you wrote it, not to be particularly funny, although you might agree it's amusing, but people just think it is a riot?

Paley: Right, I often have that experience. I think that's because of what people expect—I know that if I have a story which is really rather complicated and serious, people expect it to be funny. So I have to begin by saying, "Now, this is not going to be funny"—you have to just sort of say that, to spare them the embarrassment that they would feel when they have roared through the first two paragraphs and find six people lying in blood in the third. I do it for them as much as for anybody—as for myself.

I don't really intend to be funny. I don't, and there are certain stories I've done where I see that there are very easy laughs, and if there ever is some edition of some kind, I would take them out. I really don't like that at all. On the other hand, you really can't—if that's how you see it, you know . . . I have a story about, "Conversation With My Father," in which my father keeps telling me: "All you do is tell jokes." And it was true—talking about family reactions, this was one of the things that he would always kind of bug me about. He'd say, "Okay, yeah, more jokes, you think that's funny, right?" And I'd say, "No, I didn't say it was funny. If people laugh, I can't help it—I didn't say it was funny."

Michaels: A lot of writers have special books that they keep with them all the time, particular books that they re-read and re-read. Do you have such particular books you'd like to tell us about?

Paley: The reason I'm even bothering to answer this question is that I used to, really, keep certain books with me. But I don't, no, I don't keep certain books with me. I always hope there's a Bible in the room, and that serves.

I'm not really a big reader, as we say—now, to that extent. As a young woman I just read all the time, but mostly I read poetry, and if I kept books of any kind around me, it was usually not—I'm not saying fiction, and I'll go back to that in a minute and I'll explain to you why—it was not books of stories, or novels. It would be poetry that I kept around me, and didn't go anywhere without.

I just want to go back to that. You know, in that little black brochure for the Conference, one of the things you talked about was storytelling, and I started to write you a letter because I liked that beginning in that brochure so much. And then I saw you were going to talk on "The Art of Fiction," so I got mad. Not that mad, you know. But what I disliked was—what I don't like is the word "fiction." I think it's a false word, and it's led to "non-fiction." I mean, you're either a storyteller, an inventor in language or event or whatever, or a poet of storytelling—or you're not. I guess I'd use the example of Maxine Hong Kingston, who for *The Woman Warrior* got a non-fiction award. Well, that really got me sore, because that really was a great work of storytelling. But see, non-fiction is supposed to sell better than fiction, and novels are supposed to sell better than short stories, and so on down the line.

A person telling their own story is also storytelling, and the truth of the matter is that telling your own story is great for once—you know, you want to tell it, tell it. But the fact is that the job of the storyteller—you know, the task, as an imposed task—that task is the task of the story-hearer. It's wonderful to tell what happened to you at this and this time, and at a certain point, like when you're ninety, you should do that—you know, you probably by then have amassed so much experience and so many interesting events, and you have such a view of the world, you should absolutely do it. But the job—I keep using that word, maybe you should change it—but the interest is really to tell the story of the people, of the life of your time. I mean you have to keep saying how it was. And even if you're writing a story about the history of the past, like Maxine did—almost all of it, and even in her new book, is just telling "This is how it is now because of how it was then." A lot of people cannot begin to speak out of their own throats until they have listened enough, and heard enough the stories of others. Again, nothing wrong with telling your own story—tell it! But the story you tell, really, is not all that interesting, usually, unless something very specific is happening. But if you speak for others—if you really perform that great social task (I have a lot of useless sentences like that)—you'll really begin to be able to tell your own story better.

Interview with Grace Paley
Kathleen Hulley / 1980

From *Delta: Revue du Centre d'Etude et de Recherche sur les Ecrivains du Sud aux Etats-Unis* 14 (1982): 19–40. Reprinted by permission of Nancy Blake, *Delta* Editorial Committee.

The interview took place at Paley's home in Thetford, Vermont, August 1980.

KH: What do you think are the central concerns of your stories?

GP: I don't know. I used to know. The critics will think about that. I just keep doing the work. . . . Actually, I do know that. I'm interested in generational relations. I'm interested in how people live at this particular moment in time and history. I'm interested in the lives of women in particular. I read a lot, but I don't think about it. If you think about it too much, it falsifies, you push yourself in some stupid direction.

I *am* interested in form, despite the conversation that we had before, when I said that the real experiments were in subject matter. That really is a class idea . . . a Marxist idea. But I do agree with you that language and subject matter must come together. Still, you have whole periods when blacks are not written about, or they're written about as slaves. And if you're a black person, you'll say, "Where the hell are all the black people? Why aren't they writing about my life?" And then some black people will start to do it. And they'll pay attention, and suddenly realize that they have a speech and that language is part of the story. Language is what the American language is about. What I write about is a coming together of all sorts of other languages . . . Russian and Yiddish . . . English.

KH: Voice is very strong in your stories. Mrs. Raftery in "Distance," for instance.

GP: I don't pretend to have the real Irish lingo. Whatever I say comes from what I hear. It comes from the speech of my city. But that has to go through my American-Jewish ear.

KH: So the voices telling the story are your voice?
GP: Not my voice, my style.

KH: But there is a quality of being told that pervades your stories.
GP: I hope so. I want to be a story-teller when I grow down. But I believe that we are all story tellers.

Kathleen Hulley / 1980

KH: You said in your interview with Lennie Michaels at Berkeley that good story writing is good story hearing, good listening . . .

GP: I meant good listening. You have to hear, especially if you write short stories. You have to hear how people really talk, and how they act. You have to pay attention. Sometimes it's language and sometimes it's not language. Sometimes it's movement. With me it's a lot of listening. I write things down all the time. Sometimes the beginnings, sometimes it's the middle of a story that I've already written the beginning of. They really come to me in the voice of the teller. Sometimes I have a story teller but I don't have a story.

KH: It's a matter of voice.

GP: A lot of it is. Until I have a story teller . . . Or it's a matter of form. Sometimes I have a story teller with a story to tell, and I still don't know how to tell it. A good example is "The Immigrant Story." I knew the story for maybe twenty five years, but I didn't know how to tell it. One day, I was going through my papers and I found this dialogue between two people, and I realized that I had the form for the story. But the form is given by grace.

KH: You talked about "grace" at Berkeley too. What do you mean?

GP: I mean that it descends on you. You find it. You work and you work and you work. And you make connections, and you make connections, and you make connections. Then suddenly you realize that you have woven or created these baskets, for the story to be, or the cup, or the plate, or the sidh, or the basin . . . or the tub.

KH: Then you feel grace is a gift that comes from outside you?

GP: No, but it's like gifts that do come from outside. You have to do a lot of work.

KH: Is that a religious point of view?

GP: OH NO! I don't like that . . . I come from a long line of anti-religionists. But, on the other hand . . . Sometimes I'm against the word, not the thing itself.

KH: What first got you interested in writing?

GP: I always wrote, since I was a little kid. I was encouraged very much in verbal gift . . . don't call it gift, just call it "verbalosity." I had an older attentive sister and brother; so I'd do a song or a poem and they would write it down. Some writers are born by being made to shut up all the time, and others are born by having their sentences liked.

KH: When did you first start publishing your stories?

GP: I didn't publish for many years . . . a couple of poems when I was very young. The stories, I began writing when I was in my thirties.

KH: Did you publish when you were in college?

GP: I didn't finish school. First I went to school, then I didn't go. I was out by the time I was sixteen and a half. I just stopped going . . . just . . . ceased. I did put a poem or two in a NYU magazine.

KH: Did you show anyone your work?

GP: I worked very much alone most of my life.

KH: How did you first get published?

GP: I had written about three stories. And I showed them to my then husband, who was very encouraging. And then one day, my kids were looking at television with their best friends. And their best friends' father came to pick up their best friends. Ken McCormick—he's an editor at Doubleday. His wife asked him to look at the stories, and he did. He said, "If you write seven more, I'll put them out." And that's how it happened. I sat down and wrote seven more over the next two years. I never published in any literary magazine. Almost every story in that first book was turned down by every magazine in the country.

KH: What kept you going?

GP: Well, I had the book coming out. I had the reverse experience of other people.

KH: You said that you can't live if you can't write. Do you feel compelled to write?

GP: No, but if I imagine being put some place without a pencil or piece of paper, (like jail, which I was once), it's horrifying. It's not that I write so much, or as if I was writing day and night. But I can't imagine not being able to put something down on a piece of paper. It's scary to me.

KH: How do you write?

GP: Every way. Whatever . . . On a back of an envelope. On a small piece of paper, on a big piece . . .

KH: How do you compose it?

GP: I don't really feel I've got something until I've typed it. I can't begin working on it until it's typed. Then I can write. Until, then, I just have bits and pieces of papers.

KH: Do you ever have times when you can't write?

GP: Mostly it's different pulls. Right now we're trying to get a lot of women down to the Pentagon to march against nuclear armament. Concentration is really a problem for me. To seize something. But when I really *have* a story I'm working on, I can work on it sitting in a train, going to Washington, any place, anywhere. It's totally absorbing.

KH: You never have "writer's blocks"?

GP: I think people have writer's block because they don't really write things down. Their minds are too linear. You have blocks when either you have nothing to write about or you are just going dead ahead. If you just write, if you realize what your mind is and that it's always working, you're always wondering, you're always curious, you're always thinking about things.

KH: Does your family life interact or interfere with your writing?

GP: Writing is difficult for women with small children. That is not my case now. I don't have to do anything special. If I screw up, I screw up. Nobody else can screw me up. If I don't get work done, it's cause I don't get it done. I'm married to a writer who *does* get up at 5:30 every morning to write and he's not fussy about things. There's no one in my way, and there is no reason why I can't work. Earlier, when the kids were small . . . Everything gets in the way of everything else. I'm not a careerist in any way. I mean I view life as a whole, and that's what interests me. And I'm interested in being as good a writer as I can. I can't live without writing, but I couldn't live without my children. And I couldn't bear not to respond to the awful things that are. I regret that I haven't written more . . . But, I don't know how with my view of how to live in this really *hopeless* world . . . how I could have done more. Except if I had had a better character. If I got up at 4 in the morning like decent writing people do. I'm energetic and lazy both. I work like the devil. Like when we worked together in California on that writers conference. I worked like the dickens on that. And I loved it. And then the next day. Well, that's not exactly true. I *did* have another reading or two after that. But after those, I really *lolled*. Tillie Olsen and I walked around for a whole half a day, just walking and talking in Santa Cruz. So, I laze around a great deal. I work very hard and then I laze. I mean really *hang out*. I sit outside when I'm in New York and talk to passing people. Some good friends, some writers, my buddies from the park, who've gotten thirty years older, just like me.

KH: At the writers conference, Tom McGuane says, "When I write I go off in my cabin in the woods and my wife keeps the kids away. I'm terrible to live with." I don't think women can do that.

GP: That's why women write shorter things. But I couldn't swear to that. I think writing a novel is different. I see Bob [Nichols] when he's been working a long long time on his stuff. And he has to be alone. I don't think all women allow the kinds of interference that I have.

KH: But you do think that interference in some ways determines *your* form?

GP: No so much. I think my shortness comes also from my having written poetry. Poetry is closer to the short story. And then it's very important for me to finish things.

KH: Why didn't you stick with poetry?

GP: I write a lot of poetry. I just never get good. Poetry is too literary, a thing which comes from my love of literature rather than from my love of people, my feeling for people.

KH: Bob is your second husband? Were you divorced from your first husband when you wrote most of the stories?

GP: No. I was married for 22 years. And have children, a daughter and a son.

KH: Is it your kids you write about?

GP: No. I write about kids, but not specifically about mine. I lived, when they were small, on the block with other women, and that's where most of my work comes from. That was where most of my interests lay. I was with other women with lots of children. One of my stories begins like that. I was in a neighborhood park, surrounded by children.

KH: Was your husband gone a lot?

GP: No. I wasn't writing about myself. My husband was there all the time. I was writing about me *and* my friends. A lot of them were alone with children. I was not. I didn't have two sons and Faith is not me. But I spent a lot of time with children.

KH: In general, then, you prefer not to write about yourself?

GP: I don't not and I don't do. I write about the lives of women and men of our time.

KH: How do you see Faith?

GP: Faith gives me a chance to speak for my people, which is my women friends. I speak for my friends through her. Of course, I'm just like them. My life and theirs is interchangeable. Our characters are different, our number of children and so forth, are different. But people are not so unlike. In fact, you write about two things: you write about what is like you and you write about what is totally unlike you. Both are equally fascinating. You say, this is like me, this is unlike me. This is another world in which many things can happen. Mrs. Raftery, for example, is totally different, a different generation, and she has a totally different way. Whereas, Ginny was really just another woman in a different apartment in the same building, and not unlike Faith. Not like me, but less unlike Faith because Faith is also alone with kids. My children had a father most of their lives, who lived in the same house with them. I lived in a neighborhood with all those people. An Irish Puerto Rican neighborhood.

KH: In "Time Which Made a Monkey of Us All," what were you trying to do with that story?

GP: There were kids like that. Kids who "dropped out" of sanity even then. Even in my generation. That story called "Friends" is really about grief for the children. "Friends" is not in the books, it's in the *New Yorker*. You should get ahold of the other stories: "Dreamer in a Dead Language" in the last issue of *American Review*. Then there are three stories in the *New Yorker*, "Friends," "Somewhere Else" which is about China and one called "Love."

KH: Many of your stories, whether you intend it or not, are full of surrealistic images. The story about Rosie . . . at the beginning she says, "Only a person like your mama stands on one foot, don't notice how big her behind is getting, and sings in the canary's ear for thirty years." Is that language you invent, or is it imagery you heard around you?

GP: People *do* talk like that. They speak beautifully. That kind of language is common to me. I could think of anyone of my aunts talking like that. The speech of people is very beautiful, and that's what I think is missing in the god-damned novel. Especially when an old person is telling their story. It's almost always beautiful because they don't fuck around. They really are telling you something. Rosie's telling all her feelings to her niece. She's justifying her life. She's saying, "I lived for love." It's very romantic and yet she's a very independent woman. For her time. She's from my parents' time, and she worked in the garment industry, like all of them did. Got theatre crazy, and worked in the theatre and then went back to the garment industry. And she had this big love affair with this guy. But the story is invented. Rose is a cross between my aunts and other people. And the actor is a typical actor, Jewish. You bring it all together so that you hear it for the first time. For that kind of speech . . . We *all* hear a lot and say a lot, more than you would think. A lot of us . . . we're cut off from our language. The language of place. You should hear the way people talk up here. It's beautiful! I'm awestruck. It's when the place is dis-placed and the language is used up, it's dead. People move around too much, and they become afraid to speak their own language. I don't see television the way most people do. I see it as a destroyer of concentration rather than of language. There's dead language everywhere. We're cut off from the truth of our tongues.

KH: That's a very physical image . . .

GP: I think we're taught to use a dead language in school. To write a certain way, a dead way. When I was a kid, we came from immigrant families, and everybody was going to be a teacher. In order to teach they had to go through a real flattening of their language. To talk something called "Hunter College English." They had these interviews in which they had to speak in a certain way, and I remember them training. Boy was I mad! I swore I'd *never* give up my own accent. But my awareness of this was very keen because they were older than I.

KH: It seems to me that language is the place where your stories start. Some stories seem to be almost pure language . . . "The Floating Truth" . . .

GP: That's funny. It's interesting about that story. I'd written the first page and I had no intention of going on with it. I read it to Jess, my former husband, and he said, "You'd better finish that. That's funny. You finish it now." That story is really about work; about doing work in this world.

KH: And language?

GP: They're all about language. But it's gotta be true.

KH: How do you mean true?

GP: I invent people, and they speak. And if they're speaking wrong, you know it. You read it aloud to yourself, and you know nobody ever spoke like that, or ever said that, or ever felt that. You know when you are forcing things. You don't know in the beginning. Sometimes you really want your people to fall in love, or to be happy, or to commit suicide. A lot of writers are crazy about having people commit suicide to end their books. But people don't usually commit suicide. It spoils it for me that in Chopin's *The Awakening,* the woman kills herself. And it's bad that Anna Karenina kills herself. I mean, some insist criticism is saying that Tolstoy had no right to have Anna kill herself. And I can agree with that. Both of them have the wrong idea. The wrong idea of how much terrible life people can bear.

KH: In one story you have characters come to life and do things that the writer didn't expect them to do.

GP: That happens to all writers. Characters begin to live their own lives. Your people, or your non-people or your vegetables, or whatever, get away from you.

KH: Regarding the integrity of your own characters, at the writers conference you spoke about the difference between ego and vanity, is this related to the truth of language?

GP: You can't fall in love with your own work. I don't mean that you have to be humble, I mean when you have too much vanity, when you love yourself too much, it's evident in your work. And that self-love, that self-admiration fights too much against the important factor of attention to what's outside. It's the quality of attention to what is outside, or even inside. It's flawed by vanity. Cause you keep changing the truth. Vanity is the destroyer of truth. But ego is what helps you think something is worth putting down. You have to have a certain sense of yourself. For a long time I thought women's lives . . . I didn't really think I was shit, but I really thought my life as a woman was shit. Who could be interested in this crap? I was very interested in it, but I didn't have enough social ego to put it down. I had to develop that to a point where I said, "I don't give a damn." Women who have thought their lives were boring have found they're interesting to one another.

KH: Is that part of what you meant when you said something about your stories taking what is dark and hidden and recreating a balance in the world?

GP: Something like that. Stories illuminate. That's the purpose of a story for me. To shine a light on what's dark and give it light. And the balance is something else . . . it's justice.

KH: What are you most interested in balancing?

GP: The dark lives of women. This is what made me write to begin with. And at the time I thought no one would be interested in seeing it. But that I had to illuminate it anyway. If for nobody else, for myself and my friends.

KH: I don't think there are many stories in your work where women are *with* men. The men are gone, or they are leaving, or just meeting . . .

GP: Well, that's the way it was, pretty much. You see the women's movement has really done a lot of good for men. I see a lot of young guys who are just totally different from the way men of other generations were brought up to be. They go into careers like child-care . . . things like that.

And I don't think that the men would have been able to do that of decency without the women's movement.

KH: Even in the few stories where the women are with men, the men go off into other worlds . . . and the women stay home with the kids.

GP: It happens like that. Women should be very careful with men. Men are attracted to women with children because they themselves want that kind of care. Maternal care. But then when they get there, the women aren't really keen to give that maternal care, since they already have kids. Then the guys get sore. Women want something else from men which the men won't give them. So the guy will do something to make the women leave. That's part of the game. In "Livid and Pallid," that maternal pride is ironic. That story is the beginning of feminism. Her sense of separation. The idea that her life really is different from the men's. That they are in a world that really was not her concern.

KH: How do you see men in relationship to women?

GP: Well, I never think about marriage. I never write about marriage. I *do* think a lot about family. I think about love and family . . . As the world changed and women became more free, there were lots of problems. On the other hand, there were a lot of problems before that. My mother was very oppressed, yet my father never could have thought of himself that way. He *adored* women. And my mother's oppression was not by him alone. We always think in terms of individuals and that is where we go wrong. My mother was oppressed by her circumstances. Coming here to this country . . . who were they going to educate? They put all their money into my father, the male. And he paid off. He took care of everybody. But that meant my mother didn't get to do any of the things she wanted to do. But that wasn't *his* fault. Another example. My family encouraged me in every way. They wanted me to be a doctor, or a lawyer, or a teacher. But society outside said, "You gotta get married and have children." My mother didn't want me to fool around with guys and screw and get knocked up. But apart from that, they wanted me to be as educated as any man. But it was society which told me, "You better concern yourself with boys."

KH: Still your women are always alone, independent . . .

GP: Yes they are alone, but it was a time when women were becoming conscious of themselves as women.

KH: In some of your stories, it seems that men resist any kind of commitment. "The Contest" for instance.

GP: That's the first story I wrote.

KH: You put that story in the mouth of the man. Why?

GP: I was thinking about women and what was wrong between men and women and I thought "Why not see how a man thinks on this issue?" So I let him do the talking.

KH: You're still rough on him.

GP: I sure was. I let him talk his own language, and let him say exactly what he wanted to say. And I've had men come up to me and say, "That was really great! You really understand him. He really let that bitch have it!"

KH: How about the guy in "The Irrevocable Diameter"?

GP: I like him. He's nice. That's . . . the other. Why should *I* always tell the story? I like the other to tell the story.

KH: Why did you place that story in his consciousness?

GP: I was trying to think of a guy who wasn't a bad guy in this situation. You know with one of those little girls who aren't bad little girls, but who are powerful. He's got a nice mother . . . They're making a film out of that story. Some people in Chicago . . .

KH: Do you think you portray the women in your stories as victims?

GP: No. I don't understand that word. In fact, some of them are better off without the men. If the men were there, *then* they'd be victims. In the story, when Clifford leaves, she ceases to be a victim. While he is there, she is. But Everybody's a victim. We're more victims of our society. And men are much more victims than women. I think. I think my women characters are very strong. Their children strengthen them a lot. I don't even think Ginny's a victim. She really likes the guy; and she refuses to be a victim. I feel that the women are very remarkable. That's what interested me in these women in the first place. How strong they were. Having a hard time is not being a victim. It's how you deal with it.

KH: What do you mean that the men are victims?

GP: Well, they were more lonesome. They didn't know what to do. They were prey to this fear that they weren't macho enough which is as bad as being macho.

KH: Yet in your stories, there's a lack of competitiveness. Not much guilt . . .

GP: I'm very short on guilt. Sometimes someone else tries to impose it . . .

KH: Yet there is suffering.

GP: All of life is tragic. Sorrow is just natural. We're born into death.

There's lots of loss going on in the world day and night. If you believe that the child is miraculous, there's sadness there too. I see my little grandchild, and I know how wonderful she is, how amazing . . . Yet, I know she's going to grow up in a world where she may not get to be six years old . . . I can't stand even saying it. So it's just regular old sorrow and misery. I mean the world may not last. Just the other day Ronald Reagan said that the arms race is necessary. He has to be insane. INSANE! And all the people listening. They have to be insane too.

KH: Well, that's always been the American way, hasn't it? You go to the local bar; you flex your muscles.

GP: It's always been the European way too. I will not knock America on that. I don't see what's so great about Europeans either. The French are doing their nuclear number to *themselves*. To their own country. Their own people better get after them. If you think the people of the United States are crazy, the people in Europe are even crazier. Because, the way America is going to work it out, the Americans and the Russians are going to fight out the war on Europe's soil. And the Europeans did it to themselves. They got all that stupid American crap right stuck in the middle of their countries. And the British buying the Trident . . . they just make themselves targets. I would have said a while ago, that we'd never get off scott free. But I think that between them, the Americans would destroy Eastern Europe, and the Russians would destroy Western Europe. And the two big fat blobs would continue. People in Europe are really stupid . . . On the other hand, there is something going on now. There is an international movement against nuclear energy, against the arms race. But the left here and there were the very last people to get into the anti-nuclear movement. But you have to accept that the world may come to an end, until you're persuaded that it's going to happen, you're just being like all the Europeans and Russians and all the other people who said, "The second world war is not coming." Or, "Hitler is not so bad." Or "They do not have those ovens" . . .

KH: You went to China?
GP: Yeah, five years ago. Bob and I.

KH: Can you tell me about it?
GP: I wrote about it, in the *New Yorker* piece.

KH: Where else have you been?
GP: Russia, Chile . . .

KH: As a tourist?
GP: China we toured. And we went to Chile. It was supposed to be

socialism happening then, with Allende. We were there just before he was killed. Just before it ceased to happen. We stayed there a couple of months. And then we went to Russia to a world peace council, a congress. I went to Russia from the War Resisters League. My most interesting trip of my life was in 1969, when I went to Vietnam. I went to bring back prisoners of war. We spent months travelling in North Vietnam. We went to the DMZ and saw what we had done . . .

KH: Can you talk about that?
GP: No.

KH: Did you get the prisoners back?
GP: Yes, the Vietnamese were sending back three prisoners every now and then for the peace movement. They weren't giving them to the American government. All they were asking was that these prisoners not be used by the Air Force again. Ha! Within six months they were all back, training new pilots. So the Vietnamese stopped sending them back.

KH: When you write do you think about the kind of relationship you want to establish between the way you tell your stories and your readers?
GP: I don't like to think about that. I write for my friends, to tell the stories of their lives.

KH: Do you consider yourself a feminist?
GP: Very strongly. But what does "feminist" mean? Feminism means political consciousness. It means that you see the relationship between the life of women and the political life and power around her. From there you can take any route you want. You can become a separatist . . . but that's just . . . those are just actions. That is not feminism. That's the political stand you take in fighting for women. You can take a very strong woman . . . We recently had a case up here in Vermont. A woman who could do everything . . . built her own house, did everything, knew everything about energy. But had absolutely no understanding of the fact that when she began to tangle with some of the power around here that she was really being fucked as a woman. She thought it was purely personal. When you think things are purely personal, that's not . . . you're not acting with political consciousness. We tried to show her that the guy was using masculine power . . . This guy was a co-worker with her, he never put her name on anything they did together. Didn't introduce her around. And she thought it was personal. But by working this through personally, you're not going to do anything at all. You'll cheer yourself up, maybe, but you're not doing anything for women anywhere.

KH: So you work mostly with women? With women for peace for example. Do you feel these issues are connected?

GP: I do, but I'm working in the anti-war movement with men too. I always will. I do see that in a lot of these issues women take a lot stronger, more intransigent stand simply because of the way we were raised. We simply weren't raised to beat each other's brains out. Maybe some day we will be. But so far, women have not been raised to feel that. They don't think it's the appropriate reaction. Most men do think it is appropriate to take some kind of stand. They stick out their fists, or their cocks, or their guns. The arms race was not created by women. Of the 40% of the scientists in this country working for the military establishment, maybe 95% of them are men. Not that women wouldn't do it . . . But so far it is not the world of women . . .

KH: Since a lot of your stories were about women with kids, does the fact that your own kids are grown up change what you write about?

GP: To a certain extent. Because I've covered that subject already, as much as I can. Also, I'm doing different things. It's hard to know yet. "Dreamer in a Dead Language," (*American Review*, 26) follows on "Faith in the Afternoon." It is another visit to an old age home (where no one in my family every lived, by the way) and the thing on China is totally different. And the one called "Friends" *(New Yorker)* is really about us all, with the children grown up. In a way, now, I feel much freer to deal with lots of different things. Women's lives are just as interesting later on, after they have kids, maybe more so. Life is just continuously interesting, but something's been written, and I've already read it, I tend not to need to write about it myself. I write stories that I need to hear. There are things I want to know about, and I don't know about. Once I read a story by someone else, I find out all about it. It's not very interesting for me to investigate the same thing.

KH: As far as what your father says about your not having a plot or characters. What do you think of that.

GP: I think I've got a lot of plot. A plot is a line that if you start at the beginning, and you walk along it till you come to the end . . .

KH: OK, you do have plot, but the spaces are not filled in. It goes fast. You don't do a lot of character elaboration or psychologizing. You say to your father something about having a mistrust of narratives.

GP: I don't like plot, it's true. It's too much of a line. It just goes a different way. It moves by pictures. Certainly "The Burdened Man" is pure plot, and the kids in the subway, and the little girl being killed is not about her being killed. It's about the guy who tells the story. In the first story in the book, the guy that loved Rosie her whole life; it's a long plot. Just because I said in one story that I don't believe in plot a lot of people say that there is no plot, which isn't true. So many things happen, like to Ginny. She leads an interesting life. I mean there's to figure out what to do and meets this guy, and he leaves. I see that as a very simple plot. What I *am* against is *thinking* about plot. And it is not the way I write. I just sort of build up a train, and all of a sudden, I look at it, and its track. I didn't look for the track to put the train on. And plot does *not* move the story along. People pull you to the next event. Life pulls you. The story of the little girl getting murdered . . . I told it from five different points of view before I figured out what was the right way. You see you do a lot of things you don't know how to do yet. You don't make a decision to do something so much as you . . . can't. You are totally unable. You don't know how. You can't teach yourself to do the other thing.

The classical things are really quite marvelous, you know. It's just they have degenerated into a kind of "well-made-story" of our time. But you could learn forever from them. Look at Maupassant's very short stories. Those wonderful short stories about soldiers. They are just beautiful. He could do everything in three pages. And academics, of course, were scared to use those to teach kids to write, cause they'd never learn how to make the "well-made-story." And there's Gertrude Stein . . . those six stories. Then I get to one of Joyce's stories. So simple. So . . . so much happening in them to ordinary people..

KH: That was something that came up at the writers conference at Berkeley. The "Ordinariness" of your stories. Ordinary is such a strange word . . . What does it mean?

GP: I don't know what they mean. I think it means that writers write about other writers or about intellectuals, or about academics. One reason I don't write about those people is that other writers have already done it.

KH: Those types are pretty ordinary too . . .

GP: Or statesmen, or heroes, or senators . . .

KH: Yet you write about life, death, desertion, loss, divorce, failure, love . . . What else is there to write about? Perhaps it is because your characters are women that others perceive your subject as "ordinary" . . .

GP: It's daily life. I wouldn't call it ordinary, just daily life . . . And I'm very anti-symbolical.

KH: But if you write you use symbols . . .

GP: Except for the symbols of language, words, and writing . . . I don't write about anything but what I'm writing about. I am not writing about meaning beyond the meaning.

KH: Still that itself becomes a consistent point of view, that creates a pattern, which would yield symbols . . .

GP: I'm anti-mystic too . . . I don't feel mystic. What I think is mysterious is life. What I'm trying to do is to show how mysterious ordinary life is. But you're right, if you're at all surrealistic when you write, you do go beyond just telling. Life in "The Long Distance Runner," I'm writing about a woman going back, but I'm also writing about a place and a time and a specific relation to it. You do mean more than you say. Which I suppose is better than saying more than you mean . . .

KH: Could you ever write a novel?

GP: Yes.

KH: Are you writing one?

GP: I'm writing a long piece. If I ever get it done. It might not be more than 35 pages. People can make their own novels out of a story, if it were told differently. But I find most novels written today absolutely inflated. And almost any of them could be told in one or two pages. It depends on your attitude to language. Most novels are too boring for words.

KH: What is your attitude to language?

GP: I think we've already talked about that . . .

KH: In terms of the short story form, you have a way of collapsing time. . In the story where the woman is talking to that guy in the playground. He impregnates her with an Italian and a Pole.

GP: I like that story a lot. One of the editors wanted me to leave it out of the book, but I really liked it. "Politics" is the title. Don [Barthelme] also loved it and stuck by me on that.

KH: It happens so fast. Or, at the beginning of "Wants," "I saw my ex-husband on the street, I was sitting on the steps of the new library. 'Hello my life,' I said. We had once been married for 27 years, so I felt justified." A whole life in a flash.

GP: That comes from starting to write later in life. Time goes by so fast. And I think you *can* cover a lot in a short period of time. It's one of the gifts of the short story. I don't think you need transitions. You're taught about transitions, but you don't need them. People's imagination has been changed a lot by television. You sit and look at some TV shows, some of the worst, some of the cheapest, and you'll see them do technical tricks with time that Don [Barthelme], Coover, Barth, and everybody rolled into one would be terrified to do. Kids say that something they read is too hard for them; yet watching TV they are making jumps and assumptions and understanding things that none of those so called postmodernists could *dare* to do. And yet, these crappy hack-writers on TV know their audience, and know that they really can pull off an awful lot of stuff.

KH: Has your writing been influenced by television?

GP: No. We have all been influenced by that use of time. You know all the arts feed each other. It's just that any more information in my stories would be extraneous and boring and only make the work much longer than it needs to be.

KH: Another thing that depresses your father in "Faith in the Afternoon" is the story of the woman who remains hooked on drugs. He asks, "What becomes of this woman?" and you say, "Well, she goes out, and she gets off drugs and she becomes a receptionist in the free clinic." That's a lot of leeway. . .

GP: When I say these stories are generational . . . the father comes from a time when nothing could change. You couldn't have three careers in your life. You were lucky if you had one. You didn't have three wives in your life; you were lucky if you had one. You made a decision when you were seventeen, and you made it for life. In my father's time you have the character to carry everything through or else you died.

KH: So that makes for a different form in writing, the old notion of irrevocability?

GP: Absolutely. Now you do have choices. As far as my father was concerned there were only one or two . . . But my characters do have limitations . . . financial and so forth. "The Burdened Man" is about a guy who has a very narrow life, which he widens for one minute . . .

KH: Perhaps that explains the timeless quality of your stories. It is more a sense of place that fixes them.

GP: It's the park that brings all the people together. Our house was a decent house, but it was really a tenement right at the Port Authority, full of giant trucks going in and out, a hard neighborhood, a Cuban brothel on the same street. It was a very mixed neighborhood, but it has a very strong street life that my kids still remember with pleasure. That was where Ginny and Mrs. Raftery are from.

KH: There you go, turning your characters into real people again . . .

GP: You know in "Conversations with my Father," that's really very much him. My father and *me*. Having an argument which is the essence of all the arguments we had about art and life . . . the different positions we had . . . discussions.

KH: You do say at the beginning of the book that he *is* real. Why did you not fictionalize him?

GP: Cause he had just died, and I wanted . . . to . . . to . . . you know . . .

KH: And you had a lot of talks about your writing?

GP: No. *That* one was about writing. But we didn't talk that much about my writing. We talked about a lot of things.

KH: But he did object to your kind of writing?

GP: He was very funny. He was a very advanced guy. He came from a Russian, socialist, Puritan background (those socialists are very puritanical!) And so he had this kind of puritanical attitude about things. He was very tough on me.

KH: He objected to your always joking around?

GP: Yes, but he was the original joker. He was *always* joking around. He had the best sense of humor of anyone I ever knew. He would tell a joke and my mother would say . . . "ach!"

KH: She was a serious person?
GP: Yes.

KH: You wrote something about her in *Ms*?
GP: Yes. That one is true. It's autobiographical.

KH: But you don't write about her in your stories . . .

GP: She died when I was about 20 years old. I lived with a lot of women. I lived with my father, but I lived with my mother, my aunt, my grandmother, and my sister. So I have a more generalized Mother-feeling. Momness is less specific for me. And then . . .

My mother's death was really very hard . . . and very terrible . . . And It's hard for me to deal with. I deal with it a little bit in "Friends," talking about dying . . . It's just . . that . . . she could have died! I have an awful lot of feeling about that. It's pretty hard. I mean she'd been sick since I was about 13. You know, really sick. And I think that's where a lot of my pain comes from. That long period when I kept trying to think of something else all the time. My father lived to be about 90. So did my grandmother.

KH: How long was it before you could write about death?

GP: Well, I'm getting older, and I think about dying more. I'm closer to people that die now. If you didn't think about death it would be unnatural. I've thought a lot about coming, now I have to start thinking about going.

KH: Does writing help you deal with death?

GP: Writing does not help me deal with anything! I don't look at the facts of life as something that you have to be "helped to deal with." Unless you just can't deal with life. If you're a person who can't deal with life, you're not going to be able to deal with death. So, I don't have that therapeutical attitude towards the things one does. I mean if I wrote a poem, it doesn't help me to *deal* with it, helps me to *think* about it. If I'm going to write something about a kid dying, I'm really doing a couple of things. I'm knocking wood about such an event. 'Cause it's totally invented, and yet could happen every day, and probably has happened several times in the New York subways. And I'm investigating something. I'm trying to understand what that event is. And what it is to the people around it. What it is to the other little boys. What it is to the motor man. What it is to the women. And what it is mostly to the mother. What that loss is. So I'm trying to understand. Not to deal with it. I'm not soothing myself. I'm as unsoothed at those deaths right this minute as I was when I began to write about them.

KH: John Hawkes gave a talk in Paris a few years ago, and he writes such horrifying stories. But he says, "I'm a comic writer" . . .

GP: He's so sweet . . .

KH: And you read his stories, and you don't laugh very much. Yet when one reads your stories, one laughs a lot. Yet you say that you're *not* a comic writer.

GP: Yes, but I know they're funny . . . He's awfully sweet, John. You wouldn't think, reading his books.

KH: You know a lot of the people writing these days . . .

GP: I do now. When I was in my first book and really up to my second, I knew very few writers. And that was just the way I wanted it. I didn't like knowing them. But as time went on, I became very close to one or two writers. They lived across from me. Don Barthelme in particular who is one of my best friends, whom I love, really, very deeply. And then I became active in the writers' organization PEN, through Don. So I've gotten to know a lot of them. I never would have believed it would happen, because I was studiously avoiding it. I spent 20 years trying to hang out where I wouldn't meet them. But now, I do have to say, that I sure do know a lot of writers. But there, I see the relationship as very personal. Hardly literary. That's a flaw in me . . .

KH: Why do you put it that way?

GP: I don't talk enough about literature. Tillie Olsen is very dear to me. When I see her and stay with her . . . or Marge Piercy . . . Two very different people. And I just don't talk about literature with them.

KH: Don't you read each other's work?

GP: Oh, I read every word! But we don't talk about it. *I* don't. They would. I do very little of that with them.

KH: You just don't like literaturizing?

GP: No, I think it comes from my early fear of academics. It's really not very valuable or interesting. But it's blunted both my tongue and my ear on the subject.

KH: And here you are about to be taken over by the academics.

GP: Well, it's only in the schools that we are read.

KH: Do you read these people whom we've mentioned—Coover, Barthelme, Barth. Do any of them influence your work?

GP: Everybody you read influences you. But I still think most of your influences are made early. When my first book was written, I'd never heard of most of these people.

KH: Barthelme says that you influence his writing . . . what you do with the sentence . . .

GP: I think that's true.

KH: What do you think he means?

GP: I don't know. He likes my work. And he's very gracious. I think a lot of what influences a writer is what you hear in the street, the language you hear, the way people talk, the way,—the rhythms, the song, the language of your childhood. When I was in Russia, I felt very familiar with them, but that was just that they put the same kind of herring on the table and the people talked like my mother and father. My grandmother never spoke English at home. My parents spoke Russian. But my family also *cultivated* a love of language, a love of poetry. I was privileged to be the child of people who had been poor working people who had this love and respect for language and who carried on an old socialist tradition from Europe.

KH: Is there any order to the stories in the collections?

GP: Yes, I arrange them very carefully. But they're not in the order that they were written at all. The first thing is I try to start out with an interesting story, but then, in general . . .

KH: Do you group them in any sort of thematic way?

GP: No, it just seems to read right. I'd go over it and over it. And you know, not have all the very long ones together . . .

KH: Rhythm?

GP: Yes, some long ones, some short ones, some heavy ones, then, some lighter.

Grace Paley: Fragments for a Portrait in Collage
Blanche H. Gelfant / 1980

From *Women Writing in America* (Hanover: UP of New England, 1984), 11–29. Reprinted by permission of the publisher.

The only time I ever belonged to an underground was when I joined the coterie of Grace Paley fans who admired her stories before they became widely known. Her first collection, *The Little Disturbances of Man*, was passed to me under the table, as it were, as a test of initiation. If I became ecstatic over the strange elliptical snappy funny stories I would be *in*. How could I resist when Paley spoke a wise-cracking smart lingo that to me was native speech? Those of us in the Paley underground in the sixties waited with proverbial bated breath for the next story, the new collection. When it arrived, *Enormous Changes at the Last Minute* showed that in Paley's fiction, and in life, there is continuity rather than final ending. The apocalyptic last minute, when possibilities are closed and hope dies, has never occurred for Paley, though it has for others of her generation who have come to believe that the world will never change and their fruitless attempts to change it must cease. This is not to say that Paley is a vapid optimist, as no one could think after reading "Samuel" and "The Little Girl," stories in which mere children gratuitously die. Paley knows about death, and about drugs, human loneliness, disappointment, violence, rape; but she has learned the secret of how to survive the knowledge as a writer and a woman in the public world. Her ever-increasing visibility makes her an exemplary figure to other women, a burden that she should find light to bear since all she need do is be her self. This "portrait" is based upon real encounters with Paley and fantasies.

Settings and Encounters, Real and Imagined

In Hanover, New Hampshire, you meet your best friends—and your enemies—at the Co-op Food Market on the Lebanon Road. Waiting at the meat counter, you tell about your children, off to school or coming home, your latest trip, skiing, maybe, or backpacking, or cruising the Greek Isles, the gossip—how terrible that so-and-so is separating or permutating, or sick, or drinking again. You leave the Co-op quickened.

You have your freshly cut meat, natural bread, a wedge of Vermont cheese, and a sense of daily life, ordinary repetitive happenings that tell of the little disturbances of man.

One day in the summer of 1975, a short, pleasant, homey-looking woman was wandering down the cookie aisle of the Co-op. She looked familiar to me, as people do in small-town places. Suddenly, I recalled other times and other settings, occasions that her presence inspired: a party in a loggy country house in Erieville, New York, given in her honor by the English Department of Syracuse University; and not long afterwards, a cocktail gathering in a Manhattan hotel room crowded with professors talking to her volubly (and probably meanly) about the Modern Language Association meeting they were attending. She wore, on that wintry evening, long black boots, a woolen plaid poncho that seemed to me then bohemian, and loose, comfortable clothes which were like her manner, easy but city-wise. Her hair was held back in a bun that carelessly let little wisps escape and fall about her face. Everything about her seemed casual, plainly and naturally there, set outside of time at a time when women teased and sprayed their hair into wires and wore glossy clothes. I see now that she had the deceptively simple style of her stories, but as with the stories, the style aroused interest and curiosity. You might be missing something in that casual put-togetherness, of her clothes or her words, in that easy surface beneath which, you will discover, lies coiled an intent to arrest, an insight into disturbance, a relentless intelligence alert to life and its enormous changes.

Pushing my shopping cart, I ran to her in the cookie aisle. I had just published a review of her new book of stories, *Enormous Changes at the Last Minute,* and I had something to offer her: my adulation—but since that was intangible, I proposed instead a cup of coffee, and we talked. We were to talk again various times over the next few years, and to me our conversations were always as elliptical as the form of her stories: something was being left out, the secret, a wonderful secret, I thought, that should be shared because it was rare and precious, and someday I was going to ask it directly of this elusively mysterious woman.

"Huh," I imagine her saying, "Me mysterious! What's mysterious about me?"

"Oh, ho," I would answer. "What isn't? You tell me. What were you doing in the cookie aisle of the Co-op? How come you're living a village life in Thetford, Vermont—your boots and poncho now a country style? You, a city-people person! Look at you and the Bronx, and you and Brooklyn and Coney Island, and all the city people in your stories. How

could you leave them, even for a summer, when they're still sitting on the stoop steps eating ice cream, or setting up their orange crates to squat in front of the house for the day, watching the world go by—your world? The city streets need you to watch the women who are sitting by the windows watching the streets. You're the one who knows them, how they yell down at the kids and throw them apples and nickels for candy. How can you stay away," I would say, "even for a year, from the Northeast Playground where your women get together and carry on playground politics that's not so different from life? What about the city parks, where you put Faith up a tree? You can't go away to the country and leave Faith behind, the way Goodman Brown did [I thought a high-class literary touch would flatter and persuade]. And the city tenements where Faith's kitchen is a world with love and death and desertion going on, and children growing up. You're the one who made Faith tell her son Richard about the city, a setting she asked him, and you asked us, to love. Where else could Richard go to school with Jews, Presbyterians, and bohemians, and a smart Chinese like Arnold Lee? Faith said. In what other setting?"

FAITH TO RICHARD:

Now Richard, listen to me, Arnold's an interesting boy; you wouldn't meet a kid like him anywhere but here or Hong Kong. So use some of these advantages I've given you. I could be living in the country, which I love, but I know how hard that is on children—I stay here in this creepy slum. I dwell in soot and slime just so you can meet kids like Arnold Lee and live on this wonderful block with all the Irish and Puerto Ricans, although God knows why there aren't any Negro children for you to play with . . . (original ellipsis)

("Faith in a Tree")

Naturally, the Critic Now Appears

Out of context, Faith's words may seem ironical—"tough and cheery" in the Paley manner, and cleverly inverted—so unaccustomed are we to praise of the city as a place to live, let alone bring up children. But in the story, Faith means what she says. She likes all kinds of kids, as Richard jealously complains. She likes the polyglot faces and personalities that tumble about her in the city's parks, playgrounds, and housing projects, in the subways and the streets. She really regrets that her son has no black children to play with, tough little boys like Samuel who, in the short story "Samuel," jiggles and hops on subway platforms, where accidentally he is killed. Samuel turns out to be irreplaceable, as is every person to someone of Paley's sensibility and profession. She sees herself as a kind of catcher in the rye, saving the heedless running children of the streets—and the adults—from falling over the cliff of time into oblivion. Rescue is the writer's responsibility, explains the narrator of "Debts," who is, like Paley, a storyteller: "It was possible that I did owe something to my family and the families of my friends. That is, to tell their stories as simply as possible, in order, you might say, to save a few lives." (Start by trying to save a few lives on paper, and you might end a pacifist like Paley, protesting the waste of lives in the Vietnam War.) Samuel dies in the subway—and the runaway in "The Little Girl" dies in an appalling way the writer cannot allow—but the stories of their death memorialize them and assert the unique value of each living boy and girl. Soon after her son's death, Samuel's mother has another child, but "immediately she saw that this baby wasn't Samuel. She and her husband together have had other children, but never again will a boy exactly like Samuel be known."

This sense of the value of life—of every individual life and of life as process and change—may be exactly what we mean by faith; and Paley's heroine, who pops in and out of her stories, growing older and treasuring both past and future, is well named. Faith believes in the possibilities of personal change, and she is not frightened or appalled by social change, the transition of neighborhoods in the city, for instance, from white to black. Jolted by a seemingly gratuitous encounter—like running into an ex-husband on the library steps or a neighborhood cop in the park—Paley's heroine will change her hairdo, her job, her "style of living and telling." Faith comes down from the tree and enters the world where there are peace marchers against the Vietnam War, and policemen who won't permit them, and children like Richard who scream and stamp their feet, strapped dangerously in skates, and protest against repression. Her son's fury transforms Faith (wise mother to be led by a child) into a woman who thinks "more and more and every day about the world."

In the story "The Long-Distance Runner" (like all Paley stories, comic and convincing though incredible, unimaginable by anyone else and yet about anyone and everyone), Faith runs backwards to her past as she revisits "the old neighborhood" to see what is new in the world: the future. Black children swarm "the houses and streets where her childhood happened," and there, "as though she was still a child," she "learns" as she lives for three weeks in the apartment where she grew up, held willing prisoner by the black lady Mrs. Luddy, whose stories and son and person she comes to love. Love makes life continuous, a process in which change does not destroy but rather conserves and carries on essential meanings and relationships: another family in the

Brooklyn apartment, another race, another color, but still mother and son and an exchange of life-giving stories, still a baby crawling around in diapers, still life and death, and humor. Still, also, the staccato city-talk of people, combination of cliché, wisecrack, and insult: fresh, as in *fresh kid* and as vigorous, new, and immediately alive.

MRS. LUDDY AND FAITH:
   The next morning Mrs. Luddy woke me up.
   Time to go, she said.
   What?
   Home.
   What? I said.
   Well, don't you think your little spoiled boys crying for you? Where's Mama? They standing in the window. Time to go lady. This ain't Free Vacation Farm. Time we was by ourself a little.
   Oh Ma, said Donald, she ain't a lot of trouble. Go on, get Eloise, she hollering. And button up your lip.
   She didn't offer me coffee. She looked at me strictly all the time. I tried to look strictly back, but I failed because I loved the sight of her.

("The Long-Distance Runner")

The Critic Continues

I find in such passages not irony, but sentiment. Expressed differently, the feelings might seem cloying or cute, but the hard-boiled elliptical style controls the emotions it exposes. In a comic outlandish way, the story evokes a sense of love, hope, faith, and interest—plain old-fashioned interest in life and its idiosyncratic open-ended twists and turns. You never know where a Paley story is heading, though you know the conventions that should rule literary events, especially the convention that stories must have an end. Belief in the possibilities of change clashes with the literary convention of closure. "She can change," insists the narrator about the heroine of the story she tells in "A Conversation with My Father." Describing his daughter as a writer, the father enumerates Paley's qualities: "Number One: You have a nice sense of humor. Number Two: I see you can't tell a plain story." The father, who knows what stories should be, having read Chekhov and de Maupassant, demands "tragedy. The end of a person": "Tragedy! Plain tragedy! Historical tragedy! No hope. The end." But though she wants to please her father, the story-telling daughter feels a responsibility to the woman she has invented: she wants to rescue her from the inexorability of plot, that "absolute line between two points . . . [which] takes all hope away."

Conventional plots bring stories to a predetermined end, but the hopeful writer who believes in the possibilities of change—and so looks for ways to skew the straight line of destiny—will try to save her characters, even those who die, from an unalterable fate. If oblivion seems an inelectable end for the ordinary women, men, and children who scramble briefly on our city streets, then remembering them in stories becomes an act of human defiance as well as of rescue. Caring for those who would otherwise be forgotten, the storyteller shields her characters and her readers from a dark nihilistic vision of emptiness, the ultimate end that makes life a meaningless drama and its actors not tragic but simply null. "Everyone, real or invented, deserves the open destiny of life," the daughter tells her father, a man of eighty-six, bedridden with rubbery legs, and approaching death. Even so, he wants to hear stories, and though he demands from them tragic denouements, stories save him from a tragic end: he cannot worm one out of his daughter, nor can he ever be extirpated from the invented "conversation" in which he exists, one that by its open-ended form fixes him forever into a context of hope. "With you, it's all a joke," he says accusingly in a funny story where nothing is a joke—not life or death or the responsibilities of art—but everything may be joked about.

Paley's joking seems a way of searching within life's inevitabilities for a loophole—some surprise opening in the concatenation of events that seem to serious and acquiescent observers inexorably linked. Refusing to follow the absolute straight line of causality, which she sees as the tyranny of plot, Paley traces loops and twists and unexpected turnings that circumvent doom. These curlicues seem comic, jokes that Paley plays on life; and whenever her twistings of plot pivot around death, as in "Samuel," "A Little Girl," and "Friends," they allow the story a last laugh, for its final turn will openly defy death by invoking art. As long as the story lives, the person whose death it describes cannot be dissolved into nothingness. This notion that art confers immortality implies the timelessness of great literature; indeed, it traditionally defines greatness. Paley's stories show courage and aplomb by slipping themselves into this definition, for by their style, form, and tone—all Bronx derived—they relinquish every sign of portentousness, every means of literary inflation, that would seem to make them equal to the grand theme of the immortality of art. Still, the stories are clearly conscious of their purposes and processes as art; and like much contemporary fiction, they call attention to this art by self-reference: by stories within stories that are invented before our eyes, and by comments on stories that define the nature of fiction and its relationship to truth.

In the story "Friends," death cannot dissolve the "lifelong attachments" that make family and friendship inviolable to time. Pressed by time, dying Selena wants to think about her dead daughter Abby, who lives on in a mother's memory: "I want to lie down and think about Abby. Nothing special. Just think about her, you know." And all of the friends, Ann, Susan, and Faith, want to think about Selena. Faith has her own way of thinking, her way of inventing stories about what happened, of finding the truth in the facts. Her wise son Tonto protests against her versions of life, just as the father in conversation with his daughter had protested against her failure "to look tragedy in the face."

TONTO TO FAITH:
Here she goes with her goody-goodies—everything is so groovy wonderful far-out terrific. Next thing you'll say people are darling and the world is *so* nice and round that Union Carbide will never blow it up.

FAITH'S FINAL WORD:
Anthony's world—poor, dense, defenseless thing—rolls round and round. Living and dying are fastened to its surface and stuffed into its softer parts.
He was right to call my attention to its suffering and danger. He was right to harass my responsible nature. But I was right to invent for my friends and our children a report on these private deaths and the condition of our lifelong attachments.

("Friends")

Love between parent and child, one of the lifelong attachments in Paley's stories, permits disagreement without a rupture of relationship. Tonto lovingly serves his mother herb tea to soothe her sorrow over dying Selena, but also he mocks her way of seeing and telling the truth about the facts of life they both observe. Like the father in "A Conversation with My Father," he preempts the critic's role by challenging his mother as storyteller, accusing her of a whitewashing optimism that glosses over tragedy and, perhaps, the imminence of doom. Faith's defense is ignorance of various kinds: of who someone really is, of whom someone might become under pressure of the times. When Tonto will not allow this (nor will the critic), Faith resorts to simple assertion of what she knows, while at the same time she challenges what Tonto, or anyone, can know ultimately about someone else, even one's daughter or son.

A BRIEF DIALOGUE:
O.K., Faith. I know you feel terrible. But how come Selena never realized about Abby?
Anthony, what the hell do I realize about you?

Come on, you had to be blind. I was just a little kid, and *I* saw. Honest to God. Ma.

Listen, Tonto. Basically Abby was O.K. She was. You don't know yet what their times can do to a person.

("Friends")

Cynicism and hope, dissolution and attachments, endings and continuities—these oppositions create the vital thematic tension of Paley's stories. They do not avoid the losses in life they seem to cancel or absorb by their unique style, a style at once wisecracking and poetic, tough and sentimental, sorrowing and comic. Though Faith wonders how anyone can really know her own times, she does try to discover their meaning, running a long distance to find out "what in the world is coming next" ("The Long-Distance Runner"); and the stories *do* know that children are killed by meaningless accidents or drugs or by the times; that women are deserted by their husbands and lovers; that little girls are beaten and raped and cannot go on living. Knowing all this, the stories distance us from loss by their wise smart-alecky tone, while they present a vision of life that would reconcile us to loss by valuing loyalty—that is, by making art an expression of faith in the meaningfulness of love for one's family and friends. After listening to Tonto, Faith accords herself the last word, insisting on her right to report in her own way on the death of lifelong friends. Despite criticism she cannot disregard, she remains loyal to her version of the ineffable facts of life and death, to her judgment that Abby and Selena are *basically O.K.,* worth thinking about and remembering and telling about even though they are, perhaps, unknowable. All one knows, all the story tells, elliptically and yet completely, is that friendships exist: they can be formed almost instantaneously between women; they last; and they survive death when friends remember each other and record their memories in stories.

Friendships in Paley's stories are inseparable from place, from the neighborhood streets, playgrounds, parks where urban congestion fosters intimacy and interest. Friendships, like geraniums, bloom in kitchens. Love runs up and down a flight of stairs and enters one flat and another in the housing projects. Paley's characters convene for coffee. They do not meet for cocktails or cookouts, for tennis games or ski parties; they do not cruise the Greek Isles (though in "Somewhere Else" they tour China "with politics in mind"). They would not run into each other in the fancy-food aisle of small-town New England co-ops. The streets of Brooklyn or the Bronx bring them together—streets where Paley formed the attachments that have been her lifelong concern as a writer.

A Writer's Writer

Grace Paley's first collection of stories, *The Little Disturbances of Man,* appeared in 1959, when Paley was thirty-seven years old. In 1974, she published a second volume of stories entitled *Enormous Changes at the Last Minute.* These two collections have established her considerable reputation as a writer—an extraordinarily strong reputation considering that her early stories consistently met with rejection, her first book disappeared from print for several years, and her style, which does not appeal to everyone, stuns responsive readers in ways they find elusive. She achieves an almost inexplicable compression in her fiction. Even her short short stories, like "Love," produce the effect of totality: they tell of life, the whole of life, and not of incidents; and the art of their telling is so consummate and yet so neatly concealed—her stories are in their own way as seamless as Katherine Anne Porter's—that she has become, like Porter, a writer's writer. Her peers have praised her publicly. Philip Roth called her a "genuine writer of prose," and Herbert Gold, "an exciting writer." Susan Sontag, perhaps selling short Paley's deliberate artistry, called her "a rare kind of writer"—a "natural." Donald Barthelme said simply she was "wonderful." For many years during the sixties, Paley was an underground favorite, one whose book was passed from hand to hand, from one reader to the next, especially when *Little Disturbances* was out of print. Now she appears in such chic magazines as *Esquire* and the *New Yorker.* The Bronx is not out of her system, but like blue jean cloth and corduroy, used originally for workingmen's trousers, it has been accepted as fashionable material by the arbiters of style.

A Woman's Person

I admire Paley as someone who eludes stereotypes, sexual or otherwise. Not prolific in her output over the years, she is not, on the other hand, *silenced.* I mean this in the way that Tillie Olsen has described silenced women: those who could and should but do not write. The spaces between publication are not blanks in Paley's life, but life itself—her life.

Paley was born in the Bronx in 1922. Her parents were Jews in flight from Czarist Russia, where their religion and their socialism placed their lives in jeopardy. In America, her father lived the Jewish immigrant success story; he studied and became a doctor (see Paley's introductory tribute in *Enormous Changes*); but he and her uncles, who gathered in the Bronx apartment kitchen to discuss life, retained their belief in socialism. She was *brought up,* to use her words, *with a lot of their particular kind of idealism: I just kind of inhaled their early lives.** In her own life she has persistently acted upon this idealism, a belief, essentially, in the possibilities for social justice—a faith that the will of *good people* like her parents might prevail. *You know the idea that you can't fight City Hall—well, you can.*

Readers who generally want more of her work may complain that Paley's political activism has usurped time from her writing, but Paley disagrees: *I don't think or talk in terms of a career as a writer, but I think about myself and most other people as leading whole lives. People really use the day the way they want to. They may not be doing the particular things I do, but they do things that are considered all right for others— like drinking for three hours in an afternoon. Tillie Olsen pointed this out to me. She said people were angry because I spent my time doing something else, but nobody criticizes the people who spend three hours simply drinking in the afternoon.*

Paley has always been a pacifist, and now the constant threat of nuclear arms proliferation keeps her busy. Her area for political activity has expanded from the neighborhood around Washington Square Park, to Washington, D.C., to the world. In 1961 she helped organize the Greenwich Village Peace Center, in which she served as secretary. In 1969, she traveled with her husband, the poet Bob Nichols, to Hanoi, trying, like her heroine Faith, to see "what in the world is coming next." Out of that visit eventually came the story "Somewhere Else," typically funny, oblique, complex, and comprehensive (see the *New Yorker*, October 23, 1978). She went to Moscow in 1973 to attend the World Peace Conference. A life now divided between New York and New England has not divided her political activities: *If you work where you are and you're serious, you have a chance for a good deal of change. For instance, out of over thirty-five towns in Vermont, over thirty voted—after a lot of hard work—to ban uranium mining in the state. Also the passage of nuclear waste through many of these towns was banned.* Alert to dangers in New Hampshire as well as in Vermont, she participated in the protest against the building of the Seabrook nuclear plant. She has not avoided jail. Perhaps at least six days in jail (served in 1966 for her sit-down protest against military force) were inevitable for someone who had *inhaled* idealism early and exhaled it everywhere—into the air of the neighborhood playground where mothers "became conscious of power structure and power itself" as they gathered around the public sandbox ("Northeast Playground"). In her

---
*Italicized passages are direct quotations from Paley in our August 1980 interview. See below, Questions and Answers.

fiction, as in her experience, women are political, aware of world events as well as of sandbox group dynamics, a fact she sometimes presents comically. Here, for example, is the ending to the story "Northeast Playground," one of my favorite passages.

PLAYGROUNDS AND POLITICS:
The afternoon I visited [the playground], I asked one or two simple questions and made a statement.
I asked [two young unwed mothers], Wouldn't it be better if you mixed in with the other mothers and babies who are really a friendly bunch?
They said, No.
I asked, What do you think this ghettoization will do to your children?
They smiled proudly.
Then I stated: In a way, it was like this when my children were little babies. The ladies who once wore *I Like Ike* buttons sat on the south side of the sandbox, and the rest of us who were revisionist Communist and revisionist Zionist registered Democrats sat on the north side.
In response to my statement, NO kidding! most of them said.
Beat it, said Janice.

By the time she was seventeen, Paley had dropped out of Hunter College—almost accidentally: *I would go to school, but I could never get up to the classroom. I could sometimes get to the first floor, but I couldn't get into the classroom. I would meet someone, and talk to them, and that would be it. You know, a conversation anyplace stopped me from doing anything. . . .* By the time she was twenty, she was married to Jess Paley, her first husband, with whom she lived for over twenty years and with whom she had a son and a daughter. Her daughter, Paley said recently (while visiting a class at Dartmouth College), knows her better than anyone else—a tribute to a mother-daughter relationship that visibly impressed the young women students listening to Paley talk about the influence of the city on her fiction. Her daughter was there too, listening. Her son has recently made her a grandmother, and like all grandmothers, she always happens to have in her purse a picture of the new baby.

She is much in demand for readings, lectures, and guest professorships. The summer of 1980 was interlaced with a flying trip to San Francisco, where she and her husband read from their works, and a two-week teaching assignment at Cazenovia College in upper New York state. She is admired and sought after by women, and she gives herself generously to their activities in the academy and in the community. The portrayal of women in her stories is original, warm, and intelligent. Women are as important to her as she is to them. Her enduring feeling for them grew naturally out of a shared daily experience of motherhood: *I still can't forget how much I learned about human life being not just with my own kids, but with other women and their children. I can never repay the debt that I have to the community of women with whom I raised my kids. I owe them a lot, and they owe me. I mean, we began in those days friendships that lasted for thirty years.* Her stories constantly repay such debts, lovingly and with interest.

During the year, she teaches at Sarah Lawrence College, dividing her time between her Manhattan apartment and her house in Thetford, Vermont. There, where children, stepchildren, and children's friends arrive and depart in unpredictable sequence, two dogs guard the grounds with deceptive ferocity. Recently, one of them was shot by an arrow. The quiet countryside allows no escape from man's disturbances, sometimes unmotivated except by archaic malice. Occasionally, Paley shops, as we know, in the Hanover Co-op, and she uses the Allen Street laundromat regularly. If you ran into her there, you would probably not suspect that she is a writer, a writer's writer, a teacher, public speaker, an active pacifist, and jailbird—though you would assume she is a housewife and mother. She would probably speak to you in the quick and interested way of her characters, and tell you right off that she is a grandmother. She says occasionally that she wants to lose a few pounds, but her life is too full, I think, and too absorbing to allow her to concentrate on a diet. Nevertheless, when she came for an interview, I prepared carrot sticks.

Questions and Answers—an Interview, Sort Of

The interview took place August 1980, not in an elegant Manhattan apartment overlooking the Hudson, and not between two sophisticates sipping drinks that clinked delicately as they spoke. We ate tuna fish sandwiches and carrot sticks and drank experimental coffee—I wasn't used to the stove—in the little dining room in the little college house into which I had recently moved. The boxes and disorder that I had warned Paley about, had tried to warn her away from, didn't bother her, she said. She liked to see how people lived. The short interview had taken a long time to arrange. I saw how busy and dispersed her life was as I tried, time after time, to catch her; and even now she was soon to elude me, running off to the White River Junction bus station to meet a stranger riding down from Montreal to interview her. Ah, well! Meanwhile, here we were, munching brain food and vitamins, and I was on the verge of exploring a mystery. How did she manage in her stories to make out of odd and minimal bits and pieces—little disturbances—a whole world?

Even more mysterious than art was life. How did she manage to make for herself—as a woman and a writer—the whole life that she thought most people lived, though many people, especially women of her background and generation, would describe themselves as truncated, silenced, somehow incomplete? She knew how to place together incompatible fragments of experience to create unexpectedly a tense but harmonious whole. It was the secret of collage.

Question: I'd like to begin by remarking that you have taken many different roads in life, while most of us, like the speaker in Robert Frost's poem, take one and then regret the other roads not taken. You are a writer, teacher, lecturer, wife, mother, political activist, feminist—the list could go on. I don't want to present you as Superwoman, and yet you've managed to follow many roads when most of us find it hard to follow one. I'd like ultimately to ask your secret about being able to make the combinations you do to achieve in your fiction and your life a sense of wholeness. Perhaps I could ask first which road, if any, has priority for you?

Answer: *I think at different times of your life, different roads, as you put it, are the road you're really on. It's not a question of preferring them; you happen to be walking on them, and there's just no way out. When your kids are small, or even when they're bigger, that's your main road. But, really, nobody travels only one road: it's not only hard to travel on one road; it's almost impossible. I think that's true for almost anybody in one way or another. Nobody lives without a personal life. What I do is not unusual.*

Question: I think many women find what you do exemplary and wonder how you do it.

Answer: *Well, you really do some things by neglecting other things, if you want to look at it in that negative way. Very often when I'm doing political stuff, I should be writing. This last couple of weeks I've been doing a lot of writing, but I did it by not going to a meeting in New York which I considered not only terribly important, but very meaningful to me. It was a convention in the southeast Bronx, which is my neighborhood, a place where I grew up and very important to me. I neglected that.*

Question: How do you decide what is politically important to you?

Answer: *I'm not really very cerebral about any of these things. I'm just pushed by the time and the weather as much as anything. A couple of years ago, not a lot of people were doing antinuclear plant work. It was something I thought about, the great terrors and dangers, and I was* upset. *I felt I had to go and do things. Today I feel other people are doing just as well and better than I.*

Question: You seem to have had a capacity to recognize very early what is crucial. How do you pick up early clues? Peace, of course, is a crucial issue.

Answer: *I think everybody thinks it is, and there's nobody who thinks war is good; but I happen to have always thought about these things. I believe in a kind of fidelity to your own early ideas; it's a kind of antagonism in me to prevailing fads.*

Question: How do you distinguish what is important from a fad?

Answer: *I'm trying to think about that. . . . One of the problems would be not knowing what happened last year or two years ago. Around Seabrook, for instance, one young man, whom I liked a great deal, had just gone into antinuclear plant work, and he was saying, "Never before has anything been done here." Well, you have to explain to people that there's a long, long history. The radical history of this country is now being brought back to the people who have forgotten it.*

Question: There is certainly a serious attempt now to recover what we have lost of our past—the radical past, women's history, the history of minority cultures. To pursue the subject of your political activities a little: what are some of the victories that you recall?

Answer: *I don't think in terms of victories. When you think how bad the world is right now, you don't think you've done anything. We're soon going to elect either Reagan or Carter, and I don't know how we're going to survive either. We're really small people fighting against fantastic powers. Still, there are local victories that make you feel you could go on from there, small victories that put you in a good mood for a year or so.*

Question: Why do you think we've come to the impasse you describe, to choices that many people consider nonchoices for the presidency?

Answer: *For one thing, the presidency has become less and less important than who owns the president—who has the money and the power to elect. Even in Vermont, millions of dollars are being raised to put in one candidate and beat another. Our country is so rich: I think terrible things come from extreme wealth and greed. And terrible things come from poverty.*

Question: To switch, rather abruptly, from one road to another—from politics to writing—let me ask you what fosters or hinders your work as a writer. Children, for instance: you have said that when your children were small, then it was clear that the road you have to take was that of a mother.

Answer: *Well, you don't have to. What I say is not how I think other people should live. I think that if people have great difficulty in being with their children, they shouldn't be with them. I'm powerfully pro-choice—not just on whether or not you should have a baby, but on how you should raise it. Some people couldn't do a worse thing than stay with their kids. It's hard for them; it's hard for the kids. For me, it was just a continuation of street life. I was fascinated by them. I mean, here it is twenty-five, thirty years later, and I still can't forget how interesting the whole thing was.*

Question: Then you didn't feel the conflict between wanting to write and wanting to care for your children that's described with such agony by poets like Sylvia Plath and Adrienne Rich?

Answer: *If Sylvia Plath could have gotten through the next year or two . . . Her period with those kids was probably the hardest, when they're very little, very demanding. Then, if you're trying to do something . . . but I can't speak exactly about that because one of the things I lacked at the time was ambition. It's not that I didn't want to be a writer; it's not that I didn't want to struggle. It's just that I was writing. I was writing at about the same rate that I was writing at other times. I was writing mostly poetry, and it wasn't that good. It really wasn't. And nothing I could do improved it. I mean, I worked on it and I worked on it and I worked on it. It stayed kind of—I won't say third rate, but second rate. And I knew it. I would every now and then write a really good poem, but I mean every now and then. I guess if you really want to write, anything else can stand in your way: going to school, having to clean the house, whatever you do. For me, having small kids didn't stand in my way any more than having to have a job. Before I had kids, I worked full-time.*

Question: Did you feel the lack of a mentor? Many young women today feel handicapped by not having women mentors, or any mentors, in the way a young man has.

Answer: *What do you mean by a man having a mentor?*

Question: He has someone, a teacher, who's interested in his career and takes it seriously.

Answer: *Well, there were great English teachers when I was a kid, wonderful women, and they encouraged me. I think they existed in high schools everywhere, women who should have been teaching in colleges* *but couldn't, you know, would never have been hired in those days. Now that I think of Hunter, and of N.Y.U., I remember there were mostly men. Of course now at Sarah Lawrence there are plenty of women, a whole bunch of us.*

Question: How did you find your medium, your unique story form?

Answer: *People ask, "What is your influence?" I think you come to think through subject material you're interested in. In my early thirties, I really become involved in the lives of the women around me. I had this subject matter really pummeling me, but I thought, "Aah, who'd be interested?" Most of the literature of the time came out of the Second World War, and it seemed to me that what I had to say was not really interesting; and so it sat in my head for a long, long time. I was reading Joyce, Proust, Virginia Woolf, Gertrude Stein.*

Question: What particular Gertrude Stein? Do you remember?

Answer: *Oh, I loved* Three Lives. *Those three things had a very strong sound for my ear. . . . When I wrote my first couple of stories, because of the poetry, I worked aloud from the very beginning. I would read a paragraph to myself and then type it, and then I'd reread it and I'd take it apart. And every day I'd reread what I wrote the day before aloud. That became my method.*

Question: You said you feared being cut off from ordinary life, the parks, the streets, the women and children—the source of what you write.

Answer: *Yes, I just loved the streets, and I love them to this day. We played in the streets all the time, and the grown-ups were in the streets all the time, and we had sandwiches in the streets, and someone would throw an apple down from the fourth floor so that you didn't have to come up. I remember all that with a great deal of affection. The streets are something I care about. I'm never averse to sitting down outside . . . with friends.*

Question: Well, it used to be a spectacle. People would take their folding chairs or boxes and sit all day on the street, just watching. It was more exciting than watching a movie. You knew all the characters and something interesting was always happening. A surprise!

Answer: *That's right. . . . Yeh. . . . Yeh.*

We sat and chewed carrot sticks, and then she ran off to meet the bus at White River Junction—in Vermont.

Clearing Her Throat: An Interview with Grace Paley
Joan Lidoff / 1981

From *Shenandoah: The Washington & Lee University Review* 32.3 (1981): 3–26. Reprinted by permission.

In April, 1981, Grace Paley came to the University of Texas at Austin to give readings, to teach, and to talk to students. This interview is a composite of our private talks and a discussion with my class studying women writers, and another creative writing class.

Many of the qualities of Grace Paley's writing voice resonate in her speaking voice. Her interest in and respect for her audience echo her narrators' respect for their characters, and the spirit of cooperation and communication between writer and reader in her short stories. Her conversation, like her fiction, always embodies the abstract in the concrete—not shunning large issues, but particularizing them with humor and tact. Life and literature are of a piece for her; being a writer is inextricable from being a mother, neighbor, friend, lover and political being. And so, appropriately, she here discusses her life and her storytelling art together with tolerance, humor and sly good sense, the graces of both her personal and literary style.

L: At your reading last night, you said that all story tellers are story hearers. Would you tell us some more about that?

P: If you're a person who doesn't pay attention, and who isn't listening, you won't be a writer, you won't even be a story teller. Those of you who are writers from the very beginning of your lives were probably unusually attentive children. You heard things that the other kids on the block really weren't listening to. You may not have known it; you didn't go around when you were six years old saying "Oh, what I heard today!" but you probably did tend to come home from school with more stories for your mother or for whoever your afternoon-listener was. If they were there, if there were people to listen, you tended to be a very talkative child. You were an extremely good listener also, which everybody doubted, always saying to you, "Will you listen?" when you knew that you heard four times as much as anybody. If there was no one to listen to you, you probably heard anyway. You were a listener and you felt crummy because you were storing up all this information all the time. There's an example in that really wonderful story in Chekhov where the son dies and the father is a coachman and he keeps going around looking for people to tell "My son, my boy died" to, to tell them what happened. And nobody is listening to him at all. Finally he just takes his horse and tells the story to the horse. I think there are a lot of story hearers that nobody listens to. I think the world is full of people that nobody listens to who have a lot to say. And then I think there are people who aren't saying anything, who are storing it all up for some moment.

L: Is there anyone in particular in your family who was a story teller who influenced you?

P: When I say a story hearer, that doesn't mean that you just listen to people tell stories. Sometimes you really are extracting them from people. You say, "Well, what happened?" And they say "Nothing." That happens in a lot of families. And it takes you years sometimes to extract stories from people in your family. But no, my father was a very good talker. And my mother as a result was somewhat more quiet. But he really was a good talker, and he spoke well about lots of things. A lot of people told stories: my grandmother, aunts, mother, sister. I don't think they thought of themselves as storytellers, but neither do most people. But almost everybody in this room, in this school, is a story teller. You tell stories all the time. So it's really one of the things that almost anybody can do. It's something that's natural. I have a little grandchild and I just know that from the first time she can put half a sentence together she's going to tell me some little story. She's already telling jokes. People tell stories everywhere in the world. When you and I were sitting around having coffee we must have told each other fourteen stories.

L: There does seem to be a quality in your writing voice of people sitting around a kitchen table telling stories.

P: Well, that's nice. I'm glad. We had a kind of family life with people around tables telling and speaking. My father talked an awful lot, when he had time, and my aunts told stories. Mostly people, as they get older, begin to defend their lives in some way. They say, I did this and this and this and why I did it. My aunt especially lived in constant defense of her life. Those are the stories people tell: what happened, and why and how.

Those are the stories I heard, and then the stories on the street. We had a very lively street life at that time in the Bronx. The descendants of those families don't realize the extent to which we lived on the street, played on the street, and the way the older people, the parents of my friends, would sit out on the street all the time. Everyone would sit out on boxes and folding chairs and talk, and that to me is also terribly interesting and quite different: they would be talking about in-laws, children, husbands, wives, what it was all about. That's what you listen for and what you expect when you are a kid: the next conversation will tell you what it's all about, if you only listen to it.

L: If we think about the particular qualities of your own story telling, isn't there a Yiddish cadence in your writing voice?

P: Yes, I do write with an accent. I did have three languages spoken around me when I was a kid: English and Russian and Yiddish. Those were my languages. That's what's in my ear, so it got through my Eustachian tubes or whatever into my throat, with several disease that also came along.

L: Did you also have more specifically literary influences from your home? You mentioned before the Old Testament.

P: My father was an atheist, but he really liked the Old Testament. I had a lot of Bible stories around; I loved reading it aloud. Sort of the way kids listen to the radio today, loud now. We used to listen to classical music just as loud. It's just what happens, I think; youngsters need to lie down in music, whatever the music is.

L: Do you consider other writers' influences on you? Or do you think of things from your life as the major influences on you?

P: You're close to that, really. Nobody whom I know now and love, no writer, is an influence, much; let's put it that way, people I love, like Tillie [Olsen], or Don Barthelme, two people whose work is very different. But the influences on me happened long ago. Isaac Babel: I never read him then. He's not an influence on me, but when I read him now, I think that he had the same grandparents I had and that those grandparents influenced him in Russia and me here. But I didn't know his work at all until long after my first book. But I love him, and he's strong to me.

L: What other writers are part of your past?

P: All the great books of English literature; we were all big readers, so we read everything. In Joyce, a certain formation of the short story. Those three stories of Gertrude Stein's, I think, are very important to me. When I began to think of short stories all those forms were interesting to me. But apart from that, I read everything a big reader reads, a nice middle class big reader.

L: Did you go to Joyce and Stein to think about the form of the short story?

P: I had read them when I was writing poetry; I read those things when I was in my teens. They were useful. I read a lot of poetry, and the poetry I read had a bad influence on my poetry. (It had to have had, because my poems weren't very good.) They were literary. Poetry was very literary in that period in a way that Joyce's *Dubliners* really isn't and maybe those other stories, those short ones of Stein's. And novels are often not literary in that sense. I read all the Russians, and I got to love a lot of writers who may have had something to do with my thinking about form. Like Ivy Compton-Burnett, but I never wrote like her. On the other hand, every now and then, just some snip of something comes. But I think the literary influences were really the styles of language at home, and conversations. I'd read a lot of poetry from an early age, so my poems were written with my reading ear. (For a year, I wrote like Auden, with an English accent.) In stories, I started listening to other voices than my own, and I began to be able to clear my own throat.

L: How did you start to write?

P: I was a good kid writer in school and in junior high and so forth. I really wrote all the time. But I didn't write stories until after I was thirty, about thirty-three or so.

L: What got you started on stories instead of poems?

P: Well, just the things we were talking about. First of all, my husband did encourage me, I have to say that. He did. But mostly, it was that I was really terribly upset and concerned about women, and men and kids and all of that. I became terribly interested in the life of women and children, how they were living apart from men. It just bugged me a lot. I had lived in Army camps with the guys during the second World War . . .

L: Was your husband in the Army?

P: Yes, he was a soldier. Everybody's husband was a soldier. I mean, that was a big war. But that really troubled me. Not so much troubles between the two of us, but more troubles among my friends and also a sudden consciousness—I won't say feminist consciousness, because I didn't know enough, but a certain female or feminine or woman's consciousness. . . .

L: From the lives of people around you?

P: Just feeling that I as a part of this bunch of women, that our lives were common and important. A lot of that came from working with women in PTA's and organizations like that, things that the early women's movement mocked and laughed at.

When I wrote poems, there was a lot of "I feel," so I made this a kind of generalized, slightly inaccurate definition for myself that when I was writing poems, it was really me speaking to the world, and when I was writing stories, it was really me getting the world to speak to me. But a lot of people do that in poetry now, as we get out of that big "I-I-I-I"—that's been the meaning of this whole country for a long time. As we got out of that, I think the poems change also. But for a long, long time in poetry, as poetry's area, place of living, got narrower and narrower, it was very hard to do anything but that. Because every other mode of expression was doing all the other things. Films were being epics and novels were taking over whole narrative areas. So the poem really was just left with this person, alone. When I was younger, I couldn't have made a story for anything.

L: How did you learn to?

P: It was sudden. You hear the expression "breakthrough," and it really was a breaking through. I had just been so distressed about—well, about the things I'm writing about: all these friendships and the guys upstairs and the women friends I was getting closer and closer to. And all of these problems: the way people live in this world and the relationships and . . . what it was all about—I just couldn't deal with it in poetry. I really had an awful lot of pressure. The first story I wrote, actually, was "The Contest." Because I was trying to figure out what made all these guys tick—this guy who was upstairs was the one really; I did my best, I got into his head and I just sorta sat there and I said, "I've gotta write this story." And then the second one was "Goodbye and Good Luck."

And before I wrote those stories, I was just stuck in my own voice. Until I was able to use other people's voices, until I was able to hear other people's voices, that I'd been hearing all my life, you know, I was just talking me-me-me. While I was doing that, I couldn't write these stories. And when I was able to get into other voices consciously, or use what I was hearing, and become the story hearer—when I could do that, I just suddenly wrote them. It was a true breakthrough. I'd written one story about eight years before and another one when I was about sixteen and that was it. I often think of how it could happen so suddenly. So I'm waiting for something else to happen suddenly. I don't know what, but something. Maybe we only get one sudden thing per life.

L: Do dreams play a very important part in your conception of stories?

P: No. I never really did a lot with that. I have some poems that come from dreams. And a lot of them relate in some way to my father, too. I mean, the four poems I've written about dreams—I just realized that, just this minute. It seems simple, I could have realized it before, but I didn't. But they are really in relation to my father.

L: How did it happen that you started publishing your stories?
P: Well, that was just luck, because I wrote three stories, and then I just showed them to a couple of friends and they liked them. And I thought, that's nice. I was happy about that.

L: What stories were they?
P: They were "The Contest," "Goodbye and Good Luck," and "A Woman Young and Old." I had a friend on the block whose kids used to look at television with my kids, and her husband was an editor and they were divorced. She was always trying to give him hard tasks. She said to him very angrily one day, "Well, the least you could do is read Grace's stories." He used to come around on Sunday; it was his Sunday to pick up his kids. He'd sit there like that, waiting for them to finish the program. So he read them and he liked them and he said, write seven more and we'll publish them. He was a senior editor at Doubleday. It was pure luck, really. But what was very interesting was that as I wrote them I would send them to magazines and they were returned, all the time. So if it hadn't been for him, I really might have stopped. Every one of the stories in *The Little Disturbances* was sent back by every single magazine—I mean every single magazine sent them back. And then finally two of them were published in *Accent*, which is a University of Illinois magazine. But all the magazines that later asked me for stuff sent 'em all back. It's hard because you keep sending stuff out and you keep getting it back. And it was a very lucky thing that I knew that the book would come out eventually anyway, so I kept going. But if I hadn't had that, I just don't know if I would have kept going. I mean you really need a lot of support.

L: How long did it take you to write the seven more after that?
P: About two years.

L: Do you think there's more support around now?
P: Yes, there is. I didn't know anybody who wrote. Actually, the truth is I didn't want to know anybody who wrote either. I really didn't. I really was scared of literary people and the literary life. And I was writing a lot of poetry, so it wasn't as though I didn't think about literature. I did think about literature. It meant a lot to me. But I really didn't want to know other writers. I just wanted to know people around in my neighborhood.

L: Has that changed?

P: Well, I do know a lot of writers. That's true. I didn't think I would, but I do. And it turned out that a lot of people that I just wanted to know on my block were also writers. Now I work with the Freedom to Write Committee at P.E.N. and the New York Feminist Writers' Guild—I mean, we're all writers, you know.

L: Have you ever lived anywhere other than New York?

P: Well, for short times, but not really lived. I have lived in Vermont a lot. I've lived there three whole years, three different, separate whole years.

L: When you talk about fiction, you connect it very closely with your life experiences. What do you think of this statement about the connections between life and art that Christina Stead wrote for a 1968 *Kenyon Review* symposium on the short story: The "ocean of story" is made up of "the million drops of water that are the looking-glass of all our lives." "What is unique about the short story is that we all can tell one, live one, even write one down; that story is steeped in our view and emotion. . . . Give writers a chance . . . (and by writers, I mean everyone, not professionals, I mean anyone with a poignant urge to tell something that happened to him once) and there will be no end to stories and what stories carry that make them vital, genuine experience and a personal viewpoint. . . . The essential for us is integrity and what is genuine. . . . That is what is best about the short story: it is real life for everyone; and everyone can tell one."

P: Well, I can't put it any better than that. That's exactly the way I begin a class, by telling everybody that they are storytellers; it is absolutely so. To go further, and to get away from the short story, because you really can't always hang out in the short story, there's the expression fiction and non-fiction. That's really taking things that are stories and saying they are not really stories at all, they are non-fiction. Imagine taking a book like *The Woman Warrior* and calling it non-fiction just because you think you can sell it better that way—because that's exactly why they did it. I asked Maxine Hong Kingston, how could they do that? How could they say that it is not story telling?

L: In a number of your short stories, and some of the best, you have continuing characters, especially the narrator, Faith. Do you ever consider putting them into a novel?

P: I could, but I wouldn't like that. Those Faith stories are part of the book they're in. You could play hopscotch, and take the book and make another book if you wanted to, but I would hate to break the integrity of those books.

L: Is Faith someone you identify with strongly?

P: Well, I do, somewhat. But when I first used her, she was absolutely not me at all. She really is my friend, up to whose house I went. I went up to see my friend Sybil, and I saw she was sitting there, and there were "two husbands disappointed by eggs." I mean that really was true, a present husband and a former husband and they were both sitting there complaining about the breakfast. And that was the first line of the story I wrote: "There were two husbands disappointed by eggs." And that was really the beginning of Faith too. Actually, from then on, it wasn't Sybil either. She began to just take on characteristics of at least four friends. She's somewhat different from me, but she's all of us, she's a collective us really, but she began with my friend Syb. I mean, Syb had one child and I had two. I have a girl and a boy, and there are two boys. Faith sort of became my women friends more than anything else . . . not a composite really, because you can't take four people and make a person. It's very hard to do. It's like cooking, I guess. But she became an invented person who lived in circumstances similar to most of the women I knew—which were not my circumstances, but which were the lives of women I knew pretty well during those years when my kids were small, and when I was very close mostly to lots of women with little kids.

L: So your stories come from real people, but not a real person.

P: Well, partly. Sometimes they're really invented, like "Goodbye and Good Luck," she's very much invented, although she comes from people of that generation.

L: Do your own kids get into your fiction?

P: All those children really represent my kids in some ways. As a mother, I couldn't omit at least one or two of my children's brilliant remarks. But a lot of them are lots of other kids talking and hanging out.

L: You have a daughter and a son, but you give Faith two sons, Richard and Tonto. Is there a reason for that?

P: Yes, I think the reason is this: I wanted her to have one boy at least, for other reasons, and I was very much afraid, at that time, if she had a daughter, that I would begin to just do Nora, who was my first child and therefore the one I spoke to the most and whose voice to this day is always in my ear. I didn't want to fall back on her a lot. But that was really the reason. I was scared, plain and simple, scared that it would be too close to home. When you asked me the other day why I gave her two sons and no daughter, it made me think about it. And actually I *knew* the reason but I'd never talked about it. But it's no secret. I have a daughter and that's the first child. And you're really very close to that first child, especially if you wanted to have her and you did. You have a lot of conversations going from about the age of four months on. A lot of talking going on. So you're very, very close. It doesn't mean that I wasn't close to my son; but I felt that if I put in that daughter I would really be sort of exploiting, using Nora up a lot, because she's very articulate, and her language is so good. I thought I would just be writing *her* and I think she would be really angry. I felt it would really curtail or hurt my imagining; I would not be able to imagine a first daughter different than Nora. I was able in that first child, Richard, to make that very close connection without it being a girl. I didn't think all that through so articulately as I'm telling it to you. It was just my feelings about it. I didn't dare to have that first little girl there.

L: Some of the new feminist psychological theories suggest that mothers and daughters often experience the kind of continuing feelings of merger that these internal voices suggest—that separations between mothers and daughters are not clear and distinct.

P: Well, it would depend. That's really the first daughter, I think. I mean, my mother and I weren't really that close. My mother and my older sister were really extremely close. It never bothered me one least little bit. I mean I had no particular jealousy of it. I was much younger and I just ended up with two mothers. Three mothers actually: a grandmother was there too and an aunt. That's four mothers. My other aunt—half a mother; four and a half mothers. So that I didn't miss that at all. But my sister Jean was as close as could be to my mother. I think it was wonderful for them. But it didn't bother me one bit.

L: The same theory suggests that women may continue to think of themselves more collectively, more in connection with other people, than as distinctly separate individuals. I would think that in literature that might lead to the kind of collective heroine your story "Friends" seems to me to have.

P: That's nice. I don't know if that's so, but I would like now that it's been said to think it myself. In that story "Friends" those women, we, *were* awfully close and we began by hanging out in the park together, but we did an awful lot of politics together. We really did have a collective existence in a way, you know. And in the anti-war movement, we were a different, older group of people. But we raised our kids a lot together, and that was the beginnings of a political period. There are a lot of people living like that now. I do want in some way to be able to speak for them, in a way that they've allowed me to.

L: There often seems to be another implicit character in your stories: the reader, a "you" to whom the stories are addressed.

P: I think a lot of story telling really comes from "I want to tell you something." Almost all stories come from that. From the very first time you walk into a house and say "I want to tell you something." That story "Friends" I really wrote for my friends; I hoped that they would read it. I wrote it toward them and also from them.

L: Are there other times in your stories that you have a specific "you" in your head that you are writing to?

P: Well, sometimes it's the people I am writing about. Like in "The Immigrant Story." I had always wanted to tell that story because I had always thought about those old people and how awful my friend had been towards them. I had always wanted to speak for them in some way. It's what we call in art what's dark; what's hidden is what we want to illuminate. When we say "This is what happened." 'If I didn't tell you, you'd never know it." Of course that's not true. Someone else would tell.

L: Your stories seem to tell a lot about—everydayness.

P: Well, that's what interests me. When I am asked—Is she a heroine?—I'm not really interested in that. I'm not interested in that extraordinary person to that extent, except to the degree that all these people are extraordinary to *me*. But how daily life is lived is a mystery to me. You write about what's a mystery to you. What is it like? Why do people do this? Every day, get up in the morning. . . .

L: How do your politics and your fiction fit together?

P: It's hard for me to say, really, if they do or not. You know, people take areas to write about. Marge Piercy chronicles for us a really specific world of young and getting older political activists. That's not ordinary everyday life, and yet it's essential. I don't say that what I write about is the only important thing. I know a lot of political people and I work a lot with them. But I just don't seem to write about them. I should, maybe sometimes it might be very interesting to do. Am I not writing about them because it's too hard, or am I not writing about them because they're not so interesting or mysterious to me? This political world seems to me too plain, somehow, and less interesting.

L: And there's more mystery in the lives of the kinds of people you do write about?

P: Yes.

L: One special kind of people who appear in your fiction a lot is children.

P: Yes. See, that interested me a lot. Women and children, and how little they're really used. You also write about things that you haven't read, things that you want to read yourself. And I happen to be very taken with kids.

L: And you don't find much about them in literature?

P: Yes, a class of women is written about in which the children are taken off by their nanny. All throughout literature women do have children, but they're taken some place else.

L: As Tillie Olsen says, few writers in the past have been mothers— have had children and written about it.

P: Yeah, right. The men wrote about it, but they carried the kids off a lot. Even though they were crazy about them. Like the Russians.

L: I have thought that women and children are really at the heart of your fiction. Men are important, but the bonds between women and men are not as continuing as those of women and children, or as the long-lasting friendships between women.

P: Well, when I first began to write, those were the women I knew. I myself was married and I remained so for twenty-five years but a lot of the women I knew were alone with children already then. Now it seems more common. And it was common in that neighborhood at that time too. Also, kids weren't in day care and so it was through the children that we women became friends, and in the park. That's where we really knew each other, that's where we made friends.

L: So you are like family?

P: Oh, yeah, sure. Not with all. Still, the other day my son wanted to go to the playground and take his baby, my little grandgirl. I got very excited about that, so I went there, and lo and behold, there was my friend Erica's son Tommy and his little boy. The two little kids were throwing balls back and forth and I had to run home and call Erica up and say, Erica, our *grandchildren* were playing ball!

L: A whole new generation.

P: Yes. And it's different than relatives you know, because there's nothing that holds you. The idea that women's friendships are new is weird to me; I don't understand it. Some of our smartest, nicest women have written a lot about the newness of women's bonds, but Jesus, my mother and all those women, my aunts, they all hung out every Saturday talking and were such a comfort to one another and they stuck by each other so.... Someone like Mary Daly doesn't even know how people live—but other women, I think they come from suburban lives or something like that, and no family. That's a certain kind of life but it's not general female life.

L: On the other hand, Mary Gordon just wrote an essay about friendship where she says friendship is real, but love is just a romantic notion, relatively recent in Western history. Since Aristotle it's been friendship more than romantic love that's at the heart of human relations. Would you agree with that?

P: The formulation of it? It's just words to me. I don't think it means that much. If you are going to marry someone, you had better marry a friend, there's no question about that. If you are going to live with someone, it had better be a friend. And you're in love many times in your life, several times in one's life. And romantic love is very . . . a lot of fun, I don't want to knock it. With all the troubles that come afterward, and it may all be a lie and imposed on us, but falling in love is peachy. And if it can happen to you, boy, that's great. And if it doesn't, then by all means, you should stick to your friends. But the best . . . It's true to say to any woman who wants to do any work in this world, and who happens to be either heterosexual or homosexual, it really doesn't matter, whatever the companion of your life is, short or long term, you'd better be friends. And you'd better be with a person who doesn't boss you around and either male dominate you or female dominate you or not allow you to be yourself in any way. I'm very pro friendship, but one needn't write articles against love (tsk, tsk). The young people today are dumb!

L: You have a nice way of writing about sex in your stories. That still seems to be a special problem for women authors. One of the characters in "Enormous Changes" says that you have to speak to a woman about sex in her own language. Women writers still seem to be working on a language for sex in fiction—rejecting some existing things, and not quite knowing what to use instead.

P: Well, I'm really not playing that game. Some people seem to have missed everything. In some article a writer wrote about how Ms. Paley writes about women and sexuality in these early stories, but the woman of today has gotten so far beyond her in writing about sexuality, that she's being left behind. And I thought, boy, that's just the direction I don't want to go. It was such a funny idea, that writing about sexuality meant to get more wildly genital, in every way. That's what she thought was the direction that one would want to go. Well, some women writers have gone in that direction, but mostly men.

L: Is there anything you're too close to to write about?

P: Well, certain family tragedies. Not all, some. Some I feel free to talk about. But certain things you just don't feel free to deal with. Or you deal with them, but nobody says you have to publish everything. Sometimes you have to write things that you're not going to publish. If you're a writer, you really got in that habit of getting all that pressure on paper. And you've done that. So I have several stories I've written about things that I really wouldn't like to publish, but which I'm perfectly willing to read to friends. There are a couple of stories where people would be terribly, terribly wounded. And I really mean that. I'm not talking about the ordinary things that people don't want people to know. I'm not being over-sensitive about that. I mean, you can have a family where they say, what! you wrote that there was a divorce! in that family! Now everybody knows! I don't mean anything like that. I mean really, things so terrifying that I had to write about them, and yet I don't really feel like. . . .

L: Mirra Banks was here this fall, and said that she was filming a couple of your stories.

P: They've filmed one story already, a story that's not in the book, it was called "Dreamer in a Dead Language." It was a visit to an old age home, the same old age home, the same visitor that's in a story called "Faith in the Afternoon." And it's another visit. The guy who played the lead, the father, was really an old Yiddish actor, and got very angry about it being called a dead language. He really got so angry about it that I didn't want him to be miserable the whole time, so we changed the title to "Jokes or Love Departed." So they made it; it's a story that's in the *American Review* (the last issue) under that title, "Dreamer in a Dead Language."

L: Do you like the movie?

P: Well, I like some of it. I like the parts the kids were in. It was filmed on Coney Island, so that really was nice—that whole boardwalk and the old amusement park. And it was very nice; I liked that, I like certain things. But I think that until people understand that film is really such an *aggressive* medium—I mean it *really* just pokes itself right in there like that. And it has to be handled a little subtly. There were parts that bothered me, and certain styles, like people, there are certain things that so embarrass me. There's one old woman who really is quite wild, and she wheels herself around in this wheelchair all the time. She talks a lot, and rather well, I think. And very clearly, and they just didn't. . . . What film does, it just doesn't let people be, you know; it's a very editing medium. People always say a photograph is objective. Well, film is editing of everything; instead of just letting this woman talk, which was bad enough, this great big, fat old lady just speak, they had the camera moving in on her, just really jamming in on her face like that, as though it needed tons of underlining. Things like that really bother me. And I think films do that an awful lot, whether people are experienced or not. I really didn't like things like that. But where they let the people just live a little bit and move around, I liked that.

L: Towards the beginning of our class, we were talking about writing, and a lot of people expressed the feeling that writing is aggressive—that when you write about someone, you violate something, perhaps some privacy or integrity of theirs. . . .

P: Well, when you write biography you certainly do. That's true enough, but what you're doing in a story—you're really not writing their life; I mean you're presumptuous if you think you are. You can't. You never know enough. What you're doing really is bringing lives together and speaking for groups of people, not for one person. Sometimes you want to write something and really honor a person. Writing something to let someone really have it, I don't think that's right. I'm against that. But mostly, when you're doing something worthwhile, or something that you're pressed to do, you're really illuminating a dark object, or person, or fact. But sometimes it *is* a nasty, aggressive thing. I mean that's not illuminating something; that's sort of like bringing in five hundred spotlights or something. And that really is not illuminating; that's really flattening out. That's a distorting act.

L: You've talked about working now with the short, short story. Can a story be too short?

P: More often it's too long. I used to think that when a story ended, people thought, well, that's it, there's no more; that would be a natural ending to things. But then I have a woman in my class right now, at this very moment, who always says that there isn't a story that ends, I want to know what happens *after* that. So that all the definitions I ever had were dashed by this woman's insistence on believing that the story is *so* much like life that you really want to know what's gonna happen next, all the time.

A story is for me . . . the word "conflict" is often used, and I don't really like that word; maybe it's because I'm a pacifist or whatever reason. I think it's just a more simple dialectic than that. I think it's two events or two characters or two winds or two different weathers or two ideas or whatever, bumping into each other, and what you hear, that's the story. And that can happen in two pages.

L: When you work on a story, do you consciously try to do something new with form?

P: Well, I don't like the word "new" because I've lived through a time when everything was new every five minutes, and it's very easy to be new. I mean, you stand on your head and then you find that people have been standing on their heads for years, so it wasn't new anyway. What happens is that you try to tell the story and then the story is complicated. Everybody is a story teller, but very often even in telling, someone is going to say, "Sister, I don't know how to tell you this story; how am I going to tell it to you? I've got to drag in my dead uncle and then at the same time there are these people in Hoboken." You really are faced with a problem of how to tell the story so that the story is known. And not all stories are simple. So you try to tell certain stories, but you need the form, that's what it is. You look for the form and until you have the form, you can't tell the story. And the form, I don't know how it's gotten; I consider it received, like grace. How to tell the story. I have a story in my book which I use as an example of that. It's called "The Immigrant Story." Well, I knew that story for twenty-five years. I didn't know how to tell it and I had to tell it not just in terms of the last paragraph which said, his mother and father came from Poland, etc., but in terms of everything that came after that which I had to put first. But I didn't understand that. It took me, really, twenty years to figure out how to tell that story so that it could be understood for what it was. That is not "new" . . . I don't think of that as "new." I just think of it as trying to tell a certain kind of story and not having the means. As far as I am concerned, the means did not exist in my literary education or in my experience so I had to wait until I had enough writing experience to be able to tell that story.

L: In your story "A Conversation with My Father," the characters discuss the problem of plot. People are sometimes critical of your stories, and say nothing happens in them, there is no plot. I wonder if perhaps that's a peculiarly woman's form of story, where a lot happens, but it's not always what's called plot.

P: Well, I think by writing that story I sort of screwed myself up, because people really don't read. I mean, a great deal happens in almost any one of those stories, really sometimes more than in lots of other peoples', enough to make a novel or something. When people say, well, she really doesn't care much about plot, all they're doing is repeating what I said in my story. Plot is nothing. Plot is only movement in time. If you move in time you have a plot, if you don't move in time, you don't have a plot, you just have a stand-still, a painting maybe, or you have something else. But if you move in time you have a plot.

L: Your stories move *around* in time—almost Einsteinian time; there's long time and short time. Do you intentionally compress time and spread it out?

P: That's the way I think. I say it has to move in time but that doesn't mean it moves dead ahead in time. It can curl around on itself, it can just fall down and slip out through one of the spirals and go back again. That's the way I see. I see us all in a great big bathtub of time just swimming around; everything's in this ocean called time and it's a place.

L: Is capturing memories or past time an important part of that?

P: I don't see it as capturing; to me it's there, in a funny way. My husband says it's that I live that way. Because I really never put things away that I need. I have letters my son wrote to my daughter when he was eight years old in my telephone book that I use today. It's not so much captured. It's as if you just put out your hand and there's your life, right there.

L: Your language seems to me like that, too; there will be things in a sentence like an adjective and a noun that come from completely different places but just sit there side by side.

P: I don't like to give up certain sayings. I was thinking of writing something about that, about hanging on to idioms and slangs of earlier times, not giving into the moment, being faithful to your own seventeenth year or something.

L: Going back to "A Conversation with My Father" . . .

P: Well, actually the story's about a couple of things. It's about story telling, but it's also really about generational attitudes towards life, and it's about history. I tend not to look at things psychologically so much, but historically, I think. And for him, he was quite right, from his point of view. He came from a world where there *was* no choice, where you couldn't really decide to change careers when you were forty-one years old, you know. You couldn't decide to do things like that. Once you were a junkie, that was the end of everything. Once you were anything, that was it. Who you were was what you were. And she was speaking really from her own particular historical moment, and in another country besides, where things were more open. So it wasn't that she was giving some philosophical attitude, or some attitude close to her own optimistic disposition, although both of those things were true. That's also true, but she was also really (although neither of them knew it, only the writer knew this), they were really speaking from their own latitude and longitude, and from their own time in history when they spoke about these things. So that's really, I think, what was happening there. And her feeling which she talked about in terms of stories was pretty much exactly the same. I mean she really lives at a time when things have more open possibility, and for a group or a class that had more possibilities and a generation in that line, because he was an immigrant and he just about got here and did all right by the skin of his teeth. So she was really speaking for people who had more open chances. And so she brought that into literature, because we just don't hop out of our time so easy.

L: Have you always felt that a lot of possibilities are open to you, that you can always change?

P: Well, I can change a lot of things. I'm not about to get younger, though. That's an important possibility that's been neglected somehow. I think there's more time than people realize. I do think so. I think for women, and men too, there's . . . see, people really come from where they grew up; what year they came to young womanhood or manhood is really important. And I've noticed that people in my family who became grownups (which is my sister and brother) during the Depression, they really have a much narrower view of what can happen, of what you can be and what you can't be and what you can do. I mean they have a very strong sense that you'd better do your homework and you'd better stay with it and you'd better move, you know. And that once you've got it, you stay there. The worst thing you can do in this world is make some sort of change. But I think that growing up into the Second World War was a much more—it sounds crazy to say this—but it really was a more open time. Not for the Europeans, it was pretty bad for them. But for America, for the people here, who were not fighting, it was a very exciting, wide-open period. So I have a sense, and a lot of people I know have a much more open feeling. The Depression ended; people began to make a little money who hadn't made any. People began to go to work; there were a lot of geographical—I guess they're called demographic now—demographic changes. So that it was very lively. So I think some of my feelings really come from my particular time and my particular place. That doesn't mean that's true for everybody at that period at all. People lost half their family, they're in a bad mood for life. But I have always felt a kind of stubbornness about doing what I wanted to do. I really wanted to have kids, and I had 'em. And I wanted to write, and I did that. I didn't want to go to school, so I didn't. And I didn't do a lot of things I didn't want to do. But I never had a big overhead or a big house or a big anything. I never got myself into straits where I was really stuck and where I had to support houses, or cars, or children in a way that would be too expensive. I felt they could get by on what I could get by on. I think people should keep a certain greed towards the things they want to do, and a certain riskiness. But that's for my time. We may be coming into a time that's going to be a lot narrower in a lot of ways, so I would hate to suggest that people live as I live.

L: I think there are a lot of women your age who didn't have that.

P: True, that's true. Yeah, because the thing that happened after the war that was really interesting was that all these women who had gone to all these colleges and so forth and so on and were very smart and had really good tweed suits and everything, the government started to, I mean the world, the society, everything, started to jam them right back into the kitchen, really pushed them right out of jobs and careers, back. And this whole business of having children (which I thought was my own idea, thought of it all by myself) really was a kind of social . . . so that I know lots of women who had four or five kids and who really felt that that's what they had to do. And that was really hard. I mean, you're right in that. But I had already become somewhat wayward before that happened. I had already blocked my chances for careers; I had already gotten kicked out of schools and stuff like that, before that all happened. So that I had no choice really, I mean in a sense I had no choice; that thing wasn't even open to me, which was a great relief.

L: Are you and Tillie Olsen friends?

P: Very good friends. We just got to know each other. I can't even remember the first time, but we have very . . . I mean, here's an example. She's about ten years older than I am, and she really grew up into the Depression, and was married at that time, and had kids at a very hard time. She went into really hard times when she was at that age, which I didn't. But we come from very similar backgrounds, really. Our families were Socialist Russian Jews mostly and we have very political feelings in common, and the sense that that tradition and that history have been really subverted and mocked, and a strong feeling for the lives of women. We have disagreements, too, I have to say, but of course I admire her an awful lot. And I think she's really *our* scholar, our own. I mean people have spoken to me and said I haven't done enough work; that I've been doing all this politics and stuff, and that's true. But she hasn't been doing a lot of her fiction work; she's been doing a lot of feminist scholarship. She's really done that for everybody, for all of us. So she means a lot.

L: She writes about silences, and the interruptions that mothers experience as part of their life and how that thwarts work, but then we were saying how she seems to use that so that she takes interruptions and makes a virtue of them in her style.

P: I think that's one reason people write short stories. I feel I was limited by that in a sense. Not that all women are. There's lots of women going out there and writing big, fat old novels right now. But I really happened to have liked a lot being with my kids, so I just wouldn't give that up; I don't give a damn. But it *is* an interruption. And my generation just took it. There's no reason why younger people should take it quite that way. I mean, I was raised to say . . . when I was growing up, I'd come in the house at three o'clock and my mother would say, "Shh! Papa's busy." There's no reason why a person can't come in the house and Daddy can't answer the door and say, "Shh! Mama's busy." No reason for that at all. And I think that can be done. But I feel that that had a lot to do with me writing short stories, and it probably had a lot to do with Tillie. She worked, too, in very responsible jobs in unions that her husband was involved in. So she had full time jobs most of the time as well. That's true. And in that she suffered what a great many men suffer too. I mean, they also have 9 to 5 jobs, or 9 to 6 or whatever, and they try to write at five in the morning or ten o'clock at night, and I don't think it's right not to recognize that fact as well. They usually *aren't* troubled by the same kind of distractive interruptions that women are. But the young fellows now, they're really getting into fatherhood very big. But, I think that's true.

L: Did you ever look for women writers, in particular, or look to find your own experience in your reading?

P: No, not when I was very young. It's not so much that I looked for women writers, but I had sense enough to know that, like Henry Miller, he wasn't writing for me. That's as far as I went. I knew that these guys, even the Beats—I thought they were nice, nice to see all those boys, and nice to see all the sexual feelings, but I knew it really wasn't written for me at all. It's not so much that I looked for women writers, as that I understood certain much admired writers, like Burroughs, weren't talking to me. There was nothing to get from them. Though at the same time I did get stuff from Proust. That talked to me, but all those ballsy American heroes had nothing to say to me, though my friends thought they were just hot shit, excuse me.

L: When did you start getting a sense of a female voice in literature?

P: Well, late really, after I was writing. My book was called *The Little Disturbances of Man*. And the subtitle was *Women and Men at Love*. And the very second edition, they wrote it "Men and Women at Love." They meant no harm by it, but you look at the first edition, the Doubleday edition; it says "Women and Men." It just got normally changed, because of the guy's ear. I didn't even see it myself, although I had been very strict and said, No, the "women" goes first.

L: Do you consider yourself a feminist writer?

P: I'm a feminist and a writer. Whatever is in here comes from the facts of my life. To leave them out would be false. I do write a lot about women and the men they know. That's who the people are and what they think about.

L: Who are some of the women writers around who are not feminists, who are simply writers, or even doing a disservice to the feminist cause?

P: I think an example would be Joan Didion. First, I have to say I dislike the word cause. I think she does a disservice to the feminist cause, to any progressive cause, and also to the clarity of language. I've read a couple of her books. I don't know anything about her except she's from California. Well, I mean, so is Tillie. Just goes to show. I think her style is very . . . sentimental really. And indirect and opaque. That's all. And we were talking about how fiction or literature should really illuminate. I mean, art in general, painting, whatever—you pick up the rock and what's hidden should be seen and known. And that's why a lot of women are doing interesting work, because they're really taking these lives that haven't been seen. And I think that what she does really is she takes these lives which haven't been seen and she puts another rock on them. So that's why I don't like her. I really don't feel that strongly about most; for instance, I think about *The Women's Room*, Marilyn French. Now, I can't read that book. I really can't. But I know that a lot of women love it. So I have to have regard for it; I mean it really must speak for an awful lot of women. Women really love it. For certain women it really says, ah, that's what it was like. But I can't read it, so I have that kind of mixed feelings. Now I know one of the reasons she has such big sales is I bought three copies trying to read it. I really mean well. And I tried the same thing with Erica Jong. But, on the other hand, there's no question but that they mean something to people. And I have to respect that fact, and feel that I'm missing something. Joyce Carol Oates? I don't read her much either. Well, I have to admit, that there's that woman and she does an awful lot of work, from a person who doesn't, you have to have a lot of regard for that. I do. There probably are pieces of work of hers that are very good, and I'd like to read those. I have a feeling she has done certain really good work, and I just haven't gotten to it.

L: Have you read Mary Gordon, who is so illuminating about Catholic culture?

P: Yeah, I read the first book. I liked it. I thought it was a very good piece of work. But for Catholic writers, you must also think of James Farrell. And *Studs Lonigan* is a wonderful, wonderful book. It's one of the most painful books. And what about this guy Powers who writes about priests all the time? Those are great stories.

L: Who do you like who's writing now.

P: I like E. M. Broner, any of you know her work? She's really interesting. she wrote a book called *Her Mothers* and another called *Weave of Women*. And she does different kinds of things all the time. I sure like Doris Lessing. Say some names to me and I'll tell you.

L: Do you like Virginia Woolf?

P: Oh, yeah. I thought you meant people this week. Oh sure. She was an important person that I read when I was young. And still is, and can be read again and again. But I remember trying to write like *Mrs. Dalloway* at one time. When I wasn't writing like W. H. Auden. And I like Brontë. Not just *Jane Eyre*, but *Villette* is a *wonderful* novel. And *Shirley* is interesting too. And I like Mrs. Gaskell. Why do we always call her Mrs? Elizabeth. She wrote *Mary Barton*. I think people are very familiar with that book. But *North and South* is really a very fine piece of work. A lot of *North and South* has that whole awful industrial growth in it, and she does naturally a lot better by her ladies than Dickens does, so it's really worth reading for that. There's a funny book called *Cranford* that has a lot of short things in it, but one of them is this scene where everybody is rushing down to get the paper which the next serial of either *Hard Times* or *Bleak House* is in. I felt like she must have felt a little annoyed about all that. But I like her an awful lot, and if you haven't read *North and South*, do.

L: Have you read Susan Sontag's short stories?

P: Susan Sontag has two stories that are absolutely magnificent. I just love her story about China. She came to our school and I made her read that story. Well, I didn't have to force her exactly; she had to read something. But I said, make sure you read "China." And then there's the other story, the one that says goodbye to everything. That's very beautiful. They're wonderful stories. I always want to see what she does. She sounds like she's going about her business right.

L: What about Alice Walker, Toni Morrison, Toni Cade Bambara?
P: They're all good. They're fine writers. Black women are really talking now because they're illuminating what's been hidden.

L: Are there any foreign women writers who have interested you?
P: Well, there's a very great book called *History* by Elsa Morante, which apparently the Italians look down on—I mean, she's Moravia's wife, how could she write a great book? But it is a great, wonderful book.

L: None of the French writers?
P: Well, not especially. I'm in a lot of communication with the French right now, from a lot of translations, of *me*, which is very surprising to me. I mean, I can't figure out what it means, because I don't really have an awful lot of feeling for them. One of my stories, "Faith in the Afternoon" is in French already.

L: How did you like it?
P: Well, I don't have a lot of French, but it sure sounded classy.

L: You're not really interested in the kind of theoretical speculations the French like, are you?
P: I went to a lot of those meetings at MLA, to try to see what's going on. I think a lot of that's interesting, but, see, first of all, for me the story exists really off the page in a way that for them, it's all lying around there on the table. And for a lot of Americans too it does. And I don't think that's the direction for literature to go. I see it getting deeper and deeper into the page, until it disappears out the back end of the book. So that's the direction it's going to take. It's not that I don't love the page. I mean I love the books. But we really have to think of the throat it comes out of. I feel it's too great a movement away from the people, if you want to put it that way, and certainly away from female life.

L: When you say it exists off the page, is that the kind of thing you mean?
P: I'm really speaking about speaking the story, or being able to say it and to tell it and to talk it. And I don't mean you can sit down and read a whole novel out loud. (Though I don't see why not. I mean I just think that there's no reason not to.) As for the story, it's not so much that you don't read it on the page, it's just that in the story itself there has to be some memory, some human memory of where it came from. Of course, most stories that the person writes are much more complicated than the

story you tell at the supper table. It's much more complicated, and it has to be attended to. But I think very complicated stories used to be heard all the time, and people really heard them. Sometimes because they heard them twice. At the same time, I love the privacy of the book and the privacy of your chair and your room and your book. That has got to not go. But that memory for me has to be somewhere in the story—that a person knew it and lived it and told it.

L: Are you thinking about tales from the oral tradition?

P: When you write them down they are different. It's not the same story. One is wrong to say that that's what the written story is; it's much more. What's changed is the time in which to tell the story. Still look how long—they had a lot of time cooking up the *Iliad*, right? They told it one way, then another way, then it got stuck in that particular way. And so we have time. We have time.

Grace Paley
Ruth Perry / 1981

From *Women Writers Talking*. Ed. Janet Todd (New York: Holmes & Meier Publishers, 1983), 34–56. Copyright © 1983 by Holmes & Meier Publishers, Inc. Reproduced by the permission of the publisher.

Grace Paley, writer, mother, peace activist, is the author of two collections of short stories: *The Little Disturbances of Man: Stories of Women and Men at Love* (New York: Doubleday, 1959 [second publication New York: Viking, 1968]) and *Enormous Changes at the Last Minute* (New York: Farrar, Straus & Giroux, 1974), and numerous poems and short pieces. She is fifty-eight years old and married to Robert Nichols, also a writer. They live in New York City, where Grace Paley was born and raised. She teaches a course in fiction writing at Sarah Lawrence College.

This interview began in Paley's long, cluttered apartment in the West Village and continued the next day, uptown at our mutual friend Sally Goodman's place, to provide against the steady stream of phone calls and visitors that flow through Grace's life. One of the interpolated visits the first day, which I have omitted here, was from Karen, one of Grace's friends, who was arrested at the Women's Pentagon Action on November 17, 1981, and who told us about her ten-day incarceration in Alderson prison.

Ruth Perry: How come you're never angry in your stories? I always admire your generosity, the fact that you never add to the stock of anger and hate in the world. The forbearance of the character Faith towards her friend Anne on the train ride home, in the story *Friends*, seems to me a good instance of that.

Grace Paley: I think what happens is humor sometimes takes the place of anger, and it may even subvert it. You know, in a way, sometimes there should be more anger, and there's humor instead.

Ruth Perry: What *do* you get angry at?

Grace Paley: Well, we did this antiwar action at the Pentagon, and we did it in four stages: Mourning, Rage, Empowering, Defiance. We began by walking through Arlington Cemetery, and when we came to the Pentagon, we walked in mourning, with a little bit of black on us here and there. And then we built this cemetery under the Pentagon for all our dead. I planted the Unknown Woman, and then there were these others. Karen Silkwood. The four little girls of Birmingham. There were many, forty or fifty of them. Someone made a marker for Jeannie Goldschmidt. All our dead. And then after that, from Mourning, they were going to go into Anger, and I didn't know how they were going to do it. But somebody walked the red puppet through, the giant red puppet from the Bread and Puppet Theater, made by Amy Trompeter, and *there* was anger. Everybody blew up. What I mean to say is, I was *very* angry. That's what I feel angry about. We just screamed at the building. People had been crying before, and now we were just bawling, just screaming at the building, telling it off, banging pots and pans, and hollering. People from the building peered out and then would go back and someone else would come out. And then after that was Empowering, when women really got all around the Pentagon, really did it, surrounded it. And then Defiance. Defiance. —We blocked the doors—then—the arrests. One hundred fifty people were arrested.

R.P.: One hundred fifty. Did they pay bail?

G.P.: No. Some of them didn't pay bail at all. You know Vera Williams? She's down in Alderson for thirty days. They put leg shackles on all the women. You know, you people from Massachusetts should send something to Tip O'Neill. Call those guys and say that you know those women on the peace action were sent down in leg chains on the very same day that the Ku Klux Klan men were acquitted of murder.

After being arrested in the November 17 Pentagon action for civil disobedience, Paley thought she might have to spend sometime in jail.

R.P.: Have you spent a lot of time in jail?

G.P.: No. No, I haven't really. I've been arrested a number of times, I've spent a couple of nights here and there but only once did I spend a week. I've never spent more than a week. If I spent thirty days that would be a lot for me. Still—I believe in the stubbornness of civil disobedience and I'm not afraid of it.

I remember one May Day demonstration. In 1971. Still wartime. We were arrested and we were in this big, sort of football field. Barbara Deming and I were walking around, arm in arm. We had been arrested together. It was very cold. Everybody was finding someone to walk very close to. Later on, one person wasn't enough, we would try to get into groups that huddled: fifteen. But at that point, Barbara and I were walking arm in arm and it was a pretty messy place, because that was the year they arrested thirteen or fourteen thousand people, just picking them up off the street, and then they didn't know what the hell to do with them. At that point we were in a football field. Later, we were put inside a stadium. And so we were walking around, arm in arm, talking to each other, and then congresspeople came in to see what was going on, and Bella Abzug came over to talk to us. She and I had always had these disagreements about the electoral work and what you can call action, direct action, and we would talk to each other about this. So she came over and she looked at me and Barbara walking arm in arm. She asked how we were. She was a congresswoman at this time. She was worried about us. We said we were all right. And then she said, "Well, I guess you're where you want to be and I'm where I want to be." And we laughed, we all laughed together.

And I want to say about Bella that she was at this Women's Pentagon demonstration. She came, she walked with everybody, she didn't look for any limelight of any kind. She just sort of walked, and begged me not to get arrested. Again, she said she thought it was a waste of time. I could do more outside. But she really was just a part of the action. That's what we wanted all of our leaders to be, just a part of the women's action.

R.P.: Do you think that women's politics are different from standard politics, less hierarchical?

G.P.: I don't believe we could have done this in a mixed group, with men.

R.P.: Why not?

G.P.: Well, first of all, a lot of the ritual stuff, the ideas, came from women who had been thinking about this way of acting for a long time.

R.P.: Well, I can see wearing black and wailing as imitating eons of Mediterranean women.

G.P.: Yeah, but I mean the whole four-phased ritual. I'll tell you another thing that struck me. Lots of young kids, young women, were arrested, and they were not well treated. They were not miserably treated, but they were grabbed and pushed and pulled. I mean, those marshals are all big, and some of them are mean and some of them nice, but pulling and pushing, you know. And those kids were all crying. And I was thinking how wonderful. And I reminded them, I said, you know, if you had twenty guys like the kind you go out with, those of you who go out with guys, if you had any of those guys here, you know they would not be able to cry? They would be tense, they would be maybe tough, they would have had in fact all kinds of feelings. But they wouldn't be bawling in anger and pain and frustration like you kids are. So I think that that freedom to feel is one of the things that this demonstration was about. The marshals kept saying to us, "You going to let these girls keep crying? Aren't you going to tell them to quiet down? You're older, aren't you? Why don't you tell them to quiet down?" And I'd say, "Let them cry, let them cry."

I don't think that in a mixed group they would have been able to do it. There would have been a few guys who would have loved the business of the wailing, guys into co-counseling or something like that. But a lot of the men are not ready, would not have wanted to do that, or would not have liked it.

And I know from my own experiences in school with women and men that there's a whole stratum of women that won't speak up when men are present. Sometimes they're the women who are most men-dependent. It's not just that they're shy, and they may be the most pro-men—but whatever they really are, happens when the men aren't there. And they really need that. They still, right now, need that part for themselves, more so than the really politically developed feminists who can be pretty strong nowadays with a bunch of guys. Although, I've seen plenty of them, when their own man walks into the room, they die. No names.

R.P.: Have you become freer yourself?

G.P.: Yeah, but I don't know what that has to do with it. I think that in almost any culture the older women really begin to have a certain power. So, I'm getting older, so I really feel freer than I ever felt. I probably will feel even more so. I think some of it comes from being part of a movement but some of it comes really from just getting older and also making my own living.

R.P.: And yet there aren't many writers—I can only think of you—who have given us images of older, freer women.

G.P.: Well, it's just because that's where I am and I seem to always be where I am. I mean, I write about other things too, but I look at my early stories of women who are suffering the loss of different guys, you know, and I see that people, young people, like them. They seem to refer to them.

R.P.: You don't relate to those stories any more?

G.P.: I relate to them a little bit, but I don't . . . I don't deeply.

R.P.: How do you know when you have a story, the germ that you know is going to work out?

G.P.: What happens with me and probably other writers as well—something really bugs me for a long, long time and I may write a page or two on it but I don't know what the hell to do next. *Something* is bugging me. That story that you mentioned before, "Friends," that was after me a long, long time. I had written the first page maybe a year and a half before I wrote the rest of it. I wanted to write about this woman and I wanted to put it in terms of a visit. The visit is invented in the sense that I went to see her pretty much by myself, but I knew that groups of friends had gone to see her at different times. We were all pretty close. In fact, because of the story, one of the women who was with her now thinks that I was there with them, but I wasn't.

But I didn't know what to do with that beginning—it couldn't just be a story about her dying and our visit. I began with "To put us at our ease, to quiet our hearts as she lay dying, our dear friend Selena said, Life after all, has not been an unrelieved horror—you know, I *did* have many wonderful years with her." I wrote that paragraph partly because she really said it, and I never forgot that language. After that, it was really a big problem. Maybe a year later, you know, I was really doing other things. Finishing up some other stories. But I would write things, different parts, not so much about her but different conversations or different small sections. And when I really began to do Anne and her son and the conflicts among the women, I realized that it really wasn't just a story about Selena but it was a story about the end of relationships, or the dying of long friendship. (I hate that word relationship. I thought I'd never use it but I did. Now I don't have to be mad at other people who do it.) Something about, you know, deep, deep friendships and what they're based on and what happens to them. But, I mean, I didn't know that especially, until . . . in a way I had to make two stories before I could make one. That very often happens. You really don't have a story until you have two stories. It's those two stories working against each other and in connection with each other that make it happen. So I had to have those people visiting her and I had to figure out who they were, I had to make them up. They are pretty much, you know, based roughly on several women but they're reinvented in different ways.

R.P.: That story ends by proclaiming your right to "report on these private deaths and the conditions of our lifelong attachments." Are the two stories that play off against each other always from private life in that way?

G.P.: No. I have two stories in a story that I wrote about China. One was about an event that happened in China where people didn't want to be photographed and the other was an event that happened in this country on the lower east side where people didn't want to be photographed. That story about what happened in China, it interested me as a story to tell, you know, to gab about, to tell everyone who said, tell us about China. But it didn't interest me as a real hard-written story until I thought about the other story and decided to tell them together. One just didn't seem enough. It could have been a little article, a small journalistic thing. But it didn't really interest me until I began to realize what it was about and how it needed the other one.

R.P.: What do you think has made women's private lives of interest? The movement? The women's movement?

G.P.: Yeah, I think that's true.

R.P.: Has the women's movement changed your sense of writing and relationships?

G.P.: No. I mean, it informed me a lot because there's a lot of writing about this stuff. I can't say I had a high political consciousness when I began to write in the fifties. I was just part of what was happening. I myself couldn't have said, oh, I'm this feminist or I'm this or I'm that. The lives of these women, really apart from their men, just happened to interest me. Nobody is not part of their time. So I was part of what was really happening, and without knowing it—especially in the women's movement. The women's movement began to develop out of the left and a lot of things I did were supported by it. I think until then that women's daily lives, domestic lives were not considered interesting and their friendships were just considered, you know . . . gabby girlfriends.

R.P.: Have you always had women friends?

G.P.: Yes. I can't understand this baloney about women not having friends. In my mother's family they were aunts or they were half-aunts or they were cousins. They were related partly but a lot of them weren't related, you know. I have a little piece reprinted in one issue of *Feminist Studies*. *Esquire* wanted me to do something . . . they were doing a thing on that . . . "Mom and Apple Pie" . . . so I wrote a piece called "Other Mothers" and really it was about this whole bunch of aunts and the women in our streets who used to sit and talk to each other in the afternoons, and the aunts in my house and my grandmother. Although it's true my father was *the* figure in the house. As my sister said yesterday, "Poppa would say 'Where's the salt?' and both aunts, my mother, and my grandmother would leap up to get it first." But "Other Mothers" was about being raised by lots of women. My mother died when I was twenty-one or twenty-two, some bad time, but I had really parted from her earlier because she was very, very sick.

R.P.: For how long was she very sick?
G.P.: Oh, she began to get sick when I was about thirteen.

R.P.: Was she at home sick? Or in the hospital sick?
G.P.: Well, she was in the hospital some, but mostly she was home. She was there and I was home, too, and I was bad to her. She had good years in the middle of all that. My father was a doctor. She had cancer.

R.P.: What do you mean bad to her?
G.P.: I was bad at school, I ran around with boys—that was natural—a girl *could* get pregnant and then what? You know, nothing serious. But she knew she was going to die, really, and she trembled for me. She really knew she wouldn't live and she just couldn't bear the direction I was obviously going in.

R.P.: Which was?
G.P.: Badness. Trouble. I had an older sister, also, who was part of that "other mothers."

R.P.: How much older?
G.P.: Fourteen years.

R.P.: Fourteen years older? Oh, she really is another mother.
G.P.: Yeah. And she is now. Jeannie, my Jeannie. So that I have a lot of these close female relationships and I always had a best friend, a couple of friends. Although my special closeness to grown-up women really happened when I had kids.

R.P.: That's all those wonderful playground stories.
G.P.: Yeah.

R.P.: Do you remember which were the first stories you wrote or the first story you published? Did those subjects differ from the subjects you later picked up?
G.P.: I didn't write stories until I wrote those stories in *Little Disturbances*. I wrote poetry. I have found one or two stories that I did write *long* before—in my teens. The first story I wrote was a very tiny story about a boy who had to stop taking piano lessons with his teacher, a story Jess told me. I didn't know why I began it. All I could think of was that piano teacher. So it was really about this piano teacher who was losing a pupil. It was a very Joycean thing. It was four pages.

R.P.: What do you mean Joycean?

G.P.: It was just very spare already. Epiphanous. Then I wrote one more story sometime in there, again with a kid in it, about a Spanish superintendent's kid and the other kids on the block—written around the period of big garbage cans and coal heat. A kid by accident rolled a can off and killed somebody, and they were looking for him. It was very simple. Neither of them was too successful. And then the next stories I wrote were "The Contest" and "Goodbye and Good Luck" and the other stories in the first book [*The Little Disturbances of Man*]. Those I wrote in my thirties.

R.P.: Then the incident in "A Conversation with my Father," that incident where your father says to you, "Can't you write stories like you used to? Like Chekhov?" That's all made up?

G.P.: Yeah—the specific occasion's invented.

R.P.: About writing?

G.P.: He'd yell at me about it. He really kept me honest.

R.P.: What do you mean by that?

G.P.: I never even thought about it before. In some ways he was very good, but in some ways I could never have done anything until I got away from him. My father was wonderful. He was humorous, he was brilliant, he was sophisticated, but he really was . . . I wrote a poem one day in which my daughter says to me, "Ma, how come Grandpa didn't become great or famous. He seems like a famous man." And I say, "Well, he couldn't because really he was just a ghetto Jew." And my brother says, "What?" My sister says, "I don't believe that." And my son says, "Jew talk." I remember my first shocks in seeing him talking to Protestants or Catholics or whatever, somebody who wasn't Jewish. He really would go shy. I would be embarrassed a little, you know. He would have an aspect of deference. He didn't have it with, say, the Italian supers; he didn't have it with them. But there were certain "class" things that he revealed. He was after all considered a middle-class doctor—he did very well, he was much loved, and had a house in the country and a big car—but basically he was really a working-class man and he really never got over that kind of deference to Anglo-Saxonism. He worried a lot whether we would make fools of ourselves. But in order to really write, in order to be any kind of an artist, one of the things you have to be willing is to really be a total jackass and to really face that. So he inhibited my freedom to be a total jackass, you know? And he would say, you'll make a fool of yourself. My sister's under the impression he only said it to her, but I've assured her he said it to me many times. My mother was not too worried about that. She had more natural self-respect.

R.P.: How many children were there?

G.P.: Three. I was the youngest by a lot. He had been a poor boy when the other two were born. He was in his early twenties, going to medical school, working in a photography shop, bringing relatives over from Russia. He had been a poor, harassed young fellow from Chrystie Street when his two older children were born—children from his real working-class time. My mother was a retoucher. My brother and sister remember that she used to wear a black hood against the light retouching plates. But when I was born he was already a very successful doctor, and free to take some pleasure at least.

R.P.: And did he encourage your writing?

G.P.: Well, everybody did when I was little, sure. You know, they were very verbal people so they liked their little kid to be a writer.

R.P.: Was your father a literary man? In your stories he's always reading and quoting someone like Pushkin.

G.P.: He was a big reader. You know, from that time, that generation of immigrants that came in 1904–1905; they were all big readers. He learned English by reading Dickens—I mean, that's how he learned English. And he really had certain very elegant ways. He had the Russian lack of articles—even in his late 80s, he would forget an article; Russians do that. But he had very elegant ways of speaking or writing or talking. He wrote letters to me or to Nora—to my daughter—"Dearest Darling Daughter." He was a very fine writer. He wrote stories I tried to publish.

R.P.: And your mother?

G.P.: My mother didn't write to us much. I mean, she wrote me little letters, you know . . . and I'm sure that she was the one who made him write the letters—"You sit down and write to Grace," or something. You know? I have very few letters from her. But I never felt she did not love me. We just had too much conflict. You know, when someone worries about you all the time it gives you the feeling that you're going to end up god-knows-where. You try to step away from that anxiety.

R.P.: Was it mostly sexual anxiety on her part?

G.P.: Yes. A lot of it that I'd get pregnant or something.

R.P.: That is one of the main liabilities for women, no question about it.

G.P.: Well, she was very anxious about that and I, of course, I was outraged by it when I was sixteen, seventeen, and younger—fifteen.

R.P.: Were your parents political?

G.P.: Yes, they were Socialists. He had been in prison before he ever came here, in Siberia, and she had been sent into exile, to Germany.

R.P.: Why was he in Siberia?

G.P.: He was a Socialist. You didn't have to do much. And then the Czar had a son, so they were both released. Everybody under twenty-one was released.

R.P.: When you grew up, were there meetings at home? Did they write pamphlets on the kitchen table?

G.P.: No, my sister and brother grew up very unpolitical. They grew up with this immigrant man and woman who were bringing over relatives, who were expanding their financial horizons, who were trying to make money, who were trying to be successful, who were getting a good record player, and who were collecting first-class classical records, and who wanted their children to play the piano and tennis, both of which my sister and brother do to this day and they're in their seventies. They play the piano. In fact, my brother Vic just beat Bob and Duncan [Paley's husband and his son] at tennis and Vic's seventy-three. They wanted me to do these things but I didn't want to. They already had kids who were doing it. So I was harassed about it—and they [her sister and brother] became a doctor and a teacher. I also think my father and mother did not talk to them so much about their youth as to me, because then they were in *their* youth. I mean, they were in their twenties and thirties. I remember when I wanted to go to Europe or something and I said, "How come you never went back there?" And my mother said, "Europe, I never want to see it again. Why do you want to go to Europe? Are you crazy?"

R.P.: Where did you go to school? New York public schools all the way through?

G.P.: Sure.

R.P.: And did you go to Hunter?

G.P.: I went to Hunter College for one year and then I had to leave. Then about two years later I went to NYU for another year. And that was it altogether.

R.P.: How come? How come you quit?

G.P.: I would get up to the door of the school and I just couldn't go in.

R.P.: Because it was boring to you? Or didn't teach you what you wanted to know?

G.P.: I didn't think. I just couldn't bring myself to go in. I did take a writing class at NYU but I was married by then and Jess went overseas. I was about twenty-two and I took this writing class and the guy threw me out immediately. I started to write a story. It had some bad words in it, you know. He threw me out. I mean he said, "Get out." I wasn't even mad at him. I just thought: I guess I don't know how to do this, I guess I'd better stick to poetry. I knew all the poets—their poems—when I was quite young.

R.P.: Who were your favorites?
G.P.: I loved Robinson Jeffers. I loved Auden, I loved H.D.

R.P.: Did you read women writers because they were women writers?
G.P.: No. I thought about Woolf. Woolf meant something to me. *Mrs. Dalloway*, I remember, was the first thing I read. I loved the style; I was very interested in the style. And I was interested in Gertrude Stein. I loved the stories. They had drama in them. And I loved Jeffers and them all; I knew those poets, all of them. In high school—and I was young in high school, I was fifteen years when I graduated—I remember I had all the anthologies and I had just found these books that my aunt had given me. There was Christina Rossetti and Edna St. Vincent Millay, too. I knew them. I was in love a lot, so I really read what they had to say.

R.P.: And were you reading them just yourself? Or did you have buddies? Or teachers, even?
G.P.: In high school I remember I had a couple of friends, and I used to read poems. But I never talked in class. It was very hard—my school life became very hard early. In the middle of a class one of my friends went up to the teacher and said, very softly, "Grace knows all these poems by heart but she doesn't want to speak." Something nobody believed of me at this point. I really went through a long silence. Not an artistic silence, but a big mouth-silence.

R.P.: Did you have any teachers who meant something to you?
G.P.: Well, I had two high school teachers who found out I liked poems. I really loved those women. I talked to them. And also they shared my politics. A boyfriend of theirs had been killed in Spain; that was the time of the Civil War. I lived a lot of politics then, during high school.

R.P.: And that really came from your parents.
G.P.: Well, it came really from the romanticism I felt about them. I felt they were heroic, and I loved that stuff a lot. Of course by that time, they were very angry with me. I remember, as a child, in high school or even into junior high, we were wearing peace, something, armbands. This was

in high school. The principal said, "As long as you wear those armbands, you can't come to class." Little by little different kids would take off their armbands, with chagrin, broken down. I knew that I would never, never, never take off that armband. It really was romantic, you know. And I remember my cousin came down the aisle of the auditorium of the school and said, "Gracie, you better come up, you better come up because you know your mother's sick, you know you're making her sicker. You're going to kill her, you know that?" So, you know, that was the general feeling.

R.P.: Do you remember who you first showed your stuff to?

G.P.: Well, I was writing, at that time, with an English accent. I was already kicked out of school, so I was about seventeen and was working in offices, because my parents wanted me to go to secretarial school. I was working in an office. And Auden came to this country and he was teaching at the New School. So I went and took the course. It was my life, my whole life in that Thursday night. I mean, it was on Thursday night. I came down to this fascinating place, and I sat in the back of this class with those other two hundred people, and he talked. I couldn't understand him. Not only was there this very strong accent, but he used to lisp a great deal. It was *impossible*. But I didn't miss a class. I really loved those poems, those early poems of his—and also Spender. That gang: Spender, Isherwood, MacNiece. So then he said, "Do you want me to look at your poems?" A couple of weeks later I went to see him and he said to me, "Do you usually use words like trousers?"—I had never said anything but pants in my whole life—"Yeah," I said, "I do . . . sometimes." "And what about this word?" he said. "Subaltern." You know, like a sublieutenant. This was the beginning of the war. "Subaltern." "Well, once in a while." That was my first experience. I was writing in English-English.

I tell that story to lots of classes, when we talk about imitation. You have to, you know. If you don't imitate anybody strong you are usually just imitating some dead center. But I did not show stuff to people. I mean, when I was a young kid, about fourteen, in the country, I had three or four girlfriends who used to sit upstairs in the attic and I'd read things I had written. But I have worked alone almost all of my writing life. I always tell people that it takes too long that way. There has to be privacy but there ought to be community.

R.P.: When did you drop your English voice and start writing in this voice?

G.P.: Let's say academic voice . . . When I wrote stories. When I wrote

"The Contest," that's the first story I wrote. You know the expression "breakthrough" is funny, but it's really a break-through. Break through what? You know. Break through my own deafness. Break through my own literary falseness.

R.P.: Did you know immediately that it was right?

G.P.: Yeah. It all sounded like I'd heard it before. It was so familiar suddenly—I mean I didn't know it was good, I didn't think, "Oh, at last I'm good," I just thought, "How come all of a sudden I can do something?"

R.P.: It was easier?

G.P.: It wasn't just that. I really had gone to school to all my reading and writing for a long time, and really to short story writers, to poets, and to literature in general. So, I didn't have problems with cutting out a lot of stuff, you know, the business of shaping and form and cutting. It's as though I somehow knew how to do it.

R.P.: That's the quality of your stuff. It's so incredibly dense.

G.P.: I really had been living my life with a kind of literary ear. But the ear was far too literary. I mean it's no accident that I wrote in high-class English. Actually when I went home that night, I understood everything. My heart sort of failed me.

R.P.: After Auden said that?

G.P.: Yeah. But somehow or other in fiction I was able to really hear with this other ear—to use both. I mean the kind of traditional educated literary knowledge of this ear and *then* the ear that really had been just listening to people all the time, and used the language of place and time.

When you write poetry—this is a false definition, but you'll see what I mean when I say it—when people write poetry it's really talking to the world, especially in poetry of our time. It's got to change, but a lot of the poetry of our time says "I . . ."

R.P.: Why has it got to change? Because it's so egocentric?

G.P.: Yeah. Hopefully, more and more they write less and less like that. But that's one definition: poetry is addressing the world and fiction is getting the world to talk to you. When I was able to get into somebody else's voice, when I was able to speak in other people's voices, I found my own. Until then I did not have a voice that could tell a story.

R.P.: Well, your stories certainly give the sense of an ongoing world. Part of this is because characters from one reappear in another. What do you think accounts for that quality of denseness?

G.P.: My feeling about trying to tell a lot. It has to be interesting to me too, you know. And I'm really not interested in writing things out and out and out. If I do, they're boring to me. It's not that I write so densely to begin with. In general, I write more and take stuff out; I realize I said too much. I think about connections.

R.P.: That's part of that early poetry training . . .

G.P.: I think it's the poetry. I think it's really going to school for that economy. At Sarah Lawrence, my students in fiction writing, I make them write poetry. They've got to write a couple of poems at the start.

R.P.: Is it possible to teach people to write? Do those kids leave your class having learned something or other?

G.P.: They must have learned something. I figure they learned as much as somebody leaving a biology class or a history class. If they're learners they'll learn. And if they're not learners they won't. I mean, that's true of any course that you take. The whole point about teaching is to keep them from following false gods of all kinds and so on, and to be honorable, and to love the language. I think all teaching is moral. I mean, where it's not, we really have—in the sciences where it's not moral, or in the social sciences where it's not moral—we have the great economists of the corporate-loving right and the inventors of neutron bombs and things like that. And also in literature you have a cold, conventional prose. It's only where you really feel a moral obligation towards literature and language that there's any hope.

Part of what you do as a teacher of writing is to weed out the kids who think they want to be writers, but really aren't interested in subject matter or aren't bugged by anything. You know, nobody needs them, nobody needs them to keep working. Lots of things for them to do. And there are sometimes kids who are not, you would say, not that gifted if you wanted to put it that way—but are really driven powerfully to speak, to write, and to investigate. In some ways they might be less brilliant than those other people. (I once talked about how one of my jobs was to keep a class of smart kids dumb.) But they so much want to understand. *They* are the kids who really are going to do the work.

R.P.: One of the striking things about your stories is the sympathy with which you handle male characters. There is a great deal of empathy, for instance, when characterizing males in sexual attitudes, lust or tenderness. You must have had good male friends when you were young.

G.P.: One of the things that made me write was that I was terribly upset about men. "The Contest" was the first thing I wrote. I was trying to think about what was going on between men and women, and the only way I could think about it was to write from [a man's] point of view. So I tried to get into this guy's head, and I wrote the story from his point of view, with him telling the story. I remember writing that first line—really it was the first line I wrote: "Up early or late, it never matters, the day gets away from me." I was trying to see women, in those stories, as men saw them, but I was trying not to see them the way I want to be seen, not to put it all in the best *or* worst light. I had been living in the army camps with Jess. It was wartime. And I loved being with the guys. I was just like any typical sort of tomboy young person; I loved being with the boys. The war was happening and it was happening to the men mostly. It was terrible. None of them wanted to go; I didn't know one boy who wanted to go. I worked as a secretary, an office worker, and I lived with the office workers. I didn't live with him, you know. I'd eat supper with him every night. I'd go on guard duty with him sometimes. It was a lot of fun—I mean I really had a good time. It wasn't until I was in my really late twenties and had these two little kids, and got over that little fence of thirty to the other side, that I really began to see they weren't so much my buddies as I thought. And it took me really a long time. And then I felt bad about it. I really did. And I began to try to figure out—to get in their heads, to try a little bit to see with their eyes. In fact there's a line in "Goodbye and Good Luck", which is the second story I wrote, where she tries to talk to him and she says to him, "A man's life is something I don't truly see." She says, in other words, "What do you want? What do you want here? What do you want to do? What do you have in mind?" She's asking him, you know. And she says "A man's life is something I don't truly see."

And at the same time I was getting closer and closer to women's lives through the kids. Specifically women without men. So those two things were happening.

R.P.: What has been the relation of your writing to the rest of your life? To marriage and family, for instance. And has that changed in time? Does it fluctuate or has it got a steady place?

G.P.: Well, I think at different times in my life it's probably been different things. I was a writer from a very early age. I feel that I would have done that no matter what else. Suppose I didn't have kids or anything like that, I might have written a longer book—that's the only thing that I can think.

When the boy I was married to went overseas, [writing] was probably the most important thing in my life. I've looked at some of those poems of that very short period in my early twenties and I can see that I was making a good deal of progress. But when he came back, I have to say that *that* was the most important part of my life. He was very gloomy, and I was very concerned about him and what was happening to him. We were all into a lot of psychology at the time. It seems to me that, had we looked at it historically instead of so psychologically, there would have been better solutions. I wouldn't have regarded it as something personal. As against me. As against his mother. As against himself. I mean I would have seen he was a young soldier coming back from three years away from his life, and not knowing what to do next. Having a degree in physics and not being able to go on with it, having to make changes. Now it seems to me that anyone who has been in the army for three years and been subject to the authority of the army, that life, would be depressed and gloomy, would be suffering a lot. It would have helped to have seen the thing historically. This is an insight that I've had about that period in the last six months, remembering it back some thirty, thirty-five years ago. But although I never *myself* got tied up in a lot of psychological ideas, it was in the air at the time, and I was part of it, so I thought inside my time. And I generally never have gotten too much away from my own time.

I was also wild about the idea of having children. I loved the idea, and wanted to, as soon as possible. And after some years we did have kids and I enjoyed every bit of it, I must say. I never felt that writing and family life were mutually exclusive. Since I didn't go to school, I never got onto a time line. I didn't have a sense that at a certain age I should do this and at a certain age I should do that. You know?

I have a basic indolence about me which is essential to writing. It really is. Kids now call it space around you. It's thinking time, it's hanging-out time, it's daydreaming time. You know, it's lie-around-the-bed time, it's sitting-like-a-dope-in-your-chair time. And that seems to me essential to my work. Some people will do it just sitting at their desks looking serious, but I don't.

Right now, the problems with this political action of which I'm very much a part are complex, and require imagination. I have anxiety about that. Not guilt but anxiety, because I really feel the world's in the balance. I don't feel essential to the world, to the solution, but I just feel my normal citizenship in this—and the pity of it all. So I just find myself using my days and my mind in a different way.

The three things in my life have been writing, politics, and family. At different times each one has taken over, has been more strong. And when the kids were little, it was really family. I didn't do a lot of politics or stuff. Family of course means children, but it didn't mean my little nuclear family. It meant the life of families, schools, parks the day-care centers. And that was the point at which I was most interested in those women and what was going on in the park. That was when I really began to think about our lives. I began to write poetry because I was being teased for thinking about all these things. But also that husband of mine at that time, Jess, who didn't like poetry much, would say, "Why don't you write a story sometime? I mean, you know, you have a sense of humor, and you like people and you talk about people all the time, you're always telling stories, why don't you write a story instead of these poems?"

So the family part of life is that without which I would not have had the other part of life. I think I would have eventually begun to use prose just to get the world to speak to me, just to get that to happen. But I probably would have written longer things because . . . that business of the children . . . I mean I don't like giving anything up for anything. I have a terrible greed. I don't like giving up writing for family. I don't like giving up family for writing. I don't like giving up politics to go to my family parties, and I don't like missing my granddaughter just because I have to finish a piece of some kind. I do it all by push; I don't work it out.

R.P.: You don't strike me as being ambitious. Is that right?

G.P.: Yes. I have very low ambition standards. I'm so pleased to have done as well as I've done. I'm amazed, I'm just delighted, it's extraordinary to me that people like those two books and read them, and that when I write something people want to see it. It's really amazing to me.

R.P.: Isn't that particularly female?

G.P.: Well, it may be particularly female, but not so many females feel like that, that I know. It's just that I give a lot of value to other things in my life. *That's it*, you know. Like, a lot of people nowadays don't want to have kids. I wanted to have them at the time more than anything. I would have given up anything—I mean when I had those children. I couldn't believe I'd had them, it was so miraculous to me. I still can't.

R.P.: Men of your age, of course, are more concerned with questions of career and ambition.

G.P.: Oh, they're dying, I mean they are *dying*. There isn't one of them I know that isn't dying. Maybe I'd feel that way if my books weren't read or something. If I'd written a couple of books and nobody bought them. There's a lot of luck in my situation that I appreciate.

R.P.: Why do you think you're so popular after twenty years?

G.P.: It's cumulative you know. In the beginning the stories were not very much distributed. I'd get letters from women saying, "Thank you" and "I know how you feel." And then the stories would go out of print again. Certain editors would reprint the book—Aaron Asher has done that a couple of times. But I don't think it found its own audience for a long time. And then I think little by little it did. That's all.

And then the women's movement happened. And that has supported every woman, not just me. I mean it's brought Meridel Le Sueur back to life and literature where she belonged. It's made her old age joyful even. There isn't a woman writer who . . . if they're not grateful to every woman in the world for hearing them, I don't know, they're nuts. We owe this moment in history a lot. We were part of it happening too. I don't think I would have happened if it wasn't on the way. The feeling of women for women was beginning to happen, not just for me, but for a lot of other people far away that I wasn't even seeing. If that hadn't begun to happen, I might have still been writing some academic poems.

R.P.: Is there a particular age range, do you think, in your audience?

G.P.: No, I wouldn't say so. It seems general somehow. Kids like it, although they are a different generation. I had a wonderful discussion at City College where a young black girl got up and said, "You know that woman you had in that story, that "Interest in Life", you know her?" I said, "Yeah." She said, "She didn't seem to learn. I mean the way she was waiting for that guy all the time. Did you think she was a hero or something?" I said, "No. I didn't think she was a hero, but she was a woman." The kid says, "Well, I think she was a dope." I said, "That's good. That means your life will be better."

R.P.: Are you friends with other writers?

G.P.: I had always shunned literary life. Just the same way that I was afraid of academic life and tried to stay away from it. But now I seem to know many writers. I've been active in PEN and I feel that community. There are people on my block who are writers I'm very fond of, and I'm very close to, friends like Barthelme and Sales and people like that. But I didn't want my everyday life to have anything to do with writers unless *they* were willing to have everyday lives, so to speak. If I can't be friends with them what's the point.

When I go to California, I spend time with Tillie [Olsen]. I mean time, like hours and hours; I stay at her house, we have taken long walks, you know. And I don't have really literary discussions with her. I don't have the knack. I mean we talk a little bit about it, but mostly we talk about women's lives, about different ideas. We have talked recently about language and Mary Daly. I guess that is literary. We've had long talks on that subject. But again I'm really more interested in political life than literary life. So Tillie and I talk about politics, women, the world. And we've done different things in our lives. She'll tell me about the thirties and forties which is terribly interesting to me. And Marge Piercy is very dear to me—a person who puts her life where her mouth is.

R.P.: Do you have any particular friends that you show your work to—stories as they come—besides Bob?

G.P.: Yeah, sometimes my friend Eva in the German department at school, or Sybil [another friend] or—you know. But I do read them to Bob, a lot of stories, when I'm working on them. If he's not in an impatient mood he'll pay attention. But he varies. Sometimes he's very incisive, really helpful, and sometimes some idea hits him and it's exasperating and I'll wish to God I had never said one single, solitary word to him. But that's his character, and I have to make those decisions when to read him stuff and when not to. Sometimes when I finish things, I bring them over to Don [Barthelme]. But that's when it's totally finished. I've sent stuff to Tillie [Olsen] sometimes—stories. I just got one of her infinitesimally printed postcards.

R.P.: Those postage stamp messages.

G.P.: Sometimes I'm so angry I don't read it for a couple of days.

R.P.: You think it's hostile, that teensie-weensie handwriting?

G.P.: It's not hostile, no. But when I write to her I write very big. I try to be an example; I write with enormous letters.

R.P.: What do you think it's about?

G.P.: She told me once that it was that she had very little paper.

R.P.: I've wondered that—if it was economy.

G.P.: I think there's much more to it than that. It could come from a wish to be really looked at seriously—like people who talk softly. You say to them, "Can't you speak louder?" And they say to you, "Why don't you listen?"

R.P.: It has always been a struggle for her to be heard, or just find the time to work. She always talks a lot about incursions on her time—interruptions.

G.P.: Yes, but she allows it. She may be resentful, but she's as bad as me. I know because I stayed with her a couple of times. I mean, anybody who gets phone calls like she does at 11:00 or 12:00 at night from somebody in some city who's in bad trouble and wants to talk to her and has her phone number . . . you know, she's around a lot. I think a lot of what she writes is really for others, she's speaking for other people, and she feels their pain keenly. People really think sometimes that she complains a lot, but she really is speaking for other people, because she herself, as I say, she knows what it means, she knows the cost. But for herself, she does allow it. She has allowed it. And she didn't in all cases have to allow it.

She feels my shortage of time terribly, for instance, and she's ten years older than I am. I'm almost fifty-eight, she's about sixty-seven. And she's put a lot of time into scholarship, which is a generous act. That has taken away from her own personal work. I made a political decision to do politics and she made a decision to do that. And who says we shouldn't? I mean, who the hell is in charge of saying that you shouldn't do that? Either you see life as a whole or you don't. It's a great big ball; everything's in it.

R.P.: Who else, of this whole batch of women writers that the Historical Moment has thrown up, do you like? Who do you read?

G.P.: I love Esther Broner, and I think she's really not known enough. That *Weave of Women* book, that's original. She really just came around from left field and took hold in a different way. It's really very interesting.

R.P.: Are you quicker to buy and read contemporary women writers than men writers? Do you have a special feeling about that?

G.P.: Well, I'm interested. But I have to say that there are certain writers that I can't like. You take something like *The Women's Room* or something like that. Now that book means an awful lot to a lot of women, it really means a lot to them. It's no shit, it's real. So I see it's very important in that way, but I have trouble reading it.

R.P.: Why?

G.P.: I can't get interested in it somehow. I bought it three times—maybe that's why its sales are so good—and tried to read it, but I just couldn't.

R.P.: I know that for myself the thing that I found hard to take is the spirit of victimization that runs through it, the way she gets off on sado-masochism.

G.P.: But the people who read it don't feel that, they feel strengthened by her saying all that. They're strengthened. they say, "Oh, this is how it is for me. This is how we were. This is true."

I'm always interested in what Marge [Piercy] does. I mean we have our differences about several things, and approaches to writing—what and who and how—but she's an amazing woman and a true writer, and she does a tremendous amount of work and is very particular about what she's doing. She's doing a certain kind of chronicling of our time. She has a book called *The High Cost of Living*. I think it's really a wonderful book. It's not well-known. And it's one of her shortest things. I think she thinks she just tossed it off.

Sometimes you come to literature that seems related to your own in some ways, but after you've been writing for a while. And then you feel terribly corroborated. Like Paul's [Goodman] stories, the ones I really love the most, I read them much later, but they made me feel very good about certain things I was doing. Or Babel. Isaac Babel. When I read him, also after many years, I said, "Wow! He had the same Mommy and Daddy I had!" You know? The other writer doesn't so much influence you as have the same historical life that you have, that you come from, the same language structures, talks English the same way—or Russian.

R.P.: How about writers like Joyce Carol Oates or Didion or even Erica Jong?

G.P.: Well, with Didion I really just feel moral, political, stylistic differences. People think she's such a great stylist, but I don't. I think she's sentimental. I mean, she doesn't overwrite. She doesn't do that at all. I will say that for her. But I don't like her attitude towards people, you know. I don't think she really illuminates them but darkens them so that we see them less by the time we're through. Maybe in the beginning we see them a little bit but by the end we really don't see them. And I don't think she wants us to. And I think that's a political thing.

R.P.: How so?

G.P.: The act of illumination is a political act. That is, the act of saying, "See, this has been in darkness. This life has been unseen, and unknown." Now, to make that decision and say, "I want to illuminate this life"—which is the act of bringing justice into the world a little bit—that's a decision you make. But if you say, "Here's a life that's lying there. Now I'd like to take a rock and slowly cover it," that's a political decision. I think people do that with language all the time. Sentimental language does that. So I think that there's a lot of that happening in her and I think that what you get at the end is sort of a rock, you know. There's a cynicism in it. Who needs it? I mean sometimes you need it, but right now we don't need it.

R.P.: Did you every read *Fear of Flying?*

G.P.: Well, that's another book that I really read part of several times and couldn't really finish. I thought it could have been done a lot faster and shorter. If she hadn't been so afraid of flying, she could have got there quicker. But again, that book was very important to a lot of women. I respect those facts, when people feel like that. I don't think it's just pure popularity; I don't think it's just that they were sold.

R.P.: You mean hype and advertising?

G.P.: I don't think it was just hype. I don't think the success of *The Women's Room* or *Fear of Flying* was just hype. I think maybe things they did after that could have been. I don't know but there could have been big advances which the publishers had to cover with a lot of hype. That's possible. But those books, those two books, really were very important for lots of women.

R.P.: How do you account for the fact that there haven't been great women writers?

G.P.: Oh, there really *have* been, haven't there? What do you mean? What's great? Great goes up and goes down. Shakespeare wasn't great for a period there. Then he got great, then he got greater, then he got greatless, then he got greater again. I think the main thing is that women have been bringing up children. They haven't had work of their own of any kind—I mean why should they, if they weren't great anythings, why would they be great writers? I mean they weren't great mercantilists either. They weren't great capitalists murdering the world. They were not in public life. And writing is an extremely public art. I just look at it from the other side. I say how amazing that Jane Austen wrote and was appreciated. There were plenty of women writing, different kinds of women, you know. George Eliot. How come they did it? How come Mrs. Gaskell really did it? How come Charlotte Perkins Gilman did it? How brave George Sand was! How come Kate Chopin did it? That's the way I look at it, in an entirely different way. The miracle is what women have done in this world. It's miraculous that they did the work they did on such a high level. Where did they do it? And wearing the clothes they were wearing? How could they even sit to do it? I mean they must have loosened something. But if they were in the family parlor, they couldn't loosen everything.

A Conversation with Grace Paley
Peter Marchant and
Mary Elsie Robertson / 1982

From *Massachusetts Review* 26.4 (1985): 606–14. © 1986 by The Massachusetts Review, Inc. Reprinted by permission.

Grace Paley has published three "slender volumes" of short stories—*The Little Disturbances of Man* (1959), *Enormous Changes at the Last Minute* (1974), and *Later the Same Day* (1985)—in all, some forty-five stories. Her reputation, however, especially among other writers, far exceeds that of more prolific contemporary writers. Calling her "one of the best short-story writers we have," Robert R. Harris, an editor of the *New York Times Book Review*, termed *Later the Same Day* "fiction of consequence," "worth the wait."

The conversation which follows took place on February 18, 1982, during a visit to the State University of New York College at Brockport. Miss Paley spoke with the novelist Mary Elsie Robertson (*The Clearing*, 1982) and writer Peter Marchant, director of the Brockport Writers Forum. She began by reading her story "Once."

Marchant: I would like to ask you the first question. How exactly did you start writing? Were you always a writer? When were your first writings and publications?

Paley: I always was a writer, I guess. I've written poetry most of my life. Some of it wasn't such great poetry, but it was poetry. I did that from the time I was a child, actually. I did very little publishing; I may have published a couple of poems at some point in my twenties, but I didn't begin to write stories until I was in my thirties. *The Little Disturbances of Man* was published as a book, really, and only a couple of its stories appeared in *Accent*, a small magazine.

Robertson: What made you shift from poetry to short stories?

Paley: Well, I really loved poetry best and I loved doing it and I wrote it all the time, but there was something really wrong with the way I was working. I never *got* it, really; I never got my own throat working, you know? I think one of the reasons was that I liked it so and I read it so much and I had a very strong literary sense, as far as the poetry was concerned; but as time went on I couldn't *think* about what I wanted to think about in poetry, about the kind of things that made me write the stories—the lives of women and men, and especially women at that time. I don't mean that can't be done in poetry; a lot of people did it, but I couldn't do it, and I had to do it in stories. It was the pressure of subject matter, which people don't talk about a lot.

Robertson: One of the things that strikes any reader of your stories is that you have command of all these voices. I just wondered, is that how a story starts for you? Do you hear the voice in your head, and then the rest follows from the voice?

Paley: You've got it! In a lot of the stories, that's what happens. It's as though in a way that's how I began to be able to write stories. I heard enough voices so I could make my own out of them.

Marchant: How did you find your way to this particular form, which seems very much you, very original? Was there any model you followed, or did you just find your way?

Paley: First, I had been writing a lot of poetry, and the short story seems in many ways more connected to poetry than to the novel. It never entered my mind—I had small kids at the time, maybe four and three—it never entered my mind in a million years that I could have the time, that kind of long forward time to do a novel. Since I hadn't been writing prose, I naturally tried to write *short* prose, when I began. The first story I wrote was "The Contest," and the second was "Goodbye and Good Luck." It was because of poetry, really, that that short form was appropriate, and something I could handle.

Robertson: Do you tend to do a lot of revision, or do you write rather quickly?

Paley: The story I just read was something I thought about and thought about and then wrote pretty quickly. The very short stories, the ones that are two and three pages long, I've done that way. Those that are five pages take me a long time. With a lot of them, I write the first couple of pages and then wait six months or a year for the rest of the story to come. I have one short story that I've been working on now for a long time—I just don't imagine when I'll finish, and it's really never going to be more than fifteen pages. I do a lot of that revising as I work, and then more of it afterward.

Marchant: It sounds as if, when you wrote those short short stories, it was partly because of the children—you had no time to attempt anything much longer. Did you write in spite of the children, or as an escape from the children?

Paley: Oh, now. I enjoyed them. No, I wrote those stories because I was accustomed to thinking like a writer; that is, I was accustomed to writing in order to help myself think. And as a poet, even when the kids were around, I always had hunks of paper in my back pocket, when I was in the park or wherever, so I was always writing. But when I sat down to write the stories, it so happened that I had been sick before that, and the kids were in day-care—I don't know what I would have done without that day-care center—so in that period I was able to begin this very hard task of working in another form. I didn't have months ahead of me, but I did have whole days for several weeks. I don't like that "in spite of the children." Life is what you live, and you do everything you can in it, you know, if you're normally greedy. There's hardly any of these things that I would've wanted to do without—the writing or the children. Maybe I had the children in spite of the writing, or the writing in spite of the children, or the politics in spite of the two of them.

Marchant: But women have been terribly hampered by the lack of day-care centers. . . .

Paley: Sure.

Marchant: . . . and social custom which has kept them in the kitchen and in the nursery, and hard at it. Do you think there's been much waste of talent that way over the last few years?

Paley: Of course! That's a very specific way of looking at it. But most of its been because of women's own horizons for themselves, and also what they do in their spare time. Men have tried to be writers and have worked in brickyards or been doctors and had very little bits of time, but they were allowed to use the extra time to write. My father, say, would use his extra time to paint, but my mother would use her extra time to do something for my father. People would think it strange, really, for a woman, if she had two hours in the evening, to go to her own room and work. It's almost as though the *idea* that a woman could be doing that work was the greatest wall between her and the work itself. So whatever time she ever used for herself was stealing it from the family, whereas whatever time a man used for himself was for the enhancement of the family.

Robertson: It seems to me that all of your women characters know that they wanted to get married, even the thirteen- or fourteen-year-old main character in one of your stories. She picks out the man and all. The women seem very sure of themselves, [in a way that] the men seem much less certain. They follow the lead of the women, often; they try to do what the women want, or in some cases they just skip out. But the women are the center, I feel, in these stories; they are the strong ones.

Paley: I don't think that's true in all of them. In "An Interest in Life," she's really trying to do everything the man wants, but she is the strong one, all the same. Partly that's because that's what I was mostly interested in—the lives of women. That first book came out in 1959, and I hadn't seen anything like that book. People write what they want to read; that's sort of a funny thing, and I wouldn't want to push it too far. But I wrote about things that I hadn't been reading about. One of those things was the lives of the women around me at that particular time, many of whom were alone, without men. That was not my case, but I did know them well, and their children. One of the reasons, maybe, that I didn't write earlier was that's what I wanted to write about and that's what I really wanted to read about. It seemed to me that coming in the Fifties, after the Second World War, there was a heavy, strong masculine literature, which was natural with the guys that had been to war. On the other hand, it made women feel, or it made me feel, that what I really wanted to write about was so trivial. Who could possibly be interested in this kind of kitchen life? I didn't really do it until there was tremendous pressure in me to do it, until the point came where I really didn't care if nobody was interested.

Robertson: *You* were.

Paley: Yeah, it was what I *had* to do. And since I had been writing poetry without publishing it, I thought I could just as soon write fiction without publishing it.

Marchant: You've touched that same chord before—that you do what you have to do, and you felt you had to write so there was no big deal, you just had to do it.

Paley: Well, it was a big—it took a lot of time. But it was something I had to do, and I knew I was going to do it.

Marchant: But you weren't consciously being an *artist*, a writer with a capital *W*? You were just trying to say what you had to say?

Paley: Despite all this interest in poetry and all, I was scared to death of the literary life, not in the sense that I was shy of it, although I was, but I didn't want to have anything to do with it. I really wanted to write but to continue to be the neighborhood person I was. You know, the local, municipal, P.T.A. politics and stuff like that.

Marchant: But politics *are* very important to you. Are women's rights your foremost interest?

Paley: To me these things are all connected, very powerfully, and I would say that feminism is strongly connected to my anti-militarism. As far as writing was concerned, I wrote mostly about women—that's where my deepest thoughts went. My early politics was all municipal; I mean, it was really related to my life, like the schools where my kids were, the street, the parks, the city in general. Then, by the beginning of the Sixties, it moved into a lot of anti-war work. I was stuck with all those things; I do less municipal work, and I miss it a lot because that's the street, that's where the life is, and I'm lonesome for that.

Robertson: Do you think of your stories as *political* stories? Do you make any distinction between political art and that which is not?

Paley: I think they probably are, just as whatever subject matter or form that anyone takes is. All of art is political; if a writer says this is not political, it's probably the most political thing that he could be doing. That's a statement of an alienation problem. I would say that my interest in ordinary life and how people live is a very political one. That's politics; that's what it is. But I can't say that I thought, Oh, I'm going to write this political story. I didn't think that at all. I just thought I'm going to write about this woman and this man and how they live.

Robertson: Yes, I agree that they are political, but they are not didactic. I'm certain, as you say, that you did not sit down to write an anti-war story; that's not it. Nevertheless, that becomes a part of the story in a very quiet way, but not in a blatant way.

Paley: That's because so many people are doing that.

Marchant: They don't seem to me directly political at all. You write about people who happen to be women who happen to be Jewish or Italian or Irish, but they're people. Or, do you think that your women don't just happen to be women? The point is that they *are* women.

Paley: It *was* very important to me to write about those women. Before I wrote those stories, I would say that I hung out with my buddies, my friends, in the park or wherever; we took the kids around, or before that I always had very good women friends; but I really would not say that until I was in my late twenties I had, say, a woman's political consciousness. So what was the beginning of that? The beginning of that is to know that your life is common with a certain class, or a certain group, so that one of the things that made me begin to write the stories—this is all hindsight, you know—was that I felt my life in common with all of these women. That was it. I have to look back at that point with some gratitude for that consciousness having happened to me, because I don't know that I would have done it otherwise.

Marchant: But where does the comic come in? Where does that derive from? You look at these characters and their views. . . .

Paley: Well, you're either funny or you're not. [Laughter] People try to write very seriously; sometimes I write awfully serious stories, and I see that they have comical sections. I don't know how I feel about that. [Laughter] My father was very funny, and my mother had no sense of humor at all, but that sort of worked to make him even funnier. My mother would always say, "Well, I have no sense of humor." That would make everybody laugh.

Robertson: In the story that you read, the character says, "Oh, well, there were the Tuesday night meetings, and I had the children; then there was the war." I know that you spent a great deal of your time and your energy during those years in the anti-war movement, and indeed there is a gap between the publication dates of those two books. Is it the war that falls between these two books?

Paley: I think probably. It wasn't so much my saying particularly that I'm making this choice, I will do this, not this. It's just where the pull is strongest for me, and there have been these three pulls of politics, family life, and writing. Right now the family pull is the smallest, really, except I love to go see my grandchild a lot. Now it's just between the other two. I really move, not in a particularly conscious way, more towards one and then more towards another. We spent a lot of time organizing something called the Women's Pentagon Action that used up a lot of time, which I considered it very important to give. Life is really just a circle, and everything you do is right in it. So I write one book less than I would've written, but I'll write another book.

Robertson: I think that's really remarkable, but I think not too many writers do have that sense that the writing is simply one part of their lives. It's a part, but at any given moment, it may not even necessarily be the most important part; it's just a part.

Paley: But it's really more important than that. When I say there are pulls, I mean the pulls are strong in either direction, and also I *have* these two books out now. Suppose I was a woman struggling just to be published? I would take another view. So I have to recognize that I have this good fortune of having produced a couple of books with the things I wanted to say about life. People who haven't done that could be in both pain and rage, and feel that everything else is against them. Of course, it's probably the publishing companies more than their families.

Marchant: But you seem not to feel regret because of the books you might have written if you hadn't been so politically active, or if you hadn't had children. You have the three "pulls," but you accept them easily: you're pulled in the way of writing, you're pulled in the way of political activism, you're pulled in the way of family, and that's the way it is. You don't feel bitterness.

Paley: It's not that simple. If you remember, I was supposed to be here a couple of weeks ago, and I got awfully sick. One of the reasons I got awfully sick was that I hadn't been writing in six months. I mean, I don't want it to be too light. There *are* those "pulls," but at the point at which you're pulled there's a tear, as you're taken from something else. So it's not that easy. As for regrets, I chose to live this way, you know. Two months ago I got sick and miserable and had to stop going to so many meetings and go away for a few weeks and I had to write and I *did*. So *that* happens. Suppose you have kids. There's a point at which they get into trouble. Well, you have to stop everything; you have to stop writing for a while, you have to stop going to meetings, and you have to pay attention to the kids, because you put them in this world. And you like them, too.

Marchant: But if you don't write, you do get physically sick; you feel a malaise.

Paley: You develop a lot of pressure at certain points. Then as you get older you do want to make sure that your work gets done. So I don't want to make it too light, but I *don't* regret having spent the time I did. And I do have to add the fact that I do have a strong streak of indolence, which probably is important to writers, because how else are you going to daydream all this stuff?

Marchant: Are you very disciplined?

Paley: No. [Laughter]

Marchant: Do you have a regular time for writing?

Paley: I try to do some work every morning. And once I have a story that I'm really working on, I work very hard. If I'm not *really* working hard on a story, I do a little bit every morning. Until it all comes together, I will probably just do other things as well.

Robertson: We talked a little bit about your working on a long thing, a novel perhaps, and your feeling that you probably won't do this.

Paley: Well, it's getting late. [Laughter] I mean, I could do it—I guess I'm almost sixty—but I don't know that I have the novelist's determination to do certain things. My husband Robert Nichols wrote a very long book, so I've had the opportunity to see someone who does it. I know the kind of thinking it takes and the amount of paper that has to be hung on the walls and characters to be taken care of; and I don't see myself doing that at all. I do see myself dealing with the same people a lot; I have a lot of the same characters, so anybody who wants can make a novel out of it in their heads.

Marchant: May I ask you what you are working on now? What were you working on in Mexico?

Paley: Well, I have a couple of long stories that I started long ago. The nice thing that happened in Mexico was that I wrote a very short story, totally, which I hadn't expected. It's the stories you don't expect that are very thrilling, in a way. And there are always those little ones that come, I guess, like poems, you know. So I'm working on those two long stories, and when I finish them, I guess I'll have a book. I have enough stories for a book, but I don't have a book.

Marchant: It sounds as if you spent a lot of time dreaming about your characters. When you say you *think* about them, you're really dreaming and listening to the characters talk. Then, you're ready, and you write them rather fast.

Paley: No, no, no. The long stories take an awful long time; as I said, they take years sometimes. "The Long-Distance Runner"—I wrote the first page and a half, and then I didn't know what the devil to do for about a year. I didn't know which way it was going, and then about a year later, I wrote the next three or four pages, and then a few months after that I finished.

Marchant: Who've been your mentors—teachers and writers from whom you've learned?

Paley: It's hard for me to say. It's really a larger subject, because I was a big reader as a child, so I read everything. It all had a lot of influence on me. I think that the form comes from literature, but the language and the subject matter really come from the neighborhood and the street and my family. That's an influence that is never given quite enough credit, I think. If certain Russian writers had some influence on me, it's only because they had the same grandparents I had. That's my feeling. [Laughter]

Marchant: Do people come into your stories recognizably?

Paley: Sometimes, but I'm not good enough to make them recognizable, thank God. [Laughter] Once in a while, you know. My father, once in a while.

Robertson: And yourself?

Paley: I'm not that woman, but I'm close to her. She lives about over here. She's mostly my friends, rather than me.

Edited from a transcription of a videotape produced by the Educational Communications Center on February 18, 1982, and sponsored by the Brockport Writers Forum, Department of English, State University of New York, College at Brockport, New York. Copyrighted © 1985 by SUNY. All rights reserved by the State University of New York. Not to be reprinted without permission.

PW Interviews Grace Paley
Wendy Smith / 1985

From *Publisher's Weekly* 5 Apr. 1985: 71–72. © 1985 by Publishers Weekly. Reprinted by permission.

Grace Paley has been a respected name in American letters for years. Her new book of short stories, *Later the Same Day* (Farrar, Straus & Giroux; Fiction Forecasts, Feb. 8), confirms her as an utterly original American writer whose work combines personal, political and philosophical themes in a style quite unlike anyone else's.

Paley's characters, women and men who have committed themselves to trying to alleviate some of the world's myriad woes, usually appear in print as activists at demonstrations, marching with upraised fists. She has given them children, friends, lovers, aging parents, financial worries, shopping lists—in short, a private life to go with their public activities. Paley's work is political without being didactic, personal without being isolated from the real world.

This striking individuality accounts for the profound impact of Paley's writing, despite what is to her admirers a distressingly small body of work. Her first book, *The Little Disturbances of Man*, appeared in 1959; readers had to wait 15 years for the next one, *Enormous Changes at the Last Minute*, and just over a decade for *Later the Same Day*. "I do a lot of other things as well," explains the author. "I began to teach in the mid-'60s, and at the same time there was the Vietnam War, which really took up a lot of my time, especially since I had a boy growing towards draft age. And I'm just very distractable. My father used to say, 'You'll never be a writer, because you don't have any *sitzfleisch*,' which means sitting-down meat."

Her father's comment is hard to believe at the moment, as Paley sits tranquilly in a wooden rocking chair in the sunny living room of her Greenwich Village apartment. A small, plump woman in her early 60s, with short, white hair framing a round face, she resembles everyone's image of the ideal grandmother (so long as that image includes slacks, untucked shirttails and sneakers). As she does every Friday, she is simmering soup on the stove in her large, comfortable kitchen; she regrets that it's not ready yet, as she thinks it would be good for her interviewer's cold. She has to content herself with offering orange juice, vitamin C and antihistamines. Many of Paley's stories express her deep love of children; meeting her, one realizes almost immediately that her nurturing instincts extend beyond her own family to include friends and even a brand-new acquaintance. It's this pleasure in caring for others that makes her activism seem so undogmatic and natural, a logical extension of the kind of work women have always done. It's more complex than that, of course—lifelong political commitments like Paley's don't arise out of anything so simple as a strong maternal instinct—but it helps to explain the matter-of-fact way in which the author and her characters approach political activity as the only possible response to the world's perilous state.

The direction of Paley's work is guided by similarly concrete considerations. One of the reasons she switched from poetry, her first love, to short stories was that she couldn't satisfactorily connect her verse with real life. "I'd been writing poetry until about 1956," she remembers, "and then I just sort of made up my mind that I had to write stories. I love the whole tradition of poetry, but I couldn't figure out a way to use my own Bronx English tongue in poems. I can now, better, but those early poems were all very literary; they picked up after whatever poet I was reading. They used what I think of as only one ear: you have two ears, one is for the sound of literature and the other is for your neighborhood, for your mother and father's house."

Her parents had a strong influence on Paley, imbuing her with a sense of radical tradition. "I'm always interested in generational things," she says. "I'm interested in history, I'm interested in change, I'm interested in the future; so therefore I'm interested in the past. As the youngest child by a great deal, I grew up among many adults talking about their lives. My parents were Russian immigrants. They'd been exiled to Siberia by the Czar when they were about 20, but when he had a son, he pardoned everyone under the age of 21, so they got out and came here right away. They didn't stay radical; they began to live the life of the immigrant—extremely patriotic, very hardworking—but they talked a lot about that period of their lives; they really made me feel it and see it, so there is that tradition. All of them were like that; my father's brothers and sister all belonged to different leftist political parties. My grandmother used to describe how they fought every night at the supper table and how hard it was on her!"

As Paley grew older, there were family tensions. "My parents didn't like the direction I was going politically," she recalls. "Although my father, who mistrusted a lot of my politics, came to agree with me about the Vietnam War; he was bitterly opposed to it." Her difficulties with her mother were more personal. "One of the stories in the new book, 'Lavinia,' was told to me by an old black woman, but it's also in a way *my* story," she says. "My mother, who couldn't do what she wanted because she had to help my father all the time, had great hopes for me. She was just disgusted, because all I wanted to do at a certain point was marry and have kids. I looked like a bust to my family, just like the girl Lavinia, who I'm convinced will turn out very well.

"There's no question," she continues, "that children are distracting and that for some of the things women want to do, their sense is right: they shouldn't have children. And they shouldn't feel left out, because the children of the world are their children too. I just feel lucky that I didn't grow up in a generation where it was stylish not to. I only had two—I wish I'd had more."

The experience of her own children confirmed Paley's belief that each generation is shaped by the specific historical events of its time. "I often think of those kids in the Brinks case," she says, referring to the surviving fragments of the SDS, who were involved in the murder of a bank guard during an attempted robbery in the early 1980s, after they had spent two years underground. "If they had been born four years later, five years earlier . . . . It really was that particular moment: they were called. In one of the new stories ["Friends"], I talk about that whole beloved generation of our children who were really wrecked. I mean, I lived through the Second World War, and I only knew one person in my generation who died. My children, who are in their early 30s, I can't tell you the number of people they know who have died or gone mad. They're a wonderful generation though: thoughtful, idealistic, self-giving and honorable. They really gave."

"The idea that mothers and fathers raise their kids is ridiculous," Paley thinks. "You do a little bit—if you're rich, you raise a rich kid, okay—but the outside world is always there, waiting to declare war, to sell drugs, to invade another country, to raise the rents so you can't afford to live someplace—to really color your life. One of the nice things that happens when you have kids," Paley goes on, "is that you really get involved in the neighborhood institutions. If you don't become a local communitarian worker then, I don't know when you do. For instance, when my kids were very little, the city was trying to push a road through Washington Square Park to serve the real estate interests. We fought that and we won; in fact, having won, my friends and I had a kind of optimism for the next 20 years that we might win something else by luck." She laughs, as amused by her chronic optimism as she is convinced of its necessity. "It took a lot of worry, about the kids and buses going through the park at a terrific rate, to bring us together. You can call it politics or not; it becomes a common concern, and it can't be yours alone any more."

Paley believes such common concerns will shape future political activism. "One of the things that really runs through all the stories, because they're about groups of women, is the sense that what we need now is to bond; we need to say 'we' every now and then instead of 'I' every five minutes," she comments. "We've gone through this period of individualism and have sung that song, but it may not be the important song to sing in the times ahead. The Greenham women [antinuclear demonstrators who have set up a permanent camp outside the principal British missile base] are very powerful and interesting. When I went there the first time, I saw six women sitting on wet bales of hay wearing plastic raincoats and looking miserable. It was late November, and they said that on December 12 they were having this giant demonstration. I thought, 'Oh these poor women. Do they really believe this?' Well, three weeks later, on December 12, they had 30,000 women there. You really have to keep at it," she concludes. "It's vast; it's so huge you can hardly think about it. The power against us is so great and so foolish."

Yet Paley has never despaired—she notes in the story "Ruthy and Edie" that her characters are "ideologically, spiritually and on puritanical principle" against that particular emotion. "People accomplish things," she asserts. "You can't give up. And you can't retreat into personal, personal, personal life, because personal, personal, personal life is *hard*: to live in it without any common feelings for others around you is very disheartening, I would think. Some people just fool themselves, decide they have to make a lot of money and then go out and do it, but I can't feel like that." Her voice is low and passionate. "I think these are very rough times. I'm really sorry for people growing up right now, because they have some cockeyed idea that they can get by with their eyes closed; the cane they're tapping is money, and that won't take them in the right direction."

Despite the enormous amount of time and energy political matters absorb in Paley's life, they remain in the background of her fiction. "I feel I haven't written about certain things yet that I probably will at some point," she says. "I've written about the personal lives of these people; I haven't really seen them in political action, and I don't know if I need to especially, for what I'm trying to do. There has to be a way of writing about it that's right and interesting, but I haven't figured it out. I've mainly been interested in this personal political life. But I refer peripherally to things: in 'Living' in *Enormous Changes*, where [the protagonist] is bleeding to death, she remembers praying for peace on Eighth Street with her friend; in 'Zagrowsky Tells' in *Later the Same Day*, he's furious because they picketed his drugstore. That's the way a lot of politics gets in, as part of ordinary people's lives, and that's really the way I want to show it, it seems to me now. What I want is for these political people to really be *seen*."

The people who aren't seen much in *Later the Same Day* are men: Jack, the live-in lover of Faith (Paley's alter ego among her work's recurring characters), is a fairly well developed presence, but the book's focus is strongly female. "It wasn't that I didn't want to talk about men," Paley explains, "but there is so much female life that has so little to do with men and is *so* not-talked-about. Even though Faith tells Susan [in "Friends"], 'You still have him-itis, the dread disease of females,' and they all have a little bit of that in them; much of their lives really does not, especially as they get older. I haven't even *begun* to write about really older women; I've only gotten them into their late 40s and early 50s."

Is Paley bringing her characters along to her own current stage of life? "I'm very pressed right now for time to write; I just feel peevish about it," she says. "But I've always felt that all these things have strong pulls: the politics takes from the writing, the children take from the politics, and the writing took from the children, you know. Someone once said, 'How did you manage to do all this with the kids around?' and I made a joke; I said, 'Neglect!' But the truth is, all those things pull from each other, and it makes for a very interesting life. So I really have no complaints at all."

Grace Paley, Voice from the Village
David Remnick / 1985

From *Washington Post* 14 Apr. 1985: 71–72. © 1985, The Washington Post. Reprinted with permission.

Grace Paley hardly exists west of the Hudson or east of Fifth Avenue. Her short stories are a kind of New York chamber music in which the instruments are the voices of the city—more specifically Greenwich Village, more specifically 11th Street between Sixth and Seventh.

She works slowly, noting the flattened consonants and the political yarns heard on the benches of Washington Square Park, the eternal kvetching in the coffee shops of Bank Street, the playground yelps on West Fourth, the spoken critiques of Ronald Firbank's novels on Christopher Street, the sirens approaching St. Vincent's Hospital, the leathery weirdness blooming around the Ramrod, the good smell of bread rising in Zito's and the pizza cooling in Ray's.

Paley is attuned to all of it. Sometimes she will do her best observing while handing out protest literature on the corner of 11th and Sixth. She is always gathering seeds. And once in a very great while, the voices and smells, the emotional strength and overheard conversation will flower into lines, then literature. Her new book of stories, *Later the Same Day*, took more than a decade to cultivate.

"I'm always making little notes, false starts, beginnings," Paley says, curling her doughy self into an old rope chair. "I wrote poetry for years before I ever wrote a story. I still work like a poet. Real slow."

Her living room is filled with rays of sunlight that make a crazy corona of her wild gray hair. She has the friendly aspect of a TV grandmom. With all her notes and effluvia scattered around her, she says, "I can't even keep a journal. I'm always losing the book. I have no discipline." Certainly not the steely discipline of a Joyce Carol Oates or an Anthony Burgess, the sort of literary industry that produces bulging books in and for all seasons.

"I can't work like that and never have," Paley says. "There have been long periods of my life when I was bringing up my two kids and playing with them at the playground or working on political things and the stories had to wait. I've let all that happen. No regrets. The stories come when they come."

At the age of 62, Grace Paley has published just three collections of stories, a total of 45 tales. But nearly all of them are remarkable for their clarity, their sense of place, their sympathies. As Philip Roth has said, Paley's stories display "an understanding of loneliness, lust, selfishness, and fatigue that is splendidly comic and unladylike."

She seems to be of a type, a New York type, ready for lampooning. The city is filled with so many people *like* Grace Paley, would-be writers who wear their concerns like sandwich boards, who struggle for a quiet eccentricity in a city where difference is merely a given. But Paley is a genuine article, unpretentious, funny, and wise. In the words of her neighbor and colleague in fiction, Donald Barthelme, she is a "wonderful writer and troublemaker."

Paley's second-floor living room is vintage Village. Bookshelves crammed with Babel and Chekhov and Marx, records piled into a Hellman's mayonnaise box, a sad rag rug, artifacts of politics, woolly pillows strewn on the floor, three empty light sockets in the ceiling. The lived-in look.

"I've been here almost forever," she says. Take "here" to mean New York, and that is true. Paley's background is richer than just the block. Her parents, Isaac Goodside and Manya Ridnyik, left Russia around 1905 and settled in New York, first on the Lower East Side, then in the Bronx. When they were young in Russia they had been Social Democrats opposed to the czar. Goodside had been exiled to Siberia and Ridnyik to Germany. In New York, Goodside helped teach himself English by reading Dickens. He became a doctor. Paley's mother took care of the house—Paley herself often escapes to sweeping and washing when her stories won't come unstuck.

"When I was little I loved to listen to my parents' stories, all the talk that went on," she says. "I loved to listen and soon I loved to talk and tell."

She studied at Hunter College and New York University but not long enough for a degree. She married a movie cameraman, Jess Paley, when she was 19 and had two children with him, Nora and Dan, now 35 and 33. Her real university was an immersion in poetry. She studied writing with W. H. Auden at the New School for Social Research in the '40s.

"I really went to school on poetry," she says. "I learned whatever I know about language and craft from writing poems. I worked at it for years and years but I was never a great poet. I didn't know what to do about it, except keep at it. When I was in my early thirties and I wasn't doing my work I was worried because what I was most interested in were the lives of the women around me and our various relationships. I just couldn't write about that in poems, and so I started trying a little prose. That was the real breakthrough."

Her first story, "Goodby and Good Luck" is the work of a natural. It's about a young woman in love with a great actor of the Yiddish theater. The story, and Paley's career, began in perfect pitch: "I was popular in certain circles, says Aunt Rose. I wasn't no thinner then, only more stationary in the flesh."

Only two of the stories in her first collection, *The Little Disturbances of Man*, appeared before the book came out in 1959. "And the magazine that took them," Paley says, "was *Accent*, a little journal in Urbana, Illinois. The way the book got published was that I had the nerve to show them to Ken McCormick, an editor at Doubleday who is the father of one of my children's friends. He saw three of them and said, 'Write seven more and you'll have a book.' "

Short story collections rarely sell many copies and for years Paley's publishers goaded her to write a novel. She tried. All it did was delay her second collection of stories, *Enormous Changes at the Last Minute*, which did not come out until 1974.

"I was dumb to try," she says. "I had a lot of pages but it just wasn't any good. Thank God I was smart enough to throw them out. I didn't stay away from the novel. It stayed away from me. It probably has something to do with how I've chosen to use my time in this world. I've allowed all the distractions."

Life—political and personal—interrupted the writing for long stretches of time. She raised her children and she has been an activist for years, working against nuclear power, the war in Vietnam, U.S. involvement in Central-America, and for various feminist causes. She frequently reads her work at political forums in the city and beyond. Yet politics have not bludgeoned her art. Her stories are often political but free of the sort of agit-prop fury that turns words to wood.

When *Enormous Changes at the Last Minute* finally was published, it attracted what the industry likes to call a "cult" audience. Which means small and devoted. The cult must be growing. Last week a film written by John Sayles and based on three stories in the collection opened at the Film Forum in New York.

The short story is enjoying a renaissance in American literature lately and Paley's publishers are hoping that *Later the Same Day* will attract a wide audience. The book has won terrific reviews in *Time*, *Newsweek* and *The New York Times*. Not that the work now is any more—or less—commercial. At their best the stories are still direct, swift and vibrant. The characters have aged along with Paley, and sometimes the voice of the book is like a wise litany. At times she picks up the Irish voices in the air, sometimes the black or Chinese. Sometimes the voice sounds much like her own, as it does here at the start of "Listening":

> I had just come up from the church basement with an armful of leaflets. Once, maybe only twenty-five, thirty years ago, young women and men bowled in that basement, played Ping-Pong there, drank hot chocolate, and wondered how in God's separating world they could ever get to know each other.

Paley makes her living by teaching at Sarah Lawrence and City College. She is divorced from Jess Paley and she and her second husband, architect and writer Robert Nichols, divide their time between the apartment in New York and a simple cabin in Thetford, Vt. They are apart for months at a time, with Paley in the city and Nichols in the country.

"I can't stay away from the block too long," she says.

Nor can she stay away from her background, her Jewishness. She is roughly the same age as those Jewish-American fiction writers—Roth, Saul Bellow, Bernard Malamud—who have described the experience of second-generation immigrants. Paley keeps her distance from them.

"I'm a woman and that makes a big difference. It separates me a lot from Bellow and Roth and all those guys. There's such distortion in their writing sometimes, the kind of stuff that gives men a bad name. It really louses them up. I think there's a lot of contempt for their fathers coming out and it doesn't do the books, or them, a lot of good. I'm delighted to be a woman."

"Faith" has been a frequent character in Paley's stories, an alter ego who first appeared in "The Used-Boy Raisers" in the first book. Faith resurfaces in "Faith in the Afternoon," "Faith in a Tree" and "The Long Distance Runner" and now is heard from in "Dreamer in a Dead Language" and "The Expensive Moment," two of the strongest stories in *Later the Same Day*.

Faith, like Paley, is now "at that lively time of life, which is so full of standing up and lying down," a feisty period in which all her experience and thinking has come to an extraordinary maturity.

"Faith is the one who does the most work for me," Paley says. "I don't think I'll ever kill her off. But I can't ever say what's ahead for my stories. I don't have any plots or plans. I'm glad to have written what I've written and I'm at a point in life where I feel a little smarter and more experienced and ready to write the best I can."

With that, Grace Paley returns to one of her welcome distractions. As she does every Saturday afternoon, she takes her place on the corner of Sixth and 11th near Ray's Pizza and Poppy's Deli, handing out leaflets, chatting with passers-by and, quite possibly, finding seeds for stories.

Grace Paley: A Conversation
Barry Silesky, Robin Hemley, and Sharon Solwitz / 1985

From *Another Chicago Magazine* 14 (1985): 100–14. Reprinted by permission.

Though she has published only three collections of short stories in twenty five years (*The Little Disturbances of Man, Enormous Changes at the Last Minute,* and this year, *Later the Same Day*), Grace Paley has built a reputation as a major literary figure—a "writer's writer." The distinction probably comes in large part from that elusive quality in her writing known as "voice"—the remarkable fluid, sure, and completely original way she has of constructing sentences and telling stories. The narrator in so much of her work sounds exactly like the favorite aunt, mother, friend, that everyone wants to have; thinking, talking, wandering in and out of the "ordinary life" she emphasizes repeatedly when talking about her work. At the center of it, always, are the people—especially the women. In her work, one feels, more than with most writers, almost no gap between the voice the page hums in the reader's mind, the voice reading those words from the podium, and the voice speaking from across the dinner table.

The following conversation did in fact take place over dinner, after her reading at Guild Books in Chicago on March 30, 1985. Barry Silesky, Robin Hemley and Sharon Solwitz ate and spoke with her that evening for *ACM*. Talking between bites, joking, turning our own questions back at us, she was that same intelligent, passionate, contentious, and above all, compassionate spirit suffusing the pages of her stories.

BS: You've been known for being a political activist, but in your work, politics always seems to be in the background, never in the foreground of the subject matter. So I wonder what you think the writer's role is in terms of addressing politics in the world.

GP: I never really think of that though I'm often asked that question. I always think that the writer's role is to get off her or his ass and to get on the street and do something. But that answer does not satisfy people. But to me that's a very important thing. I think of someone like Paul

Goodman who really felt that the thing was action. So then he could write all the love poems he wanted for the rest of his life.

I also think that sometimes things are political that people don't think of as political. At the time I began writing about women's lives, it was really very political. I didn't know it was political, I didn't think, oh, now I'm undertaking a political task. That's what was happening, only I didn't know it. I was just part of that political movement without even knowing it was a movement. So I think it often happens that people write politically without thinking that they are. So I'd say, write the truth about the world as you see it and be hung for that as well as for anything else; as well as for doing the right thing.

BS: When you look at your work over your three collections, do you see any kind of ongoing political argument that it is addressing?

GP: It's probably true, but I think you're the person to say that, not me.

RH: In the story "Somewhere Else" in *Later the Same Day* and in other stories in this book, the politics seem like this nice gentle undercurrent informed by your wit, and that seems to me to be what makes it so digestible in a way. That you're not strident about any political message.

GP: What I'm trying to write about is ordinary life as I know it, which involves politics. But it also involves ordinary life. So I tend to show politics as part of ordinary life. I tend to show it as arguments between the son and the mother, you know in the last story ("Listening"). Or among the women in the way they talk about that while they're also talking about the kids. And I guess one of the things you try to do when you write is to write the story you feel like reading somehow. So when I began to write about women early on it was because they seemed to be missing from what I was reading. In lots of literature, it's like unless someone's working with very specifically heavily political people like Marge Piercy does, it's as though nobody does any politics, as though nobody thinks at all, and it's not true. I mean in many ways a lot of that stuff enters people's thoughts.

RH: I know that you're politically active outside your writing. What are you doing now, politically?

GP: I'm not really doing anything specific right now. I'm working with some women's groups—Women's Pentagon Action, things like that, which are really affinity groups, they're not big outfits or anything. And then I've always worked with the War Resisters League and with Resist— those are ongoing things with me. A lot of it is just getting out on the street in your own neighborhood, that's what I really meant. I'm just like everyone else. I'm really distraught about Central America. I really feel that so far the American people have prevented us from going in. If it continues it'll be okay. People aren't really working hard enough. They aren't doing the day to day arduous hard political boring work. Which is a lot of fun actually. I mean being on the street is a lot of fun.

RH: A lot of people are just very unaware of what's going on in Central America too. I saw a great documentary on Nicaragua, but it was at three o'clock in the morning. I just happened to turn it on.

GP: There's been stuff though. What's interesting is that there really has been some stuff about Nicaragua.

BS: What do you think about the contemporary state of feminism? One of my colleagues at work, a woman from Italy who teaches mathematics, said when the word came up, "I'm not a feminist." She made an effort to disassociate herself from that. And I was struck by that. Here's a woman who is single, and heavily engaged in a professional career, and it seemed to me she's only able to be where she is, in large part, because of the women's movement.

GP: Here again, I think it's an American effort, despite her being European, to refuse the politics of history and the history of politics—the way in which their own lives are influenced by political currents. They say, "I'm not part of this wave, it has nothing to do with me," and I think it's painful. It's terrible when it's with older people because they really should know better. But with the kids, it's understandable because kids don't have a strong sense of history.

BS: I think part of it in her case, as well as with others is a reaction to what they see as the stridency of the more visible aspects of the feminist movement.

GP: Well, any movement is strident if it's a movement. That is to say, since there are so many noises around it in the society, it's got to talk louder or it wouldn't be heard.

BS: Are you actively involved in any feminist work now?

GP: I'm really involved in a lot of feminist anti-militarist work. I've linked things together with my anti-war stuff. Many feminists don't see it that way, by the way. There are a lot of divisions. Women say that's not feminism; feminism is equal rights, day care, battered women, abortion. But they don't see the connection between the patriarchy of militarism and the patriarchy of ordinary daily life. They don't like that patriarchy but they don't seem to mind so much the patriarchy of intervention in Central America.

I think the women's movement has done a lot for young men. I'm not telling you that because you're young or anything. Do you think so? What do you think?

SS: I had a boy friend once who was an ardent feminist. He thought that women did see men as economic objects and that was one of the things that sullied male-female relationships. He was an abstract thinker and put everything in terms of polemic. He clearly thought that feminism had done a lot to benefit men.

GP: I just see among my son's friends, I see the men with their kids, they're all guys in their thirties, and they really are a wholly different bunch. And I think it's wonderful for them too. I don't think it's just nice for Mommy.

BS: Different in the sense that they're much more involved with the kids?

GP: They're really interested. It's not just that they're doing it out of duty. They've really gotten into that process, which is a process of extreme patience that does them a lot of good.

BS: So you don't necessarily agree with Nora Ephron's comment that the one tangible achievement of the women's movement in the sixties was the Dutch Treat?

GP: That's a smart ass reply. I would have said, doing dishes. You can have really a very serious dinner party and not to your amazement any more, three guys will get up and do the dishes.

SS: We've been talking about politics and your interest which is more organic than intellectual; was there a time when you didn't think much about politics and there was sort of an awakening or were you from a family where it was part of the dinner table conversation?

GP: My parents didn't do any politics. They did when they were young. They'd done a lot of stuff in Russia but when they got here, they just paid attention to business. They tried to figure out how to make a good living, raise kids, buy a house, but they always retained their interest in what was happening in the world. There were always a lot of political discussions.

BS: So you were always involved in politics for as long as you remember?

GP: Well, political talks. My generation really grew up at a very scary time. This time is probably twice as scary, but since we didn't know this time was coming—the Second World War was coming, the Spanish Civil War was happening when I was in high school. Mussolini had invaded Ethiopia and made all those idiotic statements that are famous to this day. Like how beautiful it was to bomb the Ethiopians. The Italian kids in my school were in heaven, they were so delighted and proud they were fainting with joy. It was a scary time. Hitler was coming inch by inch by inch. I remember my parents talking about it.

BS: I'd like to talk about fiction for a while. You know, people have been talking about the new boom in short stories—

GP: That's true, there is a boom.

BS: There seems to be. Yet at the same time, the kind of short stories that are being published are much more conventional than what was being written, say, 15 or 20 years ago, or even I think than what you write, which doesn't have that traditional structure of beginning, middle and end—

GP: I don't know how to do that. If I knew how to do it I would probably do it.

BS: So you don't feel any particular aesthetic commitment to nonlinear fiction, say, versus the more highly structured fiction that is being published widely now?

GP: No, I find what you call well-made stories pretty boring. And it's not really from workshops, people think it's from workshops, but it's really not. Like there's this big prize that Sarah Lawrence gives for stories—we don't even believe in giving prizes for stories, but we're stuck with it—so we pick three stories. And we fight about it because we have a big cást of writing teachers. And the ones that win are, to me, always the ones that I didn't want to pick. And another good writer, Esther Broner, who's a wonderful writer—she has two books coming out from Indiana Press real soon, re-issues—and these stories, she wouldn't pick 'em. But the prize pickers pick 'em anyway.

RH: From what I know about prizes, so many of these things are compromises.

GP: That's true.

RH: And another thing is that, it seems with awards, I know from graduate programs and stuff like that, it seems like between the editors and the graduate programs, there's sort of a conspiracy of conformity.

GP: I think you're probably right. It's hard to say really. I mean it would be an easy thing to say, but I don't know the big graduate programs like Iowa and stuff like that.

BS: There's been a massive proliferation of these programs in the last 20 years. Probably if we had grown up 30 years ago we might all be lawyers.

RH: Or we wouldn't be writing through a workshop. I went to Iowa and I found some things both very positive and very destructive. Because there was what they call the workshop story, and if you're trying to do anything different—

GP: Well, at Sarah Lawrence we're not like that at all. We have so many differences of opinion around the place that it's hair raising to the students. As a matter of fact, it's the opposite. They get so many different opinions I think they go to pieces. I don't really know that workshops are bad or they're not bad. People have to have some community of work, and so they bide their time, that's the way I look at it. If they're lucky, they hit a good place. And if it's a bad place and they have strength of character, they cut out.

SS: Do you ever tell people things like, you'll never be a writer?

GP: No. Because I think it's mysterious. I would never tell anyone that. You get some very gifted students, and they really don't become writers because they don't have the pressure, they don't have the drive. They don't need to, there's nothing they want to learn about, there's nothing they want to investigate through the language of story. They don't want to do that, they gotta do some other things, they want to do biology. So then you have kids who are a little less so and some of them become marvelous writers. It's a great longing for truth that's involved somehow.

BS: Do you see then the expansion of small press literary activity as essentially healthy? You know some people say it's a proliferation of mediocrity—

GP: I think one of the things that happened is that through NEA grants and stuff like that a tremendous amount of poetry got printed. The money was available, and a lot of little tiny talents were coming out. I think there was a problem. The main problem was that because it was easy to do that, and cheaper—you could get about two dozen poems, and put out a something with two dozen poems. And no fiction was being printed. So you really are making decisions that you aren't aware of until after it's happened. So all of a sudden you realize that's where the money went. So one of the things that people tried to do was give some incentive to publish fiction as well. So then you have a little better balance. Things can be pushed in different directions a little bit. And all of the various forms get equal time.

BS: In your own work, are you conscious of trying to address certain concerns either formally or thematically?

GP: I'm more conscious of having addressed them than I am of addressing them.

SS: How do you begin your stories? There probably isn't one way, but do you have a ritual or a notebook you look at or—

GP: No. I usually begin with a sentence.

RH: So you don't have a firm idea of where you're going? It seems to me you used the word "investigations" before.

GP: Well I don't know usually where I'm going. Sometimes I really have a story and I don't have a form, and sometimes I have a form, but I don't have a story. An example would be a story like the immigrant story. I had that story in my mind for 20 years. I always use that story as an example. It's the best example I have. And I couldn't figure out how to tell the story. I had the plain outlines of it. And then, well, I do write these pages all the time which I don't know what the hell they're about either. And one day going through my papers I found this conversation or dialogue on history or whatever, and then I had the form for the story and a way of telling it. So that's a case where I had a story but no way to tell it.

BS: Looking back over your work do you have a sense of its having changed over time, in the 25 years since *Enormous Changes?*

GP: I think it has but in a funny way. But that's another question, that I don't think I'm the one to really address it. I'm sure it's changed; I've tried different things at different times and I've written about different countries, I've gone afield.

BS: I'm sure you've been asked this before—

GP: Ask me.

BS: But do you ever have any ambitions for anything larger, like a novel?

GP: I might. In some ways my life is more open now, I seem to have more open time. But it might be too late to do something about it. Because my mind has really been thinking short stories. If you write poetry it's the same thing. Your mind makes poems.

BS: It is true that more than most prose writers you seem to have almost a poet's sensibility of play with language. And I think that's one thing that's so attractive in your work.

GP: Well, I went to school for poetry.

BS: You didn't go to a writing program—

GP: No I really went to school to read poetry. And I read poetry mostly more than anything else. I was infatuated with poets, different poets at different times. One time I wrote exactly like Auden. I spent the whole year writing British. I was seventeen and I only wrote British.

BS: You write some poetry too, but you haven't published anything.

GP: I'm going to publish a book in November.

RH: I notice a certain terseness in your writing style, a compression of language that is like poetry, so that doesn't surprise me at all. But it also reminds me of certain writers, who I'm wondering if maybe influenced you. Like Isaac Babel—

GP: You know, I never read him before my first book. I was talking with someone about it, and some guy said something about that he had gotten a certain Yiddishness into Russian and I had gotten a certain Yiddishness into English. And I've had many people ask me that. But I didn't know him. I mean I knew him, I loved him, but I didn't know him. But when you're talking about influences, you're talking about who talked to you when you were little. And I would say we had the same grandfather. So it's an influence that's linguistic and social more than anything else.

I would say that one of my major influences was "one misty moisty morning and cloudiness of weather—". I don't think I could have written a poem if I hadn't loved that when I was a little kid. I've been foisting it on my grandmother ever since.

BS: When did you start writing fiction?

GP: When I was about 33 or 34. I really suddenly got absolutely appalled by what was happening, because of living in army camps with my husband in the military. I could see some great division between us that was painful. And I became very interested in women's lives. And partly because I had little kids and I was in the park a lot. I began to know women in another way than I always had.

RH: You said at the reading that you're very interested in promoting the short-short story. And I wonder if you could expand on that—

GP: Well, I think it's a wonderful form and it's just not exploited enough, it's not done enough. I'm always giving that as an assignment. I've noticed that when you're teaching, almost invariably you'll get more good stories out of the class than if you just gave a regular assignment. Because they don't have a lot of room. They've got to tell it. They've got to move, and they've got to bring it around.

SS: What do you tell them, less than 1000 words?

GP: No, I just tell them 2 pages. And I get 3 pages.

SS: That's even harder than 1000 words.

GP: No, 1000 is very hard. This is easier. 1000 is four or five pages. You have room to really fuck up. You have room to suddenly decide you have to develop this character or develop that. You don't have time for a lot of development. You can only do it straight. If you're talking about stories, the word development is probably the worst word in writing class. How do you develop this story? It's not developed enough. Develop this character—

RH: Because in that short-short story, the characters are in some ways archetypes and you can't develop them in a real sense.
Whose writing today do you admire, or think of as important?

GP: You know I figure a lot of people get asked that question and their mind goes blank.

BS: Well, who are you carrying around in your bag right now?

GP: I'm carrying around two novels for my City College class. I have a very good class and they really do a lot of work, so that's what I'm doing.

BS: So you go back and forth between City College and Sarah Lawrence?

GP: I go Monday nights to City and Tuesday and Wednesday to Sarah Lawrence. I just like to think about people who nobody's really talking about. I like to think of that. There's this East German writer, this woman who really should be ready by everybody. And if she was a man and from the West—West German—she would be. That's Christa Wolf. She's a really great writer, she's not just an ordinary writer.

SS: Has she been translated into English?

GP: You're damn right. And much of it put out by my publisher (Farrar Straus Giroux). She comes from East Berlin and she's written half a dozen books. Some of them are so inventive and so imaginative. Her last book, called *Cassandra,* is such a strong feminist book. She does very great things. With the novel are these four essays on how she thought about the novel. Imagine that—giving us her thoughts and her method and the pathways she took.

SS: How did you come upon her?

GP: I had read her book called, what is it, *Quest for Christa T.* and another one called *Patterns of Childhood*. What she does in every book is really look for the book. She makes this great search. And in that book she's really looking for the book of her own youth, which was as a Hitler Youth really.

RH: I think everyone was at that time. I had a teacher who was a Hitler Youth.

GP: I mean she describes it like the Girl Scouts. So I had read that. And when I went to Germany, I went to West Berlin and somebody said to me, who do you want to go see, and I said, I want to go see Christa Wolf, so we did. I went to East Berlin and I saw her.

SS: Does she speak English, or do you speak German?

GP: We both speak rotten in each other's language. But I brought a translator.

BS: Do you read much current American fiction?

GP: I do try to read it, but I'm really very behind. Mostly because of school. And it really kills me. And not only do I want to read it, but I have books sent to me. Right by my bed, the pile looks like that. And it's very hard for me to get to it. Who do you guys like?

RH: I like you. And I like Barry Hannah. And some Eastern European writers. I think we all like Milan Kundera.

GP: He writes about his prick too much. Excuse me, boys.

BS: What do you mean by that?

GP: I happen to like *The Book of Laughter and Forgetting* very much. But this last book *(The Unbearable Lightness of Being)*, it's really, it's as though he's been consumed by Western concerns. I think it's a corrupt book, I really do. I mean I really read it with great hopes because I really liked *Laughter and Forgetting,* I thought it was great. But I'm so disgusted. I mean who the fuck does he think he is?

It's not that I don't think that a person can write about sexual obsession. I think there's not much more interesting than that in a way. I'm all for it. But it's so egocentrical and false, admiring her so much for this idiotic loyalty.

BS: At the same time he's trying to use sex as a political metaphor.

GP: Yeah, but so obviously. But I still like the other book.

SS: It seemed real honest to me, the idea of the exile. The fact that he's left his home state and couldn't be happy unless he was back there.

GP: I think that's good. I think that part is fine. I don't see how people can live in exile. Except exile for my parents was great. They came here when they were 20 years old, I bet your grandparents did the same, and they sure never wanted to get de-exiled. When I told my mother and father that they ought to go to Paris, France or something interesting like that, they burst out laughing. The idea that I should want to go to Europe, a place like Europe.

SS: It's different when you're Jewish, though. Exile's a whole different thing to Jewish people. We don't get as attached to a place, there's something else that we're attached to.

GP: You're attached to surviving, that's what you're attached to.

SS: But Kundera wasn't. It's just different.

GP: But that's it.

SS: So you teach at Sarah Lawrence?

GP: Yeah, that's my school. That's the school that gave me my first job. I don't have any degrees.

SS: Do you do many visiting residencies?

GP: I don't want to leave home. I mean I'm not so young, my husband's not so young. I already don't see him half a year. I have my family. I don't like to go away.

Grace Paley Talking with Cora Kaplan
Cora Kaplan / 1985

From *Writing Lives: Conversations between Women Writers*. Ed. Mary Chamberlain (London: Virago, 1988), 181–90. Reprinted by permission of the publisher.

Grace Paley was born in New York City in 1922, the daughter of Russian Jewish immigrants who had arrived at the turn of the century. She grew up in the Bronx. Her parents spoke Russian and Yiddish at home—as well as English. Her formal education ended somewhere in mid-college years. She began to write fiction in the Fifties, extraordinary, vivid tragi-comic stories centering on city life in the neighborhoods she knew. Her stories appeared in *Esquire, The Atlantic* and *New American Review*. She has published three volumes of short stories, all critically acclaimed, *The Little Disturbances of Man* (1959), *Enormous Changes at the Last Minute* (1974) and *Later the Same Day* (1985), and one volume of poetry, *Leaning Forward* (1986). Grace Paley has a son and a daughter, and has taught literature at Columbia University, Syracuse University, Sarah Lawrence College and City College in New York. She has been actively engaged with left-wing politics much of her life and given a great deal of time and energy to anti-militarist movements and women's movements. She lives both in Vermont and New York City. I talked to her in April 1985 in her New York apartment, in the neighborhood where some of her stories are set.

C.K.: I want to focus our conversation around the relationship between politics and writing in your life and work. Perhaps that means starting with your latest collection of short stories, *Later the Same Day,* because there seem to be more overt "world politics" in it than in either of the two earlier books.

G.P.: Well, when I'm writing I don't think, am I putting politics into it or am I—taking it out. Is it there or isn't it there. I guess I think that *The Little Disturbances of Man*—which came out in '59—about women alone with kids, is really *very* political, dealing with life and language that hadn't been written about so much. *Later the Same Day* is about more political people. A lot of political writing—even the best that I can think of—is about leaders and big shots, about the class they rose from, how they're moulded and melded, how they destroyed or were destroyed by their country and so on. I don't think I have a gift for writing about leadership, so my general tendency, and my interest anyway is in writing about ordinary political people I think they've been abandoned in many ways, as though they don't exist. The fact that there are a lot of people who are just normally political is a hidden fact in this country. Nobody wants to know it, and they try to pretend that there is only private life, and that people don't even talk politics, which they really do. So you find lots and lots of books—it's as though men and women never have any conversations except about their extremely private life, as though that's the only thing that's interesting. But the ordinary political person is, I think, worth shedding a little bit of light on, because that woman or man is a regular citizen. I mean that's all he is, she is.

C.K.: Your stories make it clear that there's a political practice that's part of everyday life.

G.P.: Yes. Mothers bring up sons, which is often a political act of warsome nature, or often today—a feminist act of humanizing the male child, and there's the young and the old, and there's the historical experiences of the old. Newness of the young. Then there's always the world moving in on all these people, and they just seem to know it. No big secret.

C.K.: Many of the stories in *Later the Same Day* are about a lost generation of children.

G.P.: Well, I don't think they're lost—I've called them in a story "Friends" the "beloved generation of our children"—who were I guess all Sixties kids—youngsters really now in their mid-thirties. An unusual number were killed in car accidents (just part of U.S. statistics) or went to war—Vietnam—or drugs. Of course most survived. But I think about them all because I knew them growing up; you really have a very tender feeling for a large person you knew as a two-year-old.

C.K.: Many of the stories suggest that these events, what happens to these kids and their parents, are not reconcilable, they can't be turned into tales with an implicit moral, they're just part of—

G.P.: —Revolutions—

C.K.: Yes.

G.P.: I agree with you.

C.K.: Did you decide, when you started writing, not to write the well-made story?

G.P.: Well, I didn't know how to write the well-made stories. I tried, God knows. I just failed miserably, so I just wrote the way I could. I made honest efforts to write a typical novel, but I failed, I just couldn't do it. I can't write longer things—I try to write everything the right size, length and width—and depth, for what it is.

C.K.: One of the things I sometimes feel on reading your stories, is that because of how they move in time, they encompass as much as most novels.

G.P.: I hope so. I seem unable to just let things go, in a sense. But the novel—it really sort of cuts between time zones so at the end of the story you actually feel you've had many years of someone.

C.K.: Yet you've said that you think most novels are too long.

G.P.: Well I think it's really true, a lot of writers inflate; they want to write a novel and they do write a very long book, too long for its true size.

C.K.: How did you come to your own way of writing?

G.P.: It took a long time in the sense that I wrote poetry for a long time, I didn't write stories, but once I sat down to write stories I wrote stories—I mean I wrote the stories in my book.

C.K.: You've said that the poems came out of literature, were very "literary."

G.P.: Right, I think that was true in the beginning. I mean the reason I began to write stories was that the poems up to then had been too literary, it really was a problem. I think writing the stories loosened my poetry and made it easier.

C.K.: A lot more poetry has snuck into the stories in *Later the Same Day*.

G.P.: I have a book of poetry out now [*Leaning Forward*]; I have a graduate student who also had a press and who was interested in poetry, and every now and then I'd read a couple of poems, and she said, "I want to put out your poems." So I visualized you know, a collection of ten poems—a little chap book as they say. Well, little by little by little by little—

C.K.: A lot of poems. It seems to me that one route to women's history has always been women's fictions, a way of writing to women as well as about them.

G.P.: Oh, sure. It's true for Black history too. Though I can't say that I thought I was writing to women or for women or anything. I knew I was writing *about* women, and I felt that might be troublesome.

C.K.: Why?

G.P.: At the time when I began to write, I thought nobody would be interested, that's all. That's what I mean by trouble. And in my first book I was still so shy that my major public statement would be to second the motion at the P.T.A. I mean that would be as brave as I could get. That would take a lot of courage.

C.K.: Your two main women characters that run through your fiction, Virginia and Faith, are single parents for much of the time, and you weren't. How much are their lives yours?

G.P.: Not interchangeable. My life and theirs are different. But the characters are like people who could become my friends, very close friends, if I met them. Virginia's street, I lived in that street and neighborhood for a long time. There were a lot of women alone with kids and I became very, very interested in how they lived. I myself was beginning to develop lots of anxieties about relations between women and men.

C.K.: You've said that none of the women are victims, and that seems right. Do you think women take strength from that aspect of the stories?

G.P.: Well, I read "An Interest in Life" in City College about five years ago, and a young Black girl got up and said to me, "Do you think Ginny is some kind of heroine?" I said "No, not specially, I just think she's a pretty brave person, but," I said, "what do you think?" She said, "I think she's a dope, wanting to go back to that guy." So I was taken aback a little bit and I said, "Well, if you think she's a dope, all I can tell you is I think you're going to have a better life than she has."

C.K.: The stories have a lot of unease about men, but they're not anti-men, are they?

G.P.: No, and I've always liked the men I've lived with. I mean apart from love.

C.K.: The war doesn't figure much in your stories. It's a sort of absent place.

G.P.: It's interesting, you're actually right, and yet it certainly is a very important part of my life. I mean there are Jewish stories there, about what happened to the Jews. I feel very seriously Jewish. But you're right, the first book came out in the late Fifties and I was really looking at something else. It seemed that the men had been covering the war. I have things I really should write about because I had a lot of fun living in army camps. My husband didn't (have fun). He went to the Pacific, Okinawa. Both my husbands. Bob was in the Philippines, Japan.

C.K.: All three collections talk about how women stay on the block and men go roving around, taking off, coming back when they feel like it. In "An Interest in Life" Virginia's husband joins the Army—

G.P.: Right, but there it's cynical, it's the way men get away from women. That one was written after the Korean War, a war that really went right by him. In fact if there's any bunch of guys who should feel bad, it's the Korean War class. You know the fellows who were in Vietnam feel very injured by the attitude of people towards them, which I think they're wrong about, and then the Second World War guys, everybody knows, a lot of boys. But the Korean War, nobody talks about that at all and a lot of boys died there, the guys who'd just missed the Second World War. I meet these guys who are now about fifty-five, sixty years old and they did the Korean War, and they're really not that much younger than me.

C.K.: Just as the early books brought women, the neighborhood and families into fiction in a new way, *Later the Same Day* brings international politics into the stories differently. You've travelled to Chile and to China, for instance. How have your own political activities and experience shaped the writing?

G.P.: Wherever you go, if you're a political person, you see the politics of the place. I haven't written too much about travels. We lived in Chile just before the coup, but my husband has done most of the writing on Chile. I haven't really used a lot of these experiences yet. I've written poems about having been in Vietnam in '69. We went to China to see what was happening there, not as part of any government group or anything like that. We went to Chile to see how socialism was working; if it would last. And I was in Nicaragua last June.

C.K.: What has come out of the trip to Nicaragua?

G.P.: I've done a lot of speaking. Some poems one wants to say to the American people—I said this when I was in England a lot—we would be in Nicaragua today, right now if it was up to this administration, and it's the American people that have prevented it. You know, over 50,000 Americans have been to Nicaragua, have helped out, worked with the Nicaraguans, are building houses with them, are working in their hospitals. That's what's going on and that's this crazy United States. Those efforts, and the organizations of sanctuary that have been set up here, which show some of the fantastic progressive energy—among American religious groups on the left too—need to be publicized in Europe. The superficial view of this country abroad is that nothing is happening here, and that's a view that our media wants to press on Europeans also, but there are pockets of activity all over the country; it's a big country. Tremendous actions taking place everywhere; that's one of the reasons that up to now we haven't really invaded. The government would have been in there in five minutes, but the American people didn't want it. It's important to speak in Britain about this—I love to hear about actions in other countries. It gives you some goddam solidarity and hope!

C.K.: What other kinds of things have you been doing politically?

G.P.: I've been working with some people on some feminist pieces. As progress is pushed back, as the administration and media gives up on affirmative actions for women and Blacks and other minorities (which is in contradiction to what I said thirty seconds ago) you find there's no money for health clinics, for housing—for kids—it's all going to military expenditure. And when that "moving back" on women's issues happens it happens in all sectors. Even in our own left movement, you find people saying: "Oh well, but thank God, we don't have to think about the women today. We were burdened with that last year, but this year we don't have to think about them so much." So that feminist position, that particular analysis that addresses patriarchy, begins to get lost. You've got to make sure it's still there and solidly present in people's thinking.

You've got to keep your eye on so many things. It's hard. That normal American emphasis on individualism and pride and religion—positions that seem anti-political, are very political really. They come from the ideology and structure of bourgeois capitalism—a wholly private emphasis. The general mode is one of thinking individualistically. It's the only value; it becomes *the* value.

C.K.: These latest stories argue against that by integrating the ongoing political concerns of people with their so-called private lives, so that the reader can hear how they are spoken together. Friends and lovers argue about love and politics in the same conversations, without the public topics simply being metaphors for the personal relations. China, civil rights, Chile, U.S. policy, adultery, children and parenting are all threaded through—part of the same fabric of daily exchange. There's also, and I thought this is more true of your recent work, more self-conscious writing about writing. Could you comment on that?

G.P.: I don't know where to push that. Almost from the beginning when a child tells you a story, she'll say, "I want to tell you a story and I'll tell you this." It's often a very talented story about a story.

C.K.: A lot of these stories seem to say: "It's not what you think it is."

G.P.: Right. I mean, a story is made very often of two stories, until you have one story sort of half-contradicting another or corroborating another, one with the other. Like, the story about China, "Somewhere Else," it's really two stories, but separately each story would be less interesting, and two stories together really make a third story. And every story is completed by the reader.

C.K.: Quite a lot of the politics that your characters are involved in are locally based, in the city. Now that you live in Vermont as well as New York are you still so involved in that?

G.P.: Less in New York. A little bit in Vermont. I'm not here enough. When you have a kid, the school's next door, the parks—all the things are part of the city's life. It's hard to do local political work here for me right now; I'm not part of local organizations, but local work is the most interesting work. I miss it a great deal. I've never been happier doing politics than when I did local stuff. Even the peace politics we did was very local—the anti-Vietnam War actions. Out of our neighborhood organization we really created events that took on a citywide and nationwide strata. We did something called "Angry Arts" which we initiated and pretty soon the whole city was doing it and then it was organized in Philadelphia and Baltimore. So you can start locally, and what you do can roll over . . . The Women's Pentagon Action—not quite so local—a Northeastern women's action was repeated in the West. Japanese women—Italian women called to talk about methods of organization.

C.K.: Yes I miss that, living in Britain. That particular kind of community based politics seems harder to get going. When I was a young mother there I was shocked that parents weren't supposed to take such an active interest in the schools. The teachers thought the worst possible case was America where parents had so much say. You were supposed to run jumble sales and sell cakes and that's all.

G.P.: Well that's the way things used to be and a lot of the P.T.A.'s fought successfully for a different role. To shift the subject slightly—my granddaughter's first-grade class (she's six years old) asked me to come talk to them—the teacher invited me to speak to the six-year-olds about women's history—it was women's history week or month something like that. I think I was asked because the week earlier—the teacher told me—she'd been telling the class all about the accomplishments of mankind, how remarkable mankind was etc. My granddaughter worriedly asked, "But what about womankind? Didn't they do anything?" The teacher laughed, "Is your mother a feminist?" "Oh no," Laura said, "she's a nurse." I guess the point I want to make is a small hopeful one. One of the horses history rides is language. Fifteen years ago, maybe ten, in my fifties, I wouldn't have noticed the word mankind at all. And here in 1986, a six-year-old person heard the word in all its meaning.

An Interview with Grace Paley
Melanie Kaye/Kantrowitz and Irena
Klepfisz / 1985

From *The Tribe of Dinah: A Jewish Women's Anthology* by Melanie Kaye/Kantrowitz and Irena Klepfisz (Boston: Beacon Press, 1989), 322-29. Copyright © 1986, 1989 by Melanie Kaye/Kantrowitz and Irena Klepfisz. Reprinted by permission of Beacon Press, Boston.

Grace Paley was born in 1922 in the Bronx. A mother of two, grandmother of one, she has been active in the anti-militarist and women's movement for many years. She is the author of three collections of short stories—*The Little Disturbances of Man* (Viking/Penguin), *Enormous Changes at the Last Minute* and *Later the Same Day* (both, Farrar, Straus & Giroux), and a book of poetry, *Leaning Forward* (Granite Press). She teaches at Sarah Lawrence and at City College, CUNY, and lives sometimes in New York City and sometimes in Vermont, where we interviewed her in September, 1985.

When we talked on the phone the other day, you said you were going to go to Synagogue for Yom Kippur. Have you always gone?

No, I haven't. I used to take my grandmother. We lived in the Bronx. And the *shul* was about two doors away. It was the same kind of little private house—we used to call them private houses in the Bronx—the same kind of house as ours. The *shul* eventually, when the neighborhood changed, became an Iglesia Pentecostal. I used to take my grandmother, but I never attended services and my parents were very anti-religious. They laughed at religion. I mean they wanted me to take my grandmother because they wanted me to take *her*, but if I had become serious, they would have been amused.

And I can't say lightly amused. My father came here in 1905. He was already a young man of 20, so he must have been born in '84. And he hated religiousness. And so did my mother. My mother even more maybe. My grandmother was not orthodox. She did not insist on a kosher home. But we didn't insult her. I don't think she was very insistent either. She wanted Passover. She wanted the holidays. She wanted Saturday. She wanted to go to synagogue and she did. But my parents obviously had made their rebellion against all that in their youth. And this grandmother—whom my father loved deeply, by the way—was the person they rebelled against and they won. And she was in their house. So that's the way it was.

When you go now, why do you go?
Well, I have gone to services *here* [in Vermont] the last 3-4 years. And I think probably part of the reason is that when I'm in New York I feel I'm *in* a continuous Jewish community. So for me there's a communitarian reason really. And I think if the rabbis were impossible, you know I might not. But they've been Hillel rabbis related to the school, which means they need to be kind of open, receptive, you know. They're sometimes willing to stick their necks out politically and at the same time they're deeply religious. At least Rabbi Michael Paley is—no relative. And I'm interested in what the community is here.

When I talk about the religious attitude of my family, people like to say words about Jewish self-hatred. But there was *none* of that. There was *no* wish not to be Jewish. There was *no* desire to pretend we were something else. In fact, along with his opposition to religion, my father had biblical feeling and knowledge which he shared with me. And this was true to such a degree that I just grew up liking things Jewish, kind of pleased with myself for having had the sense to be born into this family instead of some other. When I left home and lived in the Midwest, it would be one of the first things I would tell people, really—at least in the beginning.

Then what happened?
Well, what happened is I learned more about anti-Semitism in a very real sense. But I still did it. Announced who I was—I mean, I liked it.

What was your sense of what it meant to be Jewish when you were growing up?
Well, it meant to be a socialist. Well, not really. But it meant to have social consciousness. It also meant that we were related to those generations of the Jewish Bible. We had common history. Our neighborhood was solidly Jewish. Next door there could be somebody who wasn't. That would be a very exotic person. The whole block didn't have more than two people who weren't Jewish. So my idea of the world was that it was totally Jewish. And the people to be worried about and pitied are the ones outside. So there is a sense that the stranger is the one to be remembered. The reason that it's repeated in the Bible so many times that we were strangers in Egypt is really to make us behave decently. This seemed to me very much a part of being Jewish. And it wasn't a

matter of hospitality, which is as American as apple pie, so to speak. It wasn't hospitality; it was a normal sense of outrage when others were treated badly, and along with that the idea that injustice not be allowed to continue. Blacks, for example. When I was a little kid, I said the word "nigger," my big sister hauled off and socked me. When I tell her this, she's absolutely amazed. She really doesn't remember it. But those are the feelings that seemed to me very important, that seemed to me for some peculiar reason related to being Jewish.

Was it connected with anything specifically Jewish?
No, just that all the Jews I knew were people who were concerned about the fate of the world and what to do about it. And not that they weren't upwardly mobile. They were, surely. I mean, my father came here when he was 20, without a word of English, and he became a doctor within the next 6 to 10 years. He learned English. Actually he also learned Italian. And they liked to do well, and they didn't do much politics. They read the paper. They talked at every meal about the world, but they didn't do much. They *had* been active in Russia in their youth, been dangerously active, imprisoned. But not here. And my uncle, a young anarchist in his 20s, was deported in Palmer Raid days. But it just seemed to be related to this business of your attitude towards others, how you were to deal with the other. I learned that expression recently: "the other." How to deal with the other.

You've been an activist for a long time. Did that seem to you like a Jewish thing to be also?
I have to give a talk which I'm nervous about in Houston, Texas, at the Jewish Y. And I'm going to call it "Thinking Globally, Acting Jewish." And yet I've learned a lot from other groups. I learned a lot from Christian pacifists. But it seemed to me they had learned a lot from Jews without knowing it. I mean they do walk around saying everything out of Isaiah even putting lots of it into Jesus' mouth. Like it's theirs alone.

Really. Like they invented ploughshares.
Right. Right. They started the ploughshare movement. And, of course, we're the ones who till just recently haven't had much army or too many weapons either. Well I think a lot about that. I don't know to what degree this is Jewish or not Jewish. I mean there are other influences in one's life, like being born female.

At the conference in Greenfield a year ago on Non-Violence and the Jewish Tradition you were saying you had thought more about being Jewish lately.

I never *didn't* think about it. I wrote stories about Jews and I still do. But this business of going to temple here in Vermont—which isn't even a temple, it's the chapel of the school—has to do really with being in an entirely different community. My present husband—Bob's not Jewish. Very few people around here are. So, my going comes from a very simple longing to see my own people. I made Vera [Williams] go with me. She was visiting me. I said, you'll really be surprised. I know if I'm interested, she'll probably be interested. So we went. And the Rabbi kept trying to say humankind instead of mankind. He really was working on it. We both felt a kind of softness towards him. Every now and then he slipped. And the Cantor was a woman and she sang absolutely beautifully. She sang so beautifully that people didn't want to sing with her. They really wanted to hear her, to receive her. So I think that's it, just a real longing to be with your own people and to be with them at a very profound point in their year, in their life, in their thinking.

A lot of people we've talked to said that Israel's invasion of Lebanon in '82 was a real jolt. People who for years hadn't thought about their Jewishness were sort of forced to start thinking about it in relationship to Israel. Did that have an effect on you?

Well, since I think a lot about politics, it had an effect on me. But it didn't have a jolting or a changing effect. It wasn't so much a surprise as a new reason for sorrow and disgust. I was pleased at the services that year that this young fellow really spoke out very strongly.

Sometimes I think that the Left has really made some terrible mistakes. I was talking about it the other day—the way the people in Nicaragua can separate the *people* of the US from the *government*. And that is partly a result of a decision by the Left. It's not just a strategy decision, it's true.

It's a decision which the Left made in Vietnam, which was to divide the country. A very sensible, simple thing to do, to see us as opposed to the government. True too. It did not weaken the people of Nicaragua or Vietnam. So, I've never understood why my sisters and brothers on the Left haven't been able to do the same in relation to Israel. And if they'd done it a long time ago. I think things could have been different. If they had pointed out again and again: the people and the government, I mean, the difference at that time. A big majority of the American people were not yet against the war in Vietnam when the Vietnamese said, "We know you're not the government." There were maybe nine people on assorted street corners in '62, '63, '64 and the Vietnamese were already talking like that, right? So it's not as if you would have had to say the *majority* of the people in Israel are against this. Enough of them were in opposition. Why it wasn't done I—I know why it wasn't done.

Why?
Anti-Semitism. [all laugh knowingly]

Has that changed at all with the Left? Gotten worse? Or do you think it's the same?
No, I think in some ways it's better. In the women's movement press, too. You were really both very useful and really strong and influential. And I think a lot of women began to think seriously about anti-Semitism. Just because women started to stand up, others suddenly realized they had legs. The work the two of you did perked up a lot of people I talked to. I was really surprised in some cases by a new understanding in certain women that certain attitudes were plain anti-Semitism. Some suddenly said *un huh*. On the other hand there were quite a lot of people that didn't see it at all.

For a lot of Jewish women, Israel was sort of like a relative that you felt embarrassed by, that everybody was always going to identify you with.
Right.

That was sort of the level at which the understanding operated—just embarrassment and shame. Have you every worked politically on Israel?
No, I haven't done that, directly. As an anti-war worker, I've included Middle East concerns.

You just came back from Nicaragua fairly recently and you were talking about the connection between religion and the government.
Well, it's a Catholic country, seriously so. The people believe. I went to one of the liberation churches. It was very lovely and wild; they did a lot of wild singing and Indian music with flutes and drums, and guitars. And the priest spoke beautifully. He compared Nicaragua to Jesus. He said Jesus was killed because he refused to abandon the poor. And that's what Nicaragua's enemies wanted her to do on pain of death. Like Christ, Nicaragua would never abandon the poor. In Nicaragua, religion is connected to local work, the life of the oppressed. The Pope, though, has to convert the whole world. That's his job. In doing that, he has to behave a certain way to the powerful. But in a poor country, people can just believe. They have the moral ideas of the religion which are perfectly good, nothing wrong with them. Christian ideas, the basic ones. It's just that most Christians never use them.

Do you think it was a mistake to link politics with religion?
Oh, you know the Communist Party in Nicaragua is absolutely opposed

to giving in to the religious groups. They think the Sandinistas are far too deferential to the religious groups. And they speak up about it. And I became aware of that because one of the women in our group was obviously a Communist Party person, and she talked at length about this. And I saw why. I mean, in the same sense that my father. She was born and raised a Catholic and she hated every bit of it. She despised the religion as oppressive, just as my father and mother thought Judaism was. I was just looking at this article in the *New Yorker* on Hasidic Jews. And there's this general sentimentalization of them, and they really were what my father hated, ran away from.

This is switching the topic. But do you remember in Greenfield we were sitting at a table with a bunch of young women, who said they wanted to get together as Jewish women to talk about racism. And yet they had never talked about themselves as Jews.

You know in my lifetime, Jews have been very close to Blacks, really have had very close relations, and I just happen to be reading this book *When and Where I Enter* [by Paula Giddings]. Anyway, I noticed it's full of these Jewish names of people who were working in that movement. Well, some of these kids missed those years. A lot of us have thought about racism. In a sense, I've thought about it since I was 5 years old when my sister smacked me. And my thinking about it was Jewish thinking. So that in a way I think these Jewish women are "thinking Jewish" when they say that they want to think about racism. And I think it's a good thing. They feel they're talking from that Jewish base. They don't think they've skipped. They're in it. But I know what you're talking about. It's natural because they're young that they assume that nobody has thought about it yet. And it's also weird. In some groups I've worked with, a couple of young women would come in and say: "Start thinking about racism. We're all racist because we're not talking constantly about racism." It probably never entered their minds that many of us *had* been talking about it for years, acting on it for years, and that it was not a new subject for us at all, had always been one of deep concern. But it *was* new to them.

I just got this letter from the American Jewish Committee, which is helping to start up group meetings of Blacks and Jews. I think for most Jews who live in New York there's a real sadness about this terrible split that's happened. This craziness, you know, this nasty anti-Jewishness among Blacks and anti-Blackism among Jews. It's so painful, I think that a lot of people feel that. I went to a few meetings of Jewish and Black women. And it's interesting that *women* really wanted those meetings and initiated them.

I knew a lot of those kids [in Greenfield] because I've worked with them in the Women's Pentagon Action and in Not In Our Name. I was interested to see them in Greenfield. One of these women from here in New England was a really great, stubborn, inspiring war tax resister. And not only was she there, she knew all the prayers before supper, prayers after supper, etc. That's what I found surprising.

That they knew so much about the tradition?
That I didn't even know they were Jewish. And that I had worked with them. I figured they were kids mostly of middle-class families that had retained some of the ritual and been raised to be *bat mitzvah*, to go to Hebrew Sunday School, and learn the prayers. So they had learned those forms and maybe rebelled against them a little, stored them away for a few years to do other political work. And that's where I met them. And they had moved towards feminism because of their disappointment maybe with sexism, which would be very natural for young women of the late '70s. I mean they would have been really angry if they'd walked into a *shul* and had seen how women prayed. So I think they were re-evaluating their Jewishness. And trying to think of it in these new terms. They certainly knew more than I knew.

Both the women and the men at that conference talked about having worked with people in the movement for years—mostly the peace movement—and not having known they were Jews. Do you think people were afraid to say they were Jews—or it just didn't come up?
Well, it does come up, it can if you want it to.

But now, suddenly, they were all at this conference because they somehow wanted to be.
The push may have come from Lebanon. It may have come from the sense that something's going wrong, the tradition was not meant to be like that. I mean there was one woman there who had really worked hard with the Women's Pentagon Action, was seriously non-violent, active in the lesbian-feminist peace movement and fiercely, very fiercely. And with a few Yiddish words thrown in. But there she was at the conference. If you live long enough you really become patient. People improve. If they're already wonderful, they become slowly more wonderful.

Grace, did you speak Yiddish at home?
We spoke mostly Russian. My mother and father talked Russian. My grandmother talked only Yiddish. I was able to talk a little Yiddish.

But you spoke to them in English?
Mostly. I understood Yiddish, street talk Yiddish.

Where did your parents come from in Russia?
South Russia. It used to be called Donetz. It was also called Stalino and before that it was called Usovka. It was named by an Englishman named Hughes who owned a steel mill.

Was your background, your Jewishness an influence on your writing?
I think that a lot of my writing has a kind of Jewish Russian accent. I think its language and its feeling is. But when I first began writing people said I was being influenced by Isaac Babel. Well, I'd never read him. But I realized what the influences might be—that he probably had the same grandfather I had and the same great-grandmother. And what I'm influenced by is sound and feeling which has nothing to do with literature—in the beginning. It's just ordinary speech, ordinary stories, inflections and tunes. A tune is a language, so to speak. So I think it was more like that. I felt the power of Russian writers because we read them at home. And then Jewish storytelling through my parents, through my father, a certain kind of storytelling you know, and that's not literary. But it becomes finally literature.

A kind of parenthetical style where you sort of get everything in.
Yes, you don't omit anything. I mean it really is a way of talking about everything at once, while making some absolutely trite remark. You can't talk about anything without bringing in the world. It's out there.

How old were you when you started become active politically?
Well, I guess I always was a little bit. I have this memory—I just remember in junior high school or high school—very early. Something came up about a pledge not to go to war or something like that. I was right there, right away. And so I began to do that very early.

Were the first people you did that with in your neighborhood? Were they also Jews?
Oh, yes.

This is in the Bronx?
Yes. In high school, I would say almost all. I had a very good friend in junior high who wasn't Jewish, now that I think of it. but almost everybody was, and in high school kids were either Jews or Italians.

When did you first start working with non-Jews? When did you go out of the neighborhood?
Oh, well I tell you, I learned a lot from non-Jews. And that happened during the Vietnam War really. I'm just trying to think. In school, most of my friends were Jewish. All the boys. If a boy wasn't, he'd be so

interesting everybody would fall all over the place. So exotic. I remember calling my best friend, Evi, on the phone and telling her that these two guys had just come over to the house, and I didn't think they were Jewish. She came down right away. It turned out they both were, and I married one of them.

Actually during the war [World War II] I left New York, and I got married young when I was nineteen and I lived in army camps, and most of the boys were not Jewish—Jesse's friends you know. They were very interesting to me. I got to know them little by little. You know it was another world, so I was interested in it. But politically I began—[working with non-Jews] around the time of the Vietnam War. The PTA—that was a good organization. As soon as I began to work locally, I worked with non-Jews. Since I lived in the Village, the people were very mixed. And the non-Jews were politically active too, at least the ones I knew. We Jews were kind of global, but the Christians had a better local sense. Many came from small towns. They believed you could fight City Hall and they did. And I learned from them. And then I got to know people in the pacifist movement. And those ideas were brand new to me. I think I was always basically opposed to war, militarism. But I didn't know there were real ideas about those things, political philosophies that were in opposition to my old socialist-centered self. And I would say that this began to happen around '60 and '61. But then again later, one of the first women's consciousness-raising groups—a very early one that I joined, I'd say three quarters of the women were Jewish. Again in the beginning of any movement there always seemed a preponderance of Jewish women.

You said you're talking more with Jewish groups right now. Do you feel that you need to talk more to Jewish groups or that there's a special thing you want to convey to American Jews?

Well, I feel both those things, I feel that I haven't worked among Jews enough in a sense. I feel that I've lived among them all my life and that I've fought with them and so forth. But I haven't worked with them in any organized kind of way. I mean if I've joined an organization, it hasn't been usually a Jewish organization. I'm a member of New Jewish Agenda, but I don't really work with it specifically. So I feel a little—I feel I have a bad conscience.

Grace, is there anything else that you want to say about Jewish women and Jewish identity?

That word identity has been hard for many women who live secular lives and maybe harder for religious women and also feminists. But the women's movement has made a big difference. I don't know who it hasn't helped in this world. It's given a lot of Jewish women courage to stay Jewish and fight. And fight for those ordinary rights. R-i-t-e-s. Rights to have rites. That really seems important. It meant a lot to us to have those young women at the conference [in Greenfield]. I haven't yet said that it's very possible that I'm able to come back to this, to go to the *shul*, to do it wholeheartedly, to feel I have a natural place in that community—it's possible I'm able to do all of this because of the women's movement and its influence. Because of the way a lot of Jewish women took hold, women much more religious than I. Without their courage and what they did, I might not have begun to go to this temple. I might not have done that.

It's ironic because when you think about women who are religious, they're usually labelled conservative. Yet, they're the ones that made the push.
They're the ones that did it.

So that the "progressives" could come in and feel comfortable.
That's really true. I hadn't thought of it that way either.

Often when we think about Jewishness and the women's movement, we feel anger for the anti-Semitism. We don't speak much about the Jewish women who are feminists, who pushed and fought in the Jewish community.
Yes, who make those changes for *us*. For *me* certainly. I certainly would never have persuaded my daughter to go to services, or Vera. The connections are always surprising.

Grace Paley on Storytelling and Story Hearing
Jacqueline Taylor / 1986

From *Literature in Performance* 7.2 (1987): 46–58. Reprinted by permission.

Since the appearance of her first volume of short stories in 1956, *The Little Disturbances of Man: Stories of Women and Men at Love*, Grace Paley's work has never been out of print. 1985 saw the publication of her third volume of short stories, *Later the Same Day*, and a first volume of poetry, *Leaning Forward* (Penobscot, Maine: Granite Press). Paley composes at the typewriter, reading aloud to herself as she writes. She also requires her writing students at Sarah Lawrence College and City College of New York to read aloud to each other. Clearly, Paley is an author who explicitly acknowledges the connection between the written and spoken word. On the sunny morning of March 15, 1986, we met in her Greenwich Village apartment for an interview. At the kitchen table, fortified by cups of coffee and slices of the homemade bread I had brought along, we talked for an hour and a half.

Jacqueline Taylor: *Since I'm especially interested in the relationship between writing and speaking in your work, I thought we could start by talking about your writing technique. You've described the process you begin with as reading aloud, typing, and reading aloud again.*
   Grace Paley: Well, what I usually begin with is either someone else's language or my own. I usually begin thinking of language very strongly. I think it's partly because I began by writing poetry.

   JT: *So you begin with words in mind; you have somebody's language in mind when you begin?*
   GP: Yes, in a funny way, I can't find my own way of speaking until I have other voices. It's almost other voices that give me the strength or the permission or whatever to go through with it.

   JT: *When you read your work aloud as you are writing, what are you listening for?*
   GP: Well, I'm listening for everything at once. I can't even tell you exactly, but I think what I'm listening for is whether it's authentic,

whether it's true, whether it's true to the language of the speaker, which may not be me. It could be someone else.

JT: *And it's easier, initially, if it's somebody else's voice?*

GP: Well, it's the difference for me between writing poems and fiction. I would say that in poems it's you speaking out, but then in fiction you're trying to get the world to speak to you, so therefore it's very often other voices.

JT: *I was going to ask you about that. How do you know when you start whether you're going to write a story or a poem? Some of your stories are so short and so lyrical they're almost little poems.*

GP: Well, I think we worry too much about what form is which. I've noticed that heavy fiction people really don't like those little one-page two-page stories. I mean the reviewers, the fiction reviewers. Now if it's poetry reviewers, they usually like them, but if they're fiction reviewers, they usually say, "This thing wasn't developed, you know. Why doesn't it go somewhere?"

JT: *It doesn't quite fit into their categories.*
GP: Uh-huh.

JT: *When you teach, you have your students read their work aloud to others.*

GP: Yes, I do, and I not only have them read aloud, I don't have any copies.

JT: *So they have to get it with their ears.*

GP: Yes. You know, we always think of the person who is *reading* as the person who's being taught. I mean that piece of work that's being taught. That's not true. The whole class has to be taught. So for me, the class, one of the things they're being taught is listening. And it's really almost a political thing for me to pay attention to what's going on. And they get awful good at it; that's what's really interesting. I mean much better than me because I came to all this, I came to thinking about it really late. But they really *hear* a story, it amazing.

JT: *So you favor* hearing *the story as a way of* getting *the story.*

GP: Well, it's one of the ways; I'm not so particular. I mean anyone who has loved reading books also knows the joy of simply being able to get into an armchair or a bed or some private place where you simply enter another world. So I love that too. But I think for writers especially, which most of them want to be, that business of paying attention to the word, to the sound, and to the meaning of the story is very important; so that's what I want them to learn.

JT: *In my performance studies classes, I teach literature by having students do readings of it. And they have to attend to it much more closely that way.*
GP: They do. And it's slower, it slows it down. Because the eye is such a speedy thing. The eye goes zzt, zzt, zzt, you know? The ear says, "Wait."

JT: *Also, when they have to perform a work for an audience, it belongs to them more.*
GP: Well, I don't care about that so much. There's too many "my's" in our society, I think.

JT: *Yet if students don't know they like literature, it helps them feel a connection to it.*
GP: Right. Well, especially reading other literature. We do that too. I begin every class, for instance, with the reading of poems, of something somebody thinks is beautiful. Like sort of a ritual, like saying grace, or thank you God, or something. Somebody comes in and picks up a poem and reads a poem by George Herbert or reads a poem by almost anybody. Somebody read two pages of Faulkner yesterday. I want them to read something they love. So at least two poems are read at the beginning of class—or fiction.

JT: *Do they do this voluntarily, whoever wants to read, does?*
GP: Yes, if nobody wants to, I'll have a little something. But almost all the time people do. In fact, I only read something once because I was dying to read it. And then one day a week whoever wants to, comes to my office, this is no more than four or five people tops, and we just read.

JT: *Your own work or somebody else's that you love?*
GP: Somebody else's.

JT: *Oh, I like that a lot.*
GP: We try to read old things because that's not done. I mean it's done in the English department, but among writing students, they're very hep on what was written last week, but a lot of them really need old tunes in their ears.

JT: *You've said elsewhere that the story really exists off the page and that we have to think of the throat it comes out of. Is that in a way suggesting that the story really lives in the throat, in speech?*

GP: I wish I had it here, I wish I could show it to you, it's a piece out of Jerome Rothenberg's book, *Technicians of the Sacred*. It's just one page, and it's a page in which everybody talks about what poetry is, and the Aztecs say something, and the New Guinea people say something, and the Bush people say something, and one of them says, "The magic of the generations, the magical knowledge is stored in our bellies and can escape only through the larynx."

JT: *Oh, that's wonderful.*

GP: Yes. It's right up (or down) your alley.

JT: *Yes. I'd love to see it.*[2] When did you start doing public readings of your work?

GP: Soon as they asked me. (Laughter) The poets were doing it already.

JT: *Yes, there aren't as many short story readers out there.*

GP: Yes, but I love to read any time I am asked to.

JT: *Do you find that when you read for an audience you learn different things about your work than when you read it for yourself as you are writing?*

GP: Well, there are certain things. For instance, I have some humor in my work sometimes, and some of those parts really get very cheap laughs when they're read aloud; so I don't read them aloud. I'll just leave the sentence out. Read alone on the page, they're OK, I *think*. But read aloud, they're wrong. I mean, people will laugh, right away at a point where it's not to be laughed at.

JT: *So you have some works you're interested in reading for an audience, and others—*

GP: I read everything, but it's just those little sentences, maybe three in all those books, that I will change. No more than that. And for all I know, I could take them out altogether, if they don't work. I haven't really wanted to take them out. But I know I don't like to read them because I don't like what happens to people's faces when they hear them.

JT: *What are the stories where this happens?*

GP: There is a little story called "Friends."[3] It's a sad story, and there's a place where she says, "You know the night Abby died, when the police called me and told me. That was my first night's sleep in two years." That I say. But I don't say, "I knew where she was," because it's too intense to be said aloud. There must be things like that.

JT: *Maybe that laugh is to relieve tension.*
GP: Right, that's a very good point. But they wouldn't do it alone, I don't think.

JT: *When we were speaking on the phone about this interview, you mentioned that although you favor reading works aloud, you're against performance.*
GP: Well, I don't like to read with a lot of expression; I don't like to read as an actor. I don't like to take actors' parts. I don't like to overinvent the characters. I want the people, just as they do when reading alone, to have some relation to make. It's almost what I don't like about the theatre; it's so overdefined: "How can I totally define it so that the listener can't escape *my* definition?"

JT: *So you're really making a distinction, if I understand you, between a reading that grows out of the work and one that seems to be imposed on the work.*
GP: Yes.

JT: *I've heard you read on two occasions. Once some years ago in Dallas at Southern Methodist University.*
GP: Oh yes, I remember that.

JT: *And then last year at Guild Books in Chicago. I think the persona you use when you read is wonderful for your stories. You're an excellent reader of your own work.*
GP: Well, I like to read. I love to read. Once I found myself getting very specific about the character, and I pulled it down a little bit.

JT: *Your reading has the same kind of down-to-earth, matter-of-fact, here-it-is quality that I find in your fiction.*
GP: I'm glad you say that because I want that to be there. Poetry is read now, it seems to me, in such a false way, you miss the poem sometimes. I mean the reader reads it as though each line is drifting off to heaven.

JT: *I've noticed that often when poets read their own work the rhythm really predominates.*
GP: Well, that's good though. See, the poets should be *always* reading aloud. I've never understood why in poetry classes they do give out all these copies; I *never* do. I mean, I can see somebody arguing in fiction that it's complex, but poems, in a class, it seems to me, should be read aloud *four times*. You have a poem, you don't get it, *read it again*. You have a poem, you don't get it, *read it again*. Poems, which are after all,

most of them, like a page long, especially the short ones, should really be just read three, four times for the—you notice what I'm doing with my hand—for the rhythm, for the chant, for the music, if there is music in it, which often there is not, but there should be.

JT: *1985 was a big year for you. Your book of short stories came out, the volume of poetry, and also the film,* Enormous Changes at the Last Minute.[4] *I was curious about what you thought of the film adaptation.*

GP: They did three stories. I liked the first one, "An Interest in Life."[5] The first one is excellent. It couldn't be better; I couldn't imagine it better. I couldn't have done it. It really used the story well. In fact, when I look at that story, I will always think of the film because it's not far from what I would have imagined. That's not true. I would not have imagined Ginny looking exactly like that. I saw her looking differently in my mind, but since I never described her, it's up for grabs, you know? Ellen Barkin was just wonderful. Then the second story, "Dreamer in a Dead Language"[6]: there were complications because it was cut and recut and recut; so there were a lot of technical problems. It was a very difficult story to put into film, and why they listened to me and did that first, I do not know. It was a very hard story. But they did it, and they did the best they could, and there are parts that are wonderful. I like the woman in it, and I like the children. But I think for some people it is not satisfying because it has a lot of technical problems, including the sound. The third one, "Enormous Changes at the Last Minute,"[7] I had the most problems with. People liked it. But to me, it's not my story.

JT: *I noticed in the reviews that the narrative voice is gone. It's hard for me to imagine how the stories could survive without that narrator.*

GP: Well, "An Interest in Life," when I look at it, it's as though it was written in scenes almost, and some of the interior thinking either becomes language or it works or they give it to her as a line to say to somebody. But there is a problem with the last story because of these songs I wrote. There are a lot of songs in "Enormous Changes." It ends with a song, and without that song at the end—I had to fight to get them to put one of the most important songs in it:

Who is the father?
Who is the father?
Who is the father?
    I! I! I! I!
I am the father.

I had to argue with them a lot to get that in. But they did get it in, thank God.

JT: *So you were really involved in the production?*
GP: No, I wasn't. I was very little involved. And in the best one I was the least involved of all. Maybe because I saw how it was going.

JT: *You have mentioned in the past that poetry was the school you went to to learn to write fiction.*
GP: Right. That's true.

JT: *I wonder if you could talk about what that means.*
GP: It means that mostly I just read poetry and mostly I just wrote poetry, and that's all. That was the homework I gave myself.

JT: *That may explain, in part, why your short stories seem for the ear. Among the many reasons that I love your work is that it so much exists as speech; as I read it to myself, I can hear the voices. I notice that you sometimes describe yourself as a storyteller rather than as an author or writer. Would you talk about why you choose the word "storyteller"?*
GP: Well, I'm wrong in a way because obviously my stuff is written. When you think of storytellers who tell stories, they're really quite different. But mostly I use "storyteller" because I hate the word fiction.

JT: *Because it suggests it's not real?*
GP: No. No, I think it just divides from nonfiction. You know things come out as nonfiction, and yet they're somebody's true stories. A lot of oral histories. Those are stories. What makes a piece of fiction? What makes fiction is a person telling it to me. And what makes a story is a certain amount of bringing together two stories in some way. So it really exists on a lot of levels. I mean a kid comes home from school and tells a story, says "Ma! I gotta tell you something!" And that's the first impulse of a little storyteller. "I gotta tell you something. I want to tell you something." And proceeds to tell the story. Now the mother receives it in two ways. First, she knows the kid, and then she listens to the story. If it's true or false, it doesn't really matter. But the life of this little child and the voice of this little child coming together with the story tone, becomes the story.

JT: *I love that moment in "Ruthy and Edie" when the granddaughter has just learned "Remember dat?"*[8]
GP: Yes, that's my granddaughter.

JT: *I thought it might be.*
GP: She says, "Grandma, member dat? Member dat?"

JT: *It's as if she has awakened suddenly into storytelling.*
GP: Right.

JT: *In "Debts," the narrator comments that she owes it to her family and the families of her friends "to tell their stories as simply as possible, in order, you might say, to save a few lives."*[9]

GP: Right. I tried to tell it simply, but I got complex. (Laughs) Good intentions anyway.

JT: *I wondered if that was the narrator voicing some of your own motivation as a storyteller.*

GP: Well it is. Yes, it is. The different stories about an aunt are my aunts. And it's not even their stories exactly. That first story is *not* the specific story of my aunt, but it's my aunt in various places. I mean it's for her, really.[10] And then the little tiny story, three books later, so to speak, is her, twenty-five years later: "In This Country, But in Another Language, My Aunt Refuses to Marry the Men Everyone Wants Her To."[11] It's the same aunt; I want to talk about her.

JT: *You've expressed, not only in talking about your own work, but even in talking about other people's work, a value that involves hearing the unheard voices.*

GP: Yes, really what's hidden. Illuminating what's hidden, I think I call it.

JT: *I find your fiction remarkable in that respect. I went back this year to your first book,* The Little Disturbances of Man. *In the 1950s there was no large social movement framing women's concerns, and yet you were writing fiction about people and events that no one thought were fit subjects for fiction.*

GP: In a way what *made* me write fiction is that I was really thinking an awful lot about women's lives, and I wasn't able to get it into poems somehow. I was thinking. I was in my thirties—early thirties to begin with, the book came out when I was thirty-seven or thirty-eight—I was thinking about it, and I became very worried—not frustrated—worried, you know, about my friends and the men my husband knew, who were around an awful lot. You see where that school is, we lived there before the school was built. We had one big room that we lived in with the kids and everything in it. They were always there for supper, talking, talking. And I felt what I hadn't felt before in my early twenties; I felt this split, really, between myself and them. They were talking differently, and I was *not* one of them like I had assumed when I was eighteen or nineteen, one of the gang. So that separation began to happen in my mind, and I didn't do it. And then I had the kids, so I was really beginning to spend much more time with lots of women. So I got to know women better and better, although I had always had women friends, but I got to know them better. So I would say that I was part of what was happening, that is, women were beginning to think just as I was. I began to write about it very quickly, but people were beginning to think about it. Tillie Olsen's book came out the year my book came out, or the year after.[12] So there were really a lot of other voices beginning too. Some of them were beginning to speak politically only, not in literature, but it was beginning to happen. And in the next ten, fifteen years, it all happened.

JT: *In "Listening," the final story in your latest collection, you introduce Cassie, the friend of Faith, who complains that Faith has omitted her lesbian life from all the stories she has told.*[13] *It seems to me that that does at least a couple of things. It suggests that even though all along you've been telling stories that haven't previously been heard, you're still alert for the voices that you yourself have not been hearing. It also seems to function as a little promise to your readers that we're going to get Cassie in the next volume.*

GP: My friends hope so. We'll get her a little anyway. It's true, you know, I was working on that story, and I came to a point where I didn't know what to do next. I had already known it was about listening. I sort of knew that because it began with hearing those stories of those guys talking. It began with thinking about telling stories, like he says, "Why don't you tell me women's stories?" and she says, "Forget it." So it's really about listening. Then Richard overhears her and comes into the room and says, "I heard you talking about all this metaphysical shit." It's all about listening. I didn't know what the heck to do, and then it suddenly really came to me. I'm such a big-shot about listening, but here I've been living/working with all these women who are as close to me—they're my real pals, I teach with a couple of them. And I've worked with them in the last ten years, you know, in politics and Women's Pentagon Action and different actions. And here I'm such a big-shot listener, and I haven't been listening!

JT: *It was a wonderful moment in the story.*

GP: I've heard it, but I didn't listen. You hear, but listening is another matter. So it suddenly came to me that's what the story is about.

JT: *Cassie's remark undercuts the authority of the narrator.*

GP: Right. It also does something else. I try to think about what it did. Some people said to me, "Oh, then you are Faith telling the story." I said, "No, Faith is the person who has been telling all of these stories. It isn't me." It's a complicated idea. My question, when I finished it, was how does it sound? I was a little nervous about how it would sound technically, how it would work. But it seems to be OK.

JT: *That scene has been quoted a lot in reviews. Women seemed to relish it.*

GP: Oh my friends, everybody said, "Did *you* ask her that question? Was it *you*? Did *you* say that to her?"

JT: *The titles to both* Enormous Changes at the Last Minute *and* Later the Same Day *suggest that life is full of surprising twists, turns, continuations, and interruptions. Do you think this might be a more prevalent theme in women's work, and do you think the circumstances of your own situation—writing in between all the other parts of your life—are related to the recurrence of this theme in your work?*

GP: I don't think so literally, in a way, but I do know that it's been part of *my* woman's life and many of the people I know, this activeness, this pulling away. But there are people who are women who get a tremendous amount of very solid work done all the time and constantly and without interference. I know how they work. I've seen them in their rooms working. I've seen the way their rooms are, and if you've seen the way my rooms are, you know that it's just not working right yet.

JT: *But you have all these other important things going on all the time.*

GP: Yes, well it's a decision, how to live, really. How shall I live on this earth?

JT: *I think much that's in your stories couldn't be there if you were living a different kind of life. For instance, the sense of urgency you feel about the condition our planet is in gets into your stories and becomes a part of what you have to say.*

GP: Well, that's good. I'm glad it does.

JT: *I want to backtrack to something you mentioned earlier. You said your friends were asking each other who had made Cassie's remark to Faith. It seems that that linking of Grace and Faith is very common. And yet Faith is not the narrator of all those stories although critics sometimes write about her as if she is.*

GP: Yes. Not only that, her life is totally different from mine. I lived with my first husband, my children's father, for about 22-23 years. And I've lived with my present husband already about 14, 15 years, at least, and I probably will for the rest of my life. I'm just a long-term person, and Faith is not particularly that. Nor are my children quite like them. I deliberately made them different from my kids. But I really knew a lot of children. I had all these kids around the house.

JT: *That Richard is so wise. I fell in love with him in the first story of yours I ever read, "Faith in the Afternoon."*[14]

GP: Oh yes. I love to read that story. But it's long, so I have to just read it at certain places.

JT: *But in some of your stories, the details of the narrator's life are much closer to your own. Sometimes the narrator seems to have written what you have written. In "Debts," for instance, and "A Conversation with My Father."*[15]

GP: Well, "Debts" and "A Conversation with My Father" are really not Faith's stories; they're really my stories. Those are particularly my stories.

JT: *Another narrator who can't be Faith because she has been married too long is the narrator of "Wants."*[16]

GP: Right. That's not Faith at all.

JT: *Faith and her friends are getting older. Do you think it's fair to say that as they do, their concept of what's included in the neighborhood is changing? It seems to me the neighborhood is getting larger.*

GP: Well, they get to travel. One of the women goes to all the socialist countries. Also, "Somewhere Else" is really not—it could be Faith—but it's really not Faith's story.[17] It's really a story about having gone to China. It's a true story, and yet it's Joe's story. And I think Joe ends up being Ruthie's husband.

JT: *Yes, in a later story. It's kind of fun trying to keep up with these characters and all their connections.*

GP: Well, sometimes it gets mixed up—I don't know what year it was in. So I decided not to worry about it. I just want to pretty generally imply the connections, but it doesn't have to be exactly right.

JT: *In your three volumes of short stories, you've chronicled the growth and change of a central group of women and created a neighborhood. You really haven't written a serialized novel, and yet there is that continuity between the stories. Do you think perhaps you've created a new form?*

GP: (Laughs) Maybe. Well, writers make worlds, everybody makes a world. The first world I ever saw when I was a kid reading was Galsworthy. Any book that has drama, any book that has all these characters in it, you really like that, it's nice. So I was writing short stories, and I still liked that idea. I liked that; it seemed to me it was a world. It just seemed to be right. I think what short story writers do is, whenever they write any short story, they give people different names and stuff like that.

JT: *But it's the same people?*

GP: But it could very well be the same people. I mean, it's just that they don't realize they can do it. You know, you have to have permission very often to do certain things if you're not certain about them.

JT: *I think it has become one of the secondary appeals of your work. We want to know what has happened to Faith, what has happened to Ruth, what has happened to Richard, what has happened to Tonto. What will be next? What are they up to? And does this fit with how we knew them when they were younger?*

GP: Right.

JT: *What draws you back to Faith and her friends? Do you keep finding you have more to say about these characters?*

GP: Yes. I mean, when I have more to say about them, I use them. And when I don't, I don't. I have more to say, really, about some other characters. I have more to say about the antecedent characters of my family's family. I think when people get older, they really think about the past a lot. They think about the wide future and the narrow past, really the tunnelled past, way back. There's more to be said yet.

JT: *I want to talk about your humor. It's not unusual, even in literature by women, to find that women are the butt of the joke. Society might be seen as wrong to place such impossible demands on women, but women are more wrong for their inability to cope with those demands. Maybe they go crazy or they can't function as superwomen, so they somehow fail. But in your work, the women are fine; the world is crazy.*

GP: Well, it's true, isn't it? (Laughter)

JT: *Yes, in my version of events.*

GP: When you talk about my humor, a lot of it is related to women, and a lot of it is Jewish, plain old Jewish humor from around. Where the Jews make these jokes in which they are presumably the butt. In which they allow themselves that. But they're not. Like the joke Faith's father makes in that story where he says, "Give me another globe." That's a typical Jewish joke, where the Jew says, "Well, it's probably my fault, but still, give me another globe."[18]

JT: *So in a way, you're using this strategy that Jewish people have developed for making themselves central in a world that defines them as marginal, and transferring it to women.*

GP: Well, to some degree. I think you put it in a very clear way. I could never have said it like that. I mean you would think that *all* oppressed people would understand all other oppressed people. However, this is not so. (Laughs)

JT: *It also seems to me that it's your very existence as a member of two marginalized groups—women and Jewish people—that allows you to see so much.*
GP: Umhmm. And also very verbal people.

JT: *As you can probably tell from my speech, I grew up in the South.*
GP: A little "verbality" there.

JT: *Yes. Our backgrounds are extremely different. And yet I relate so strongly to your work. I've asked myself, why does this writer, who has lived most of her life in New York City, who grew up as the daughter of Jewish socialists, speak so strongly to this person who grew up in this tiny little town in the South, the daughter of a Baptist preacher. I think the storytelling is key, that whole emphasis on orality. My family sat around and told stories and told stories.*
GP: Well, it means a lot to me what you've just said because it goes along with my idea that the more specific and regional you are, the more you speak to everybody. If you try to speak to everybody, nobody will listen. But if you really speak out of a specific place and time, somehow or another it's interesting to others, and they pull out of it what's close to them.

Notes

1. Joan Lidoff, "Clearing Her Throat: An Interview with Grace Paley," *Shenandoah*, 32 (3, 1981), 25. "I went to a lot of those meetings at MLA, to try to see what's going on. I think a lot of that's interesting, but, see, first of all, for me the story exists really off the page in a way that for them, it's all lying around there on the table. And for a lot of Americans too it does. And I don't think that's the direction for literature to go. I see it getting deeper and deeper into the page, until it disappears out the back end of the book. So that's the direction it's going to take. It's not that I don't love the page. I mean I love the books. But we really have to think of the throat it comes out of. I feel it's too great a movement away from the people, if you want to put it that way, and certainly away from female life."
2. Trobriands, New Guinea, Appendix A: Statement on Poetry; Jerome Rothenberg, ed., *Technicians of the Sacred* (Garden City, New York: Doubleday, Anchor Books, 1968), p. 359.
3. *Later the Same Day* (New York: Farrar Straus Giroux, 1985), pp. 71–89.

4. Directed by Mirra Bank, Ellen Hovde, and Muffie Meyer. See review in the "Literature in the Media" section of this issue.
5. *The Little Disturbances of Man* (New York: The Viking Press, 1956), pp. 79-101.
6. *Later the Same Day*, pp. 11-36.
7. *Enormous Changes at the Last Minute* (New York: Farrar Straus Giroux, 1974), pp. 117-136.
8. *Later the Same Day*, pp. 115-126.
9. *Enormous Changes at the Last Minute*, pp. 7-12.
10. "Goodbye and Good Luck," *Little Disturbances*, pp. 9-22.
11. *Later the Same Day*, pp. 107-108.
12. *Tell Me a Riddle*.
13. *Later the Same Day*, pp. 199-211.
14. *Enormous Changes*, 29-49. I misspoke here. the story I was in fact thinking of was "A Subject of Childhood," from *Little Disturbances*, pp. 135-146.
15. *Enormous Changes*, pp. 159-167.
16. *Enormous Changes*, pp. 1-6.
17. *Later the Same Day*, pp. 17-60.
18. In "Dreamer in a Dead Language," Faith's father tells this joke: "There's an old Jew. He's in Germany. It's maybe '39, '40. He comes around to the tourist office. He looks at the globe. They got a globe there. He says, Listen, I got to get out of here. Where you suggest, Herr Agent, I should go? The agency man also looks at the globe. The Jewish man says, Hey, how about here? He points to America. Oh, says the agency man, sorry, no, they got finished up with their quota. Ts, says the Jewish man, so how about here? He points to France. Last train left already for there, too bad, too bad. Nu, then to Russia? Sorry, absolutely nobody they let in there at the present time. A few more places . . . the answer is always, port is closed. They got already too many, we got no boats . . . So finally the poor Jew, he's thinking he can't go anywhere on the globe, also he can't stay where he is; he says oi, he says ach! He pushes the globe away, disgusted. But he got hope. He says, So this one is used up, Herr Agent. Listen—you got another one?"

An Interview with Grace Paley
Kay Bonetti / 1986

This is a print version of an interview which is available on cassette from The American Audio Prose Library, PO Box 842, Columbia, MO 65205. 1-800-477-2275. Free catalog available. ©1986 by The American Audio Prose Library. Reprinted by permission.

The following is an interview with Grace Paley conducted by Kay Bonetti for the American Audio Prose Library in April of 1986 at the Fales Library in Greenwich Village, New York City, where Grace Paley has lived for the past 38 years, raising her children and earning a reputation as your friendly neighborhood activist, starting when her kids were small and she banded together with other mothers in the PTA to keep city buses out of Washington Square Park. And to her students at Sarah Lawrence College, she's an extremely popular teacher of creative writing. But to some of those folks in the world at large, Grace Paley is the gifted author of three volumes of some of the most highly praised short stories in the language. And she's famous, too, for having replied when asked why she writes short stories instead of novels that "art's too long and life's too short."

In Grace Paley's stories traditional plot and narrative are mostly ignored. They have perhaps been best described as elaborate introductions to the people who inhabit them. Grace Paley's parents were Ukrainian-born social democrats. And her physician father, Isaac Goodside, came here in 1905 with his wife Manya after being released out of a Siberian prison camp. So it's safe to say that Grace Paley, born in the Bronx in 1922, the youngest of three children, came by her strong political and social consciousness quite naturally. And she describes her East Bronx childhood as the daughter of the neighborhood family doctor as quite happy and secure despite the fact that they were pretty much as poor as everybody else on the block. It was also extremely fortunate in terms of her development as a writer in that she grew up in a rich atmosphere of three languages—English, Russian, and Yiddish—with parents who were in love with the arts.

Bonetti: I'm intrigued by your description of your upbringing. Why did your family think that you were a dud?

Paley: Well, I guess what happened is that I was a very smart little girl, and around towards high school I began to act like a very dumb little girl. And then when I went to college I left after about a year, and it looked like I just was not going to fulfill the great promise they thought that I had. At the time, I was writing a lot of poetry, and I always did. I never didn't write, and I never didn't read. So they always had some kind of hope that I would return. Well, they were immigrants, and they wanted me to have a profession. And they believed that girls too should learn something. And they thought I should be a teacher or a social worker or something that seemed right for my character. And they couldn't understand why a great curtain fell over my mind every time I went to school.

Bonetti: Were you the youngest child?

Paley: I was the youngest by a great deal, by fourteen or sixteen years. My brother became a doctor and my sister became a teacher.

Bonetti: The ideal?

Paley: Well, yeah. They were the children of my parent's youth, when they came to this country. And so they really were the children of poor people originally. And I was sort of a child of the middle class. So by the time I was born, the family was leading another life. But they were those other children, and they knew they had to do well. And also they grew up into the Depression. And I have noticed that almost anybody I know whose young womanhood or manhood happened in those years, those early thirties, those people always had enough anxiety to keep them at school, first of all because there were no jobs, and then they had enough anxiety to really push them through to anything. Whereas I came into that young womanhood through those years, but really actually into the Second World War, which was a horrible and euphoric time. And there was work of all kinds, and I simply wasn't the least bit worried. I wasn't afraid of being poor because my family was fairly comfortable. And I didn't mind, really, doing crumby jobs, office work, which is what I did. but I was very anxious to get on with life and marry and have children and do all the grown up things that the youngest child often wants to do. That seemed to me really great. And also I left home, and I married at nineteen. And I left home and lived in army camps, which I loved. My husband didn't love it because he was a soldier, but I liked it because I had the great pleasure of living in barracks and living among large numbers of young men. And at the same time I did not live under their discipline. I had my own life.

Bonetti: When did you start getting serious about the lives of women?

Paley: Well, I'd always had best girl friends. I was a very tomboyish girl, like a lot of little girls with a lot of energy. And I just loved things of boys and felt myself, as a matter of fact, a boy, which a lot of little girls do. But at the same time I always had two or three, one beloved best friend of my life and another two or three extras that I love to this day. But I really was not that interested in girl's lives because I knew girls' lives. And it wasn't until I had children and I began to spend a lot of time in the park with women, and began to have this common trade with women, which is child raising. We were sort of in the same line of work. We were interested in the same sort of things. And living in the Village as I did here, I lived among a lot of women who were really alone and without men, whose men had left, a lot of them, or who lived in all sorts of peculiar circumstances. And they were my friends, they were my buddies, and they were my pals, and I worked with them. I began also to do a lot of political work, and that also continued with these same women as time went on. And it began when the children were babies, so I had a lot of continuity, I think, in that respect. But I really began to be worried about the lives of women, and that's how I began to write stories. I guess I was in my thirties, and I really didn't like what was happening between men and women. I had been really rather fond of men, and I was getting very discouraged about them and sad, and in many cases angry. And I guess there was no movement then really to latch onto in any way, or I might have really not written. I might have, since I tend to activate myself or get out, just gone out and done other things. But anyway those are the things that really troubled me, and that's what I was really interested in. You really write from what you don't know. You write from what you know, but you write into what you don't know. And those lives were what I did not know.

Bonetti: You have often said that you are not Faith.

Paley: No, no, I'm not Faith. I have lived with my children's father for about twenty-five years, so I am not Faith. Nor was he any of the men in there. Faith could be someone who was my dear friend. I could have invented her or whatever. She lives within a few feet of my head some place.

Bonetti: Is she in any way your alter ego? She has been described as . . .

Paley: Well I don't even know what alter ego means, really.

Bonetti: But a lot of the opinions . . .

Paley: She does a lot of work for me. Let's put it that way.

Bonetti: Well, that's what I wanted to know because a lot of the pronouncements that are made about "Grace Paley thinks this," "Grace

Paley's stories reveal that" are, in fact, things that Faith says in the stories, things that Faith tells. Is she reliable in that respect?

Paley: Sometimes. Not in every respect.

Bonetti: Oh, really?

Paley: Yeah, not entirely. I mean sometimes she really does some dopey things, but in general, I agree with her on most things, like I do with most of my friends.

Bonetti: Is Faith the teller of all those stories? Evidently not.

Paley: No, no, she's not a number of them. Well, she certainly doesn't tell the Zagrowsky stories; she's really a kind of an annoying person in it. The first Faith story is in *The Little Disturbances of Man,* and it's really not about me at all. It's about my friend who is my best friend now, and I did go up to her house and there were these two husbands disappointed by eggs. I think it's called "The Used-Boy Raisers."

Bonetti: It seems like you've given her some of your childhood memories though, haven't you? In the stories about your father or her father you have said in the introduction that it's really your father?

Paley: Well, that's true, but actually, my parents never lived in an old aged home, you know.

Bonetti: Oh, they didn't?

Paley: No, never. My father lived in his own apartment until the day he died, and he died in his own apartment. He lived alone there. He wouldn't live with anyone. My mother died in her late fifties, so he was alone a long time. And so it's nothing like that, but the character is a lot like that, the father in the old age home who is writing poems. Well my father wrote stories, and mostly he painted pictures. So a lot of that is about him, but he would not have moved into a place like that.

Bonetti: The story "A Conversation with My Father" is that in fact a Faith story?

Paley: I don't really think so. I think it's not. I think it's really a conversation between a writer and her father. It really is a typical conversation I might have had with my father, the typical arguments we would have back and forth about the whole thing, not in that order. Nor did I ever write such a story for him, but we would argue about those things. And he really felt exactly like that about me. So if I tended toward a little overcheerfulness. . . . He felt like that when I flunked out of school. That was just the beginning. I remember them saying, "You have no insight. You have no foresight. You don't know what this is going to mean to you." And they were absolutely right. I was about sixteen or seventeen, and I was perfectly satisfied with myself. I didn't think or worry the least about my future. I felt it was there, so therefore it had to be all right. And so they were right in many respects. But anyway the feeling that I wouldn't look at reality was really something that he felt. And it came from that particular period.

Bonetti: But do you think it's true of your stories, that you don't really face tragedy?

Paley: No, I don't think it's true at all. I think I face it.

Bonetti: Do you ever have the sense that anyone could justifiably criticize you for writing stories that are too much the way you would like the things to be rather than the way things really are?

Paley: Well, I don't know. People can criticize you for anything.

Bonetti: But that construct that you make, though, at the end of ["A Conversation with My Father"] you said, "That woman did live across the street from me."

Paley: Well, that's different. In that story, the argument was a very interesting argument. It was a historical one basically. We were both right. In my father's time, coming from where he did, you really had to make your decisions early and you were stuck with them. And the idea that anybody at forty could change their lives, and the fifties being even more ridiculous, that's one of the reasons they were so horrified with what I did. They felt very much that what I did at sixteen or seventeen was going to affect me for my whole life. And they were right. Inside their world that was true. Look at England, I mean, look at other countries. And its even true here where the kids really are slated and directed and set in straight lines toward their destiny. But for a middle class kid like me, it simply wasn't true. And that's what I was saying. I am saying that there was more room here in this country—and it still is true—for class mobility.

Bonetti: Is there any sense that you write to demystify the preconceptions that people have about city lives and everything, everybody being alienated and isolated from one another?

Paley: Yeah, I think you're right. I would never have said it. I would not say, "I am now writing out of this," you know. I wouldn't say that, but I think there's something in it. And you write for a lot of reasons. You write to say "I want to tell you something," you know, on the simplest level. You write to say "I don't understand this, I am going to try to understand it. I don't know and I'm trying to understand it." And then you write to memorialize certain things, the people, to remember them. And you write really in praise also as well as in fear like in the knock-wood stories. You know, "I hope this doesn't happen." Like there's a story, "Samuel." I regard that as my knock-wood story, 'cause I wrote it just watching little boys playing between the cars.

Bonetti: One of the things that's been said about your stories is that they live in the language, that the language is the whole reason for being. Are you conscious of that as one of the impulses out of which you write?

Paley: Sure. I think that's a great impulse. I don't mind that at all. That is to say, I would not think that was a bad thing about them.

Bonetti: You want to memorialize the different speeches of the city?

Paley: Well, it's not just that. I think there are a lot of funny things that language does. And sometimes when I am just writing ordinarily without dialect or anything like that, I think about language a lot, like in the story "The Story Hearer." There is no dialect there at all, but there's a lot of stuff about language. I think about language a lot. There's old language that I sort of fool around with. And there's a lot of word play, partly because there's a lot of play. There has to be play in everybody's work. You know there is a lot of play and variety or else there's nothing, or else it's wrong. Writing that does not have play in it is often half dead. So there's a lot of that. And I am interested in what language can do. And I do like the way people speak. And I do believe that when people are speaking about what interests them, they speak well. I don't think they speak dumb or dopey or whatever. I mean to listen to people speak about what concerns them, you'll really hear wonderful speech.

Bonetti: In some of the early reviews that I read or the reviews of your earliest collection, *The Little Disturbances of Man,* a couple of reviewers raised questions about whether or not you, in fact, were Jewish because you wrote so well in all of the different idioms. I take it you would take that as a compliment?

Paley: Oh, I do, I do. But the truth is that I write in those other idioms rarely. I don't really have a lot of stories with that. I have a couple of black stories and a couple of Irish stories.

Bonetti: "Lavinia" is one of these.

Paley: Yeah, "Lavinia." And then I have that very tragic story in that book called "The Little Girl with Black Eyes," who is my friend, by the way. And he's the one I memorialize there. I wanted the story told the way he told it to me.

Bonetti: That was Charlie, right?

Paley: Yeah. And so I do want to think of that. And I love the way they speak. It's something you don't know, and you have to reach out for it and find another way of speaking. There are a lot of people who feel politically it's wrong to talk in other people's languages, but I think they're wrong. I think that if you do it with a longing for truth and a sense of the mystery of the other life you should do it.

Bonetti: How does a story start for you?

Paley: Mine all start in different ways. The two stories I happen to have read started similarly, that is in both cases, I wrote about a page, but they actually are very different. I wrote about a page and then sort of let it lie around for a long time. The second story, "Friends," I really had to figure out how to tell it. And the story I really had to tell, I had self-obligated to memorialize, not just that woman, but the whole group of women. And I had the first page for, oh, I don't know, six months. And that's generally how I work. I seem to get a whole page down.

Bonetti: Was it the first page of that story or just a page?

Paley: Yeah, it was that first page. It's not always that, it's not always the first. It sometimes ends up altogether out.

Bonetti: I was going to say, does it ever disappear?

Paley: But very often how I begin a story is how really I go on because I already now begin a story where I want to begin it. That's the one thing that I've learned finally.

Bonetti: Is it a voice or an idea?

Paley: It's a voice.

Bonetti: You hear a voice?

Paley: It's not an idea. The idea develops really from the life. And I may have some sort of an idea, but I didn't really know that "The Conversation with My Father" would really turn out exactly the way it did. I really just began to write an argument and a dialogue.

Bonetti: Can you elaborate on that wonderful phrase that "people whether they are real or imagined deserve the open destiny of life"?

Paley: Well, I really write without knowing exactly where I'm going. And there's no telling what can happen. Probably, once I'm through the middle of the story, what's going to happen is going to happen, and there's not too much avoidance. But in the beginning I really don't know which way I'm going. And I didn't know how I was going to write this story "Friends" at all. I knew the woman was dying at the very first. I told you what was happening in the very first line really, so that it wasn't some kind of mystery that was going to proceed. But how and in what way and what would happen with the other women and what was going on I really had no idea until I went on. In fact, I have learned one thing about a story, I never really have a story until I have two stories.

Bonetti: Oh, really?

Paley: So I couldn't write the story of "Friends." I couldn't write the story of Selena dying until I could write the story of the kind of quarrel and dissolution of the friendship between Anne and Faith. What was happening to the other women had to become almost as important or as important. And until I got that, I couldn't write Selena's death.

Bonetti: And you say that's often true for you in a story?

Paley: Oh, I think it's always true.

Bonetti: There has to be two stories?

Bonetti: Nothing is clearer than in "The Conversation with My Father," where the two stories are almost over-simplified, the story of the argument between the father and daughter, and then it's the other story.

Bonetti: Chekhov was mentioned there, and he was very famous for stories within stories and characters in stories that tell stories. And, of course, that's what you do in your stories. A question that I always like to ask is about early models and influences like . . .

Paley: Well, I don't really know. I read a lot, I know that. I read a great deal. I really admired "Dubliners" a lot. But I probably was writing when I read it. I don't know. I can only say really it's more poets I think of when I think of anyone. I think more of Yeats sometimes when I write than I do of anything else.

Bonetti: What is it about poetry that you think you carry into the short stories?

Paley: Well, I think it's a love of language. And considering Yeats, I really throw a lot of stuff out that I don't need. And I also am not afraid to make great leaps. I hate the word "transition." I just like to make a good jump.

Bonetti: Well, back to speaking of how a story comes to you. You hear a voice. Now, you write about this family of friends, interlocking, interrelated characters, so when you hear a voice does that say to us then that you don't get a story and then place it into Faith and her circle of friends?

Paley: No.

Bonetti: It's part of the territory?

Paley: No, it's too organic.

Bonetti: How about the references within stories to other stories, such as "Listening," which has a paragraph in it where Faith is talking to Jack and she said, "And I didn't tell him about Zagrowsky, and I didn't tell him about . . . " What was the other story? There were two stories she mentions there that in fact are in the collection. Now, how did that happen?

Paley: Well, that was really part of it. I had a whole series in my mind called "The Story Hearer." The reason I had it is I wrote the stories in it, and then I thought I would write something called "Telling" and "Listening." I had no idea what they would be. And my idea was—which never happened that way—that she would tell these stories to Jack. And as a matter of fact in that last story I have all these things happening, like he says, "Why don't you tell me the stories?" because obviously she hasn't done it. So we hear me playing a little bit with myself. He says, "Why don't you tell me women's stories?" and she says, "I don't want to tell you them, they're too private." So that's really where it happened. Now I wrote those two, the "Zagrowsky" story and that story, around the same time. And I had the first two pages of the "Zagrowsky Tells" story for about two years. And I was stuck. I couldn't figure it out, and the reason was I was telling it the wrong way. I was having her tell it. See, I was still in that idea she was going to tell the story to Jack. My idea was that she would say, "I went down to the park, and I saw him under the Hanging Elm" and so forth. Well, at this certain point, I realized she didn't know the first damn thing about him. He was the only one who knew. So suddenly the simplest thing sort of came to me in a flash, which any idiot would have known, was that he was supposed to tell the story. But that came to me two years later. So when I figured that out, I was able to write that story. But it lay around for two years with just two pages, maybe a page and a half.

Bonetti: At what point did you decide to write the two stories about Ginny and John Raftery and Mrs. Raftery? The first story shows up in the first collection, and it's told from uh . . .

Paley: Ginny's point of view.

Bonetti: Ginny's point of view. Then you wrote it later from uh . . .

Paley: Well, I guess what happened is I retained a lot of interest in those people because I lived over there on 15th Street and 9th and 10th Avenue for about five years. And I felt I hadn't done justice to them, to the old woman, and I was sort of curious about her. And there again I really began with this first line, with the first paragraph. And I wrote that really before I realized that I was writing her. And I said, "My God, this is Mrs. Raftery, I've been thinking about her." So I proceeded to go a little further with it, but very tentatively. I was rather scared of it, but I knew a lot about her. I mean, I knew a lot of the things that were in there. The fact of the matter is, the other story, "An Interest in Life," is very much made up. It's a typical kind of story, made up. And yet it seems probably true. It probably happened right then and there. But I knew more about the old woman than I did about them actually, as it turned out.

Bonetti: Surely you are a writer who works in some way for the ear consciously in your writing process?

Paley: I do. I write aloud. I work aloud. I don't know what I'm doing until I read everything aloud. I read aloud. I believe in the story. I love to read. I read a lot. I think fiction people should be reading much more than they do. They've let the poets take over. Actually, they've begun to read, they really have, and it's a great thing. But we really owe a lot to the poets who went out in the fifties because they weren't selling any books. They really went out and began to make their voices heard. And I'm grateful to the Beats for that. And then whenever I can, I read stories. The story was meant to be told, and I just don't like it lying around being a text all the time.

Bonetti: I'd like to talk to you about the women's movement a little bit. Recently, the PEN International Conference happened, and it was widely publicized. And amazement was expressed that the thing that happened, that the women were criticizing there, namely, that essentially women really just weren't used in this conference as well as they should be. You've expressed amazement that that could be happening in 1986. Do you think it is amazing?

Paley: I think it is amazing, and I think it's amazing for PEN especially, because PEN has a lot of women working in it. It has a lot of women working on committees, and influential, and it was surprising. We could have seen it was going to happen because in a way there were six women less on the executive board than there were the year before. It's a big drop. It's a big drop because it means a big increase on the other side, so you really have a difference of thirteen. So you might have seen something like that happening. But I think what happened there was no conspiracy. They hadn't gotten together to say you're not going to have women. It was like a big absentmindedness, like some cloud went over before the eyes of the people who were working.

Bonetti: Do you have any opinions about the whole question of women's literature and the study of women's literature as women's studies?

Paley: Yes, I think it's a wonderful thing. I think it's really marvelous. And you think you never thought of it before, but I take a look at some of the things I wrote when I was younger, and I see that I sent them out under as androgynous a name as I could. They're under G. Goodside Paley or something or G. G. Paley or something. And a lot of women did that.

Bonetti: Do you ever feel that there's any truth to the fear that by putting things in black and ethnic studies, women's studies, to quote Tillie Olsen: "Sad is the country that requires women's studies, black and ethnic studies."

Paley: Uhn hnh, Yeah. But that's the way it is, and I think we still do. And what's interesting is, I do teach, and I go to a lot of universities. And you find that if there isn't a woman's studies, certain subjects are simply left out. Where there's not political consciousness, where there's not real consciousness of these things, they're forgotten easily, like "Whew," the men say. I've seen this in the radical movement. "Hunh, we don't have to think about that any more. What a pressure that was on our heads, to have to think about all this all the time, about making sure we had enough women and enough blacks on this thing. At last, the pressure's off."

Bonetti: Do you think there is a female creative principle which is different from a male creative principle or anything like that?

Paley: I don't really know. I've tried to figure those things out. But I do think there's certainly subject matter. And there's interest. And there's a sense of what's worth writing about and what isn't. And women think that a lot of stuff is worth writing about that men don't.

Bonetti: Do you think of yourself as a citizen of the world, a citizen of your community who also writes, or do you think of yourself as a writer who is a citizen of your community and the world?

Paley: Oh, I don't know. I just think of myself as a person. I think of my life as a whole. I don't think that I'm either a writer or a citizen. I think I'm a family person and a writer and a political person, and all of these things. And I'm a person who's Jewish and who's American and who's all of these things. I think of it as a whole rather. I think of it as kind of a big circle and that I'm in the bathtub of all this information.

Bonetti: And you did, after all, inherit your political consciousness and everything. When they talk about writers writing about what they know and everything, your political self is what you know. That's very much a part of your existence.

Paley: Oh, yeah.

Bonetti: I would take it you probably don't have too much patience with the folks who want to separate out art from politics.

Paley: Well, they only do it here. And the very same people who do it here don't mind if the South Americans are political, and they certainly don't mind if the East Europeans are political. They really love all that, but they don't think we should be. They have some idea that we are free of all that or that we were sort of born untouched by history or events, or any of the forces of social existence. Whereas other people in other countries, its OK for them, poor things.

Bonetti: Well, about the women's movement in more general or even outside of literature, what do you think is going to happen in the near future?

Paley: Well, we're part of this whole thing that's going on. We're in a very militarized society, and as long as we're in a militarized society, we're in a very masculine society. And as long as we're in that, we really are going to have to keep our eyes on things and really keep fighting. We just can't sit back. There is just no question about it. There is a big article in the paper about women now being in over 50 percent of the professions. Well, it turns out they're the professions where you make the least money, so it may be over 50 percent of the professions, but they're still way, way, way, way down. They're like 18 percent of the doctors and 19 percent of the lawyers, something like that, so there's a lot of falseness being printed about our condition also which has to be responded to.

Bonetti: What about the question of the female sensibility in the workplace and all that, and the debate between women being like men or changing the workplace to accommodate the woman's management style?

Paley: Yeah. I don't think about managers so much. They are really not my cup of concern. But I think that women who have some project that they are working on together really do work very well together, if they are working on some kind of equal terms. I think what people are talking about are the processes by which women live, the processes of child rearing where you really are extremely aware of a very slow event occurring, the growing of a human being and have to offer it some sort of patience and waiting. So I think that's the sensibility that people are really talking about when they think of them working differently. Wherever women really think that the main thing is to have a piece of the pie, things are not good, because the pie is really a rotten pie. It's really full of guns and death. So I would say that's not so hot. But wherever women want to make their own pie its OK, it's better. We don't really want to be equal with men so much as we want them also to be equal with us in other things.

Bonetti: What about the question of feminist criticism?

Paley: Well, I don't really pay any attention to it, stuff like that. The worst review I ever got was by a woman in *Commentary,* but that's their politics, so that's natural. They're there, but I'm older than a lot of those women, and I began to write when there was no need of feminists, when the second wave of feminism had not hit the shores really. I guess I was part of it in a sense, but I didn't know it. I was certainly not a feminist then. But I really just went my own way, and I always will as far as I'm concerned go my own way. I've read the most livid articles, but you read them by men too, so?

Bonetti: What about teaching? Is it something that you love to do or something you have to do?

Paley: Well, I had to do it. Before I taught, I was an office worker. And I made, well, of course, what I made is ridiculous now altogether.

Bonetti: Minimum wage, I'm sure.

Paley: Yeah, but I made very little money and the only skill I had was typing, and I was bad at it to the bargain. So I never could get a really good job. But when somebody offered me a teaching job, I still kept working for Office Temps.

Bonetti: Well, what role, if any, does teaching play in your writing? Does it at all?

Paley: Well, it doesn't play a hell of a lot, except that it really keeps me in touch with young people. And it's a gift. It's been really a gift to me from some authority, whoever it is in the world.

Bonetti: Teaching?

Paley: Yeah. And I've known generations now. By generations we mean every four years. I've known generations of young people, and they're my friends. I stay with them in different parts of this country when I read. And it's a great happiness to me. It's a present from life itself to me.

Bonetti: Do you believe that writing can be taught? I mean, what do you think a teacher of writing can do?

Paley: I don't know. It can be taught as much as math can be taught. I could never learn math, so you might say math cannot be taught. You need a learner to teach, so you try out and some people don't learn, so you never taught them a thing. What you can do in writing classes, a writing class does a lot of things. It's only purpose is not to make writers; it's hopeful purpose is to do that. That's the gravy of it all; that's the special joy if some of the people do that. But people really begin to understand how literature is made. They try making it, and they learn a great deal about it, and they love literature more. And that I swear by, and I know is true. And also your most gifted kid may not become the writer, because the person who will write is the person who finally is pressed, as I was when I began to write these stories, by some inner drive to do so.

Bonetti: Do you have a reader that you write for, that you tell these stories to, an audience, a hearer?

Paley: No. Well, sometimes I do. Sometimes I really do.

Bonetti: Who is that when it is someone?

Paley: I don't know. I really don't think about it.

Bonetti: You don't?

Paley: I don't think about it when I'm doing it. Some paragraphs I write, like I'll write a paragraph towards my husband. Usually I'll take it out afterwards 'cause it's long. But you tend to write things towards people. But sometimes they're memorializing stories, and they really aren't written towards people so much as for them. "Friends" was written for my friends. I really feel that is what I had in mind. "Goodbye and Good Luck" and other stories about my aunts were totally invented, nothing about their lives, but they were written for my aunts.

Bonetti: Your stories are usually seen by readers to have a very strong moral basis underneath them all. Do you feel that this is legitimate?

Paley: Yeah, I suppose so. I think a lot about what's right in the world still and how to live it. How to live in this world is very important to me.

Bonetti: Do you believe that morality in literature grows out of the quality of the mind of the writer, that that's the way it relates?

Paley: Yeah.

Bonetti: You don't sit down to write a story and say this is going to be a moral story, it's going to have a moral in it?

Paley: Oh, no. I don't even think that way. I don't sit down and say, "This is going to be a political story." I don't sit down and say any of those things. I don't sit down and say, "Well, I'm going to drag some of this politics into it." I don't do that. It's just not the way, and I'm not saying even that that's bad. It's not necessarily a bad thing to do. You could sit down and say, "I am now going to write a story that is going to really show the relation of the forces, of the power of so forth and so on." I mean, why not? That's a perfectly good intellectual and aesthetic pursuit. I happen not to do it, because I happen to be mostly interested in ordinary people, and ordinary people just lead unpowerful, ordinary, hopeful lives.

Bonetti: What do you envision for the children of the future?

Paley: Well, I sometimes wish they were more enraged. I always appear very hopeful, but I'm really quite pessimistic about the future of the world. And it just seems as though everything beginning with race hatred, woman hatred, neighbor hatred proceeds, and then the arms race continues, gets bigger and bigger. We want to get after Nicaragua, which is a teensy weensy country. We don't want to seem to make peace with the Russians. I am just very fearful for my granddaughter and all the little children in the world. I just don't see which way we're going that's hopeful. On the other hand, it seems to me that the world is worse, but the people are better. And I think, for instance, that we'd be in Nicaragua right now if it wasn't for the American people. They really don't want to do it. They really don't want to go in. And it's not our movement necessarily that's doing it. It's really the American people. And one of the horrors is that this administration may simply override the American people and their feelings, which are fairly decent at this time.

Grace Paley is the author of three collections of short stories: *The Little Disturbances of Man,* available in Penguin paperback; *Enormous Changes at the Last Minute,* available through Farrar, Straus & Giroux paperbacks; and *Later the Same Day,* also in Penguin paperback. She's also the author of one volume of poetry, *Leaning Forward,* which is available through Granite Press.

The American Audio Prose Library is a comprehensive collection of distinguished American writers reading and discussing their works. This tape was produced by Kay Bonetti and Ed Herman with special assistance from Frank Walker of the Fales Library at New York University. The music is by Francis Poulenc. For information about other writers in this series, write us, The American Audio Prose Library, at the address printed on the label of this tape. This project is made possible with financial assistance from the National Endowment for the Arts and the Missouri Arts Council.

Looking at Disparities: An Interview with Grace Paley
Martha Satz / 1986

From *Southwest Review* 72.4 (1987): 478–89. Reprinted by permission.

Grace Paley was interviewed in November 1986, during a visit to Southern Methodist University for its annual Literary Festival.

Satz: Recently, you made a nice remark quoting Muriel Rukeyser's advice on learning to be a writer, "You become a writer by listening. Everyone was once a child sitting under the piano and listening." And I thought we could begin with your own childhood. Where did you live? What was your mother like? What was your father like?

Paley: Well, I lived in the Bronx, and my parents were immigrants who came here when they were about twenty, but they were already married. Then they had a couple of kids on the Lower East Side. And then they began that particular generation's rise in the world, which brought them from Rivington Street to East 177th Street in the Bronx. My father was a doctor, and we lived in a house, the house in which the office was. And it was a very nice childhood in that sense—that the life of the household and the life of my father's office were really part of the same thing. Breakfast, lunch, and supper, I had all those meals with him and naturally with my mother, and grandmother and aunt, who also lived in the house. My brother and sister were much older, so by the time I was four my brother had gone to medical school himself and when I was seven, my sister married. So I was very much a small person among many large ones.

Satz: And listening to their conversations?

Paley: Really entranced most of the time by what was being talked about—by my father and his medical friends talking sometimes about cases, by the loud political arguments going on sometimes because my aunt who lived with us had very different politics from my family.

Satz: What were the divisions?

Paley: It was all variations on Socialist politics. But I can't say my aunt was totally a Communist. What she was was very angry to have been brought to this country because she came when she was sixteen. A very beautiful, beautiful girl and furious no matter what we said to her. We kept telling her, "Look, you would have been *dead* already, fifteen times." By 1945 there were at least four occasions on which she could have been slaughtered.

Satz: Was any of your family or your parents' family in Europe during the Holocaust?

Paley: Well, some of the family was in Russia. But some of them had come, most of them before the revolution, but some after the revolution. And then in that period of our family argument, before I was born, as my grandmother describes it, there were also Zionists. They all went to Palestine. So those people we didn't see a lot of. But we did hear from them and they were kind of contemptuous of my parents—for doing well in the New World.

Satz: Were your parents anti-Zionist?

Paley: Yes. They were socialists, and most socialists were. They felt very strongly that my relatives had made the wrong decision and they had made the right one.

Satz: And your mother? We've talked some about your father.

Paley: Well, my mother died when I was about twenty-three. That was a long time ago. And she was in general a much quieter person. She was really hard on me because like the mother in my story "Friends," she was really very sick from the time I was about thirteen. She knew, she just felt, that she wasn't going to live and that I was really going to go to Hell. So there was this kind of argument between us, most of the time, which was only resolved by my safely getting married when I was nineteen. Then her heart was at rest. But she really worried about me, more than I could bear.

Satz: My mother died, too, when I was nineteen, and a lot of my adult life has been spent trying to imagine what my mother was about.

Paley: It's true. It's very hard. And my brother who was her first child and who naturally lived with her the longest, and my sister who was very close to her in all that period, who begged me to act decent, to behave myself, even they wondered what she was simply *about*. And it's hard when you think about it because for that generation the women got together—the aunts, my mother—and they put my father through school. The women worked in shops. My father also had to work.

Satz: Shops in the garment industry?

Paley: In the garment industry, and they were photographers in Russia. My mother was a touch-up brush worker. They had a family trade. All kinds of eye-ruining industries they were in. But the women did that, and he really did pay off. That's what he said. They did that for him, and he saw to it that everybody, cousins and so forth, were all in good shape later on. But my mother, I think, really had a hard time. First of all, she was very musical. And I think she had a very deep longing for that world. She put it aside not only because of my father but, because—well this business of the extended family is very nice for children but it's hell on adults. And I don't think people understand that. I think they suffered living together, all those people.

Satz: Tell me more about that. Who lived in your house?

Paley: Well there was my father's mother. They really had a hard time because they hadn't liked each other particularly when they were all young, and it didn't improve. And on the other hand, they all loved us, my sister and brother and me. So we really got all the good of all these people. And I was able to listen to all the differences. And I was able, amazingly, to love both sides. I tried to present each side to the other. People do it between parents, but for me it was not between my parents.

Satz: You said your mother was a quiet woman, and in the past you have said that you tell the story of women whose stories have been untold. Do you have a sense of speaking for her and that generation of women, imagining and remembering them?

Paley: Well, the odd thing is that I have a few aunt stories because although my mother has this unknown quality it seemed that my aunt was very much hurt by coming to this country, even though she would've been dead if she hadn't. She was hurt in the sense that although we did live in an extended family, that was not really considered good once you came to the United States. You are supposed to just be a mommy and daddy. I don't think she thought of it that way. But that idea, which was socially there, made her feel a little bit as though she didn't belong here or there.

Satz: She was unmarried?

Paley: She never married and that also was considered *pretty bad* and also somehow her fault. Well, it *was* her fault, she didn't like anyone. She just liked my father. And so the idea that she should be really somewhere else made her very angry. Her politics seemed like Communist politics, but really it was Russian Nationalism. I mean she was lonesome for that country, which had actually killed her younger brother and produced pogroms and so forth. I think one of the first stories I wrote was "Goodbye and Good Luck." It's not about her, it's really not. But it's about her. It's about me thinking about her, a little bit about her stubbornness and so forth.

Satz: What were your family's expectations of you? You said your brother was a doctor, your father was a doctor.

Paley: Oh, their expectations of me were that I should do whatever I wanted to do. I think one of the interesting things is the way there was this method called double-think. The expectation is that you can do anything, you're a smart kid, you read a lot. You'll be an honor to the family. You'll go to school. You'll get "A's." You are already getting "A's" in fourth grade. You are going to do marvelous, you'll be brilliant, you can be anything you want to be. Of course, they think . . . what do they think of? You can be a teacher, a social worker, but you can be a doctor too! "You want to be a doctor?" You can be a doctor. But at the same time, you get this other thing, that if you don't get married pretty quick, if you put it off too long, you'll end up like this aunt or that aunt or this cousin. And you'll lead no kind of serious life. So you get both of these things all the time.

Satz: So how did you imagine your future when you were a child, a teenager?

Paley: Well I always really did everything I wanted. I always knew I would write and I did.

Satz: When you were a child you just wrote.

Paley: I wrote. And people would say it was nice writing. Very pleasant. And I did. And I loved it. And I read. Read a lot I read all the time. I knew I was going to do that. But I also loved *very much* the idea of getting married and having children and since I was the youngest, the idea of being in charge.

Satz: Did you see those two things as a conflict at any point in your life?

Paley: No, I never thought it would be a conflict. Of course I was accused always of not having a good grasp on reality especially when I didn't do well at school. Finally, I did very badly in school, disastrously, finally.

Satz: Why did you do disastrously? Where was this?

Paley: Well, it began in high school. I absolutely couldn't think about school.

Satz: Where was your mind?

Paley: I think I was thinking about boys constantly. I was doing that. I was writing a lot of poetry. I was studying some things—English. So it wasn't as though I was totally out of it. But I had a big problem in school.

Satz: You got married at nineteen?

Paley: Well, many people did the same. It was 1942. The war was coming, and we didn't feel that we wanted to face this cloud alone exactly. You certainly didn't want to face it sitting in your mother and father's house.

Satz: You know when people discuss your work, they often talk about your ironic view, your comic view of human nature. Do you understand that feature of your writing as a Jewish world view?

Paley: Oh absolutely. Oh, I think it's totally that. Well, looking at disparities. That's what humor is about. Someone who's six foot eight married to someone who's four foot ten, which can be tragic in reality, but it's comical. And to live an ordinary life in a disastrous world!

Satz: How does being Jewish figure in your own life?

Paley: Well, my family was atheist, all of them, except my grandmother. And my father and my mother really believed in their Socialist ideals. The Enlightenment crawled across Europe, and when it reached them, they were at home at last. And as far as my father was concerned, he would spit if he saw a Chassid walking down the street as well as a priest. Either one of them disgusted him utterly.

Satz: I remember my father throwing the pebbles visitors had left as a remembrance off the tops of graves in the Jewish cemetery.

Paley: Yes, it's the same thing. My father couldn't stand it. My mother couldn't either. My mother announced every time my father made a joke that she didn't have a sense of humor, and that's why she wasn't laughing. It wasn't that she was mad or anything. So she was very firm, much firmer. Living out in the world as he did, he made compromises of various kinds. But my mother was firm in her disbelief and unmoving. But, on the other hand, it was just assumed that I would walk my grandmother to the schul. And I always did. And it was *assumed* that we would have a giant Passover dinner. And we always did.

Satz: And then there was the Holocaust.

Paley: No. Forget the Holocaust. I'm older than you. It had nothing to do with the Holocaust. No, they were very Jewish-identified. That is, they felt solidly Jewish, and their lack of religion didn't make them say that we're really Americans.

Satz: And how do you feel now about that?

Paley: I've always liked being Jewish.

Satz: Tell me why.

Paley: Well I think for a lot of reasons. When I was a little kid, I liked it because everybody else was. But going out into the world, into this country, I really felt having an identity of some kind with a people who had been seriously, severely oppressed for a couple thousand years, not just last week, not since the Holocaust, but for a long, long time really gave me a very powerful and active feeling for other people and an identification whether they felt it toward me or not, which they didn't. But I certainly felt it toward them. I think that's true. And that feeling is passing.

Satz: That feeling is passing?

Paley: It's passing. It's not passing as much as it might. It's not passing as much as general affluence maybe would make it pass in other people. I don't know how to put that.

Satz: No, I understand.

Paley: But it's passing. It is. And I liked very much what seemed to me the social tradition of the Jewish family of very deep charity toward others and a feeling before my going out into the world, a feeling that they really had of helping other people, of sympathy, of empathy or whatever, and a strong social consciousness. And I feel lucky for having had it.

Satz: In "Used-Boy Raisers," you talk about Jews being the splinter in the toe of civilization.

Paley: Yeah.

Satz: And in that story also as in your story "Friends," you link Judaism and feminism.

Paley: Well, that really of course is a big problem. Of course I've never been orthodox. And when I'm in New York, I never go to temple. But I do in Vermont. And I'm very interested in it. And of course I go because it's a very open congregation. There's a woman cantor. And women read from the Torah. And I've even gotten up there and read stories. Women are very welcome in every way. And little girls read Hebrew very well. There's one little girl, I think she's an adopted Hawaiian or something, whatever she is. But every year she reads pages and pages of the most beautiful Hebrew. There are boys who read, but not half as well. So I think it's the voices of women in the synagogue that has changed things for me. I don't think I could go back to those narrow places.

Satz: With women sitting up in the balcony?

Paley: Yeah. Yeah. And the women in those little schuls that I used to take my grandmother to. I mean, they were all fainting. They had to be carted out of the schul and carried up to my father's office.

Satz: But is there a link too between the oppression of Jews and the oppression of women? Do you see them as linked oppressed groups?

Paley: I'm very interested in what you've said. I'll think about it. But I can't say I've thought that way. But I like that. I'll think about it.

Satz: Well, you've written a lot about the lives of women. And you indicate often that women and women's lives are different from men and men's lives. I was thinking that in "Used-Boy Raisers," the woman sends the men off into the world.

Paley: I wrote that a long time ago. I wrote that in 'fifty-eight.

Satz: Right. But in "Friends" also you talk about the bond between the two women smiling over their children in the sandbox, a bond "at least as useful as the vow we'd all sworn with husbands to whom we're no longer married."

Paley: Yes.

Satz: Do you think that there are aspects of women's psyches, lives, connections that haven't been explored enough?

Paley: Oh, yeah. That I think is clear. Yeah, if somebody asks me about what the difference is in writing, I don't really feel that there is that much difference, and I think as time goes on, there will be even less. I don't know whether you can insist that there is a huge difference in style because I don't see it. I don't truly see it. But I do think the subject of women's writing is different: there is experience that hasn't been dealt with. You know you go through a period where you're very annoyed with all these male writers. They were your ideal intellectuals simply because they were the literary people of your youth. And then you go through a period where you just can't stand them. I just began to read Saul Bellow's short stories. I hadn't read Saul Bellow in a long time. But I saw how good the writing was. And I read it. And I liked it so much. I liked his stories. They were so beautiful. And there were no women in it. The guys had a woman, or they didn't have a woman or there was an aunt that everybody loved or an aunt that everybody hated. Whatever. But the wives were terrible. But I thought to myself, "Well, it doesn't matter so much maybe as long as we women have a voice." But unless *we* tell about *our* lives, those stories can't be listened to. You can't bear half the truth. But as long as we women are being read, then I can accept them. But the points at which (like our big fight at the PEN club) they don't hear us, we have to say, "Fuck you. If you're going to act like that, if you're not going to let us play, we're not going to let you play either." So that it's not really women who cut men out ever. It's they who cut us out. Really. And as I say, I'm willing to accept and admire a lot of male writing but only within the probability of our telling our own stories. It's like history. It's like the whole history of mankind. It's like a film I saw recently. It was perfectly true, all that was represented was men slaughtering each other. And it's true because that's men's history, and that's what they did. So this woman said to me, "There are no women in this picture." So I said, "That's all right. Thank God!" There's a book that's just coming out by a woman named Eva Figes that you might want to take a look at. She has a couple of other books. She has a very small book on Monet. It's a piece of fiction called *Light*. Look at it if you can. It's so beautiful. It's a beautiful, beautiful book. But her new book is called *The Seven Ages*. And really what it is about is what was happening to women while history was happening over there, while history was being recorded, what was happening to generation upon generation of women.

Satz: Do you think in some ways we women haven't even seen our lives because we haven't talked about them? Some experiences because they haven't been recorded until very recently haven't even been recognized. (Oh this is just something I do but of course it's not important. Yes, of course I have this friend but who ever talks about women's friendships as important.)

Paley: Yes. Yes. Well, there's that and it's the history of what women were doing, how they were living, which comes into the present. It seems like that knowledge would give us even more understanding of where we come from. I really have a lot of feelings on this subject.

Satz: What do you think about men and women? Do you think that they can get together?

Paley: I think a lot of young guys, at least where I am, are much more tender, are close fathers in babyhood. You do see it a lot. I see my son and his young friends, all of them pushing these strollers and sitting in the park. Young guys, just talking about the babies. And I really think that talking about babies, which has been considered a woman's occupation, is probably one of the most civilizing conversations a person can have.

Satz: Do you feel responsible for that? Do you think that part of the thing is that these boys have had mothers . . .

Paley: I don't personally.

Satz: But you raised your son.

Paley: Yeah, but there are a lot of boys who were raised differently, but who have been affected by their young wives and who just hadn't realized that if they live with these women, they had to allow them to live their own lives.

Satz: Good, there is change and development. So we all should be happy in some ways.

Paley: Oh I think it's wonderful. I sometimes think the women's movement has done more for men than it has for women. I think it has lifted this burden of "macho" from their backs, if they allow it to.

Satz: You talked last night about the different callings in your lives. Do you feel fragmented or do you feel that all of the parts nurture each other?

Paley: Well, I feel both. Sometimes if I have to go to a meeting and I think it's very important and I want to stay home and write, I think—oh, shit! But I probably would go to the meeting unless I feel that my presence is totally unnecessary. Then I'll feel bad. Mostly I feel—let it pull a little bit this way and that way. It's stretching.

Satz: All the elements of your life come together, don't they?

Paley: Well, there was a time when no one in my political life knew I was a writer. I just didn't talk about it especially. They didn't know it. And they were surprised when they found out. But since then, people know. And in some ways it's better, but in some ways in the old days I would do a lot of basic grassroots stuff. But now all the time I give talks and stuff like that. And I don't like that so much. I mean I like it when I do it all right. But I did like the other very much. I do like going on the street to get signatures, the ordinary kind of thing. It is for me a very happy kind of thing.

Satz: How do you feel about the fact that because you are an eminent writer, when you perform a political act you get more attention than other women?

Paley: I feel—well, I'm not very nervous when I have to read. I like to read. I love to read. And I'm not nervous. Well, a little bit, but not really. But when I have to make a political speech, I'm very nervous because I really feel responsible for other people. I mean I can really fuck everybody up and that's something.

Satz: In your writing, you found your style early. I mean the voices.

Paley: No, I didn't. Well, early. I found it in my mid-thirties. I mean when I wrote those stories, that's the day. Suddenly. Suddenly, I heard the voices.

Satz: You were writing poetry, but not very satisfied with the poetry?

Paley: It wasn't me. I'd write like other poets. Three years I would write like Auden. And then like someone else. And it's only when I wrote stories that I could feel that I knew what I was doing.

Satz: The form of your stories is very satisfying although I think sometimes a bit confusing for readers because occasionally as a reader, you have the experience of walking into the middle of a conversation—you don't quite know what is going on because these people have been talking for a while. You don't know who is who and what they are talking about.

Paley: Right. Right.

Satz: Is that an intended effect?

Paley: Well I guess I have this idea that you should begin the story where the story begins, not two pages before with a lot of introduction and stuff like that. The fun of writing, because you know there's a lot of fun, is really getting it all to happen at once, if you can. You mentioned earlier something I had said a long time ago—that you write what you like to read. And I was really always impatient with introductions.

Satz: And descriptions probably?

Paley: And settings of scene, which were often very irrelevant to me.

Satz: Did you skip them?

Paley: Yeah, sometimes. So I begin the story where the story begins and not where I first thought of the story. So that might be it. But you can always figure it out, eventually.

Satz: Oh, yes.

Paley: But when I read aloud, I set the scene. Because when I'm reading aloud, people can't turn back, it would go past them. But they seem to get it.

Satz: I know people often ask you about Faith and your relation to Faith, Faith and Grace, and you've said in response that she's someone that has that status of a friend of yours.

Paley: Yes, she could've been a friend, but she wasn't.

Satz: But she's been around so long, she and her sons, that she must have a kind of life in your life. She is someone you know very well.

Paley: I know her well, but she has this funny mixture of sometimes taking over one of my parents and then not. Since I began her so long ago, I gave her a name I don't like, and in a way that's sort of good.

Because I didn't really like the name Faith, and I did it as sort of a joke. I thought of this family called Faith, Hope, and Charlie. I was playing around. So in a way because I don't like her name, it's better. It gives me a little distance from her. And certain other characteristics are not mine. And the father is not like my father. But what he has is my father's energy and his gift for storytelling. But the mother is really just not good. She's not like my mother or anybody else's mother. I feel that Faith is further away from me than she might be, and I'm glad of it. I'm glad of it.

Satz: Why are you glad of it?
Paley: Because I don't want to write about myself in that sense. I mean she's divorced. I lived with my children's father for twenty-five years.

Satz: Is the name *Tonto* also part of a joke?
Paley: I never know. There was some little kid in the park who was called Tonto. I picked up that name in the park.

Satz: How do you see your future?
Paley: Too short!

Satz: What are you engaged in now? What do you want to do?
Paley: I'm in this situation where I live half the year in New York and half the year in Vermont. It's a kind of gift for me that I'm developing a whole rural, I mean not small town, but rural sensibility. So it's something that I haven't digested enough yet. So I really have to digest a different kind of life, which I like a lot. You asked before whether I'm torn. I'm not torn between teaching and writing. I'm torn between the city and the country. I miss my city friends, my city buddies from my children's and their children's childhood. We've been together twenty-five years. I miss the political activity of city life. There's a lot happening in the city. And, on the other hand, there's a lot going on in Vermont, fortunately. And I'm part of that. So, I'm between the two. I get into things, but I never quite consummate the actions that I'm in, that I begin. I've begun certain things in Vermont, but I'm not going to be here for them another month and a half. And I feel terrible about it because I've started things that other people are going to have to carry on. That seems to be almost immoral. So those are problems for me, and so I don't know what I'm going to do. I have to solve my problem.

Satz: You are half a year in New York because of your teaching at Sarah Lawrence?
Paley: That's right. So I just have to figure out how to do continuous work while I live that way.

Satz: Do you write equally well in Vermont and in New York?

Paley: Equally badly. So what I really want to do is get a number of pages which will eventually constitute a book, and that's all. I don't really have big plans. I just want to continue.

Satz: I hear in everything you are saying that you are leading a very full and rich life doing a lot of good things.

Paley: Yeah, I am. My daughter is in Vermont, and my son is in Brooklyn, so I live with them equally in a sense. I have a grandchild.

Satz: How old?

Paley: Six.

Satz: Do you tell her stories?

Paley: I do, but no more than anybody else. I'm not such a good story teller. She was shocked. I'm a storywriter, and her father tells better stories. She's writing stories now. She's six and a half, and she calls me up and reads to me what she has written. That's a whole other thing, beginning again.

An Interview with Grace Paley
Eleanor Wachtel / 1988

From *The Brick Reader*. Ed. Linda Spalding and Michael Ondaatje (Toronto: Coach House Press, 1991), 185–91. Reprinted by permission of the publisher.

It's been almost thirty years since the publication of Grace Paley's first book of short stories, *The Little Disturbances of Man: Stories of Men and Woman at Love*. Fifteen years later came a second collection called *Enormous Changes at the Last Minute,* and then in 1985, *Later the Same Day*. Not much volume in three decades, but some of the most remarkably memorable stories you're likely to come across. Paley writes in an idiosyncratic style about women and their children, lovers, husbands, aging parents and friends. Many of the stories are about a woman named Faith, something of an alter-ego to Grace. The stories are told in perfect pitch.

Grace Paley is sixty-five. She grew up in the Bronx—her parents were Ukrainian-born Jews who emigrated to New York early in the century. She still has a residual Bronx accent although she's lived most of her adult life in Greenwich Village. Her second husband, a landscape architect and writer, is a Vermonter and they spend six months of the year there. When she's in one place, she thinks about what she's missing in the other. In Greenwich Village, she wishes she's in Vermont, planting or something. She took up gardening two years ago. When she's in Vermont, she thinks about all the exciting things her New York friends are doing.

Grace Paley has warm brown eyes and a shock of thick, short, white hair. She's five-feet-one. On the day I interviewed her she was wearing a pink blouse under a purple cardigan, dark purple skirt and dark stockings. A thin green-brown agate hung from a chain around her neck. When the publicity director for the 1988 Harbourfront International Authors Festival asked if she wanted the same room at the Harbour Castle Hotel she had earlier in the day, she said: "Okay, it was clean." He led us to the room. It was large, with a view of the lake, but stale cigarette smoke lingered in the air. The publicity director mentioned that one of the writers said that if he had to choose between death and living in that hotel he'd choose death. "With death as the alternative," said Paley, "sometimes you change your mind. You remember that there's a gift shop downstairs." We sat at a small table. She kicked off one shoe, looked me in the face and said: "Ask me anything."

Wachtel: Why did you start writing short stories?

Paley: I'd been writing poems for a number of years—in fact for most of my life. But they weren't doing the work I wanted them to do. So I felt I had to try to see what I could do with the story form.

Wachtel: When you say the poems weren't doing the work that you wanted, what do you mean?

Paley: I mean a couple of things. I couldn't use people in the way I was really interested in doing. I began to think about language and sentences, and using other voices. And I had also become oppressed by my worries, my feelings about women's lives. That was in the mid-fifties. I began to hang around with women, doing the mundane things that most people don't enjoy too much but which I really loved. I liked working in groups. I began to feel a great deal of pressure on my soul about women's lives. A lot of them, even then, were women alone with kids. My kids were in day care. Also it's as though some kind of sound in the air had begun to be heard by other women and by me, even though we didn't know what it was.

A lot of this began to bother me. It wasn't just a question of women. There were my aunts, my mother, et cetera. I had to find a way to write about them. My husband was really good about this. He said, "You have a sense of humor and it's never in any of these damn poems." And it's true, it wasn't. "And you're interested in people." All of this was true and I was also interested in myself as a Jewish woman, which I had not really thought about particularly or read about in literature. So all of that came together at one particular time and I began to write stories. Once I started I was lucky. I was sick that year. As a result I had to be home a lot and the kids had to be away a lot, so I had a couple of months in there—maybe two months—in which I could really carry one or two things to completion. Getting that done was important. Actually beginning and finishing the two stories in my first book—"The Contest" and "Goodbye and Good Luck"—was great.

Wachtel: What kind of voices are you referring to when you talk about the use of other voices in your work?

Paley: For me, you don't get to your own voice until you use other people's voices. I mean, you're not going to get that gift until you have paid enough attention. And maybe in the use of other voices, in that kind of dialectical experience, something happens so that your own voice comes through, almost in opposition. It sounds peculiar, but I think I'm probably right. That's what I was interested in when I wrote those two stories—one in the voice of an aunt who's totally invented and the other in a man's voice.

Wachtel: Your writing style is very original. Were you conscious of going your own way when you began writing short stories?

Paley: I was conscious in this sense. I had gone to school to poetry, I hadn't gone to school to fiction. I'd gone to school to poetry to learn how to write, so I had the habits of a poet, which seem original maybe in fiction. That's part of it: the kinds of jumps and leaps and liking of language that a poet has. The other thing was that I didn't like literary life. I was afraid of it. I didn't want to be part of it in any way, so that must have entered into the way that I began to write. I was afraid of being cut off from my own life by going into another world that was more literary. But I didn't think, "Oh, I'm being original."

I had done a lot of imitating. Not on purpose, though. I didn't even know it when I was imitating someone like Auden and writing with a British accent. Not on purpose, but because this tune was in my ear and I couldn't get my own tune going until I wrote stories. I wasn't so much aware of it as I felt something peculiar was happening. I'm probably doing something wrong, I thought. I was writing about those lives that no one would be interested in. I was putting in all those kitchen scenes that no one would care about. And I was writing in a funny way that probably nobody would like. But I had a great commitment to finish.

Wachtel: To some degree you write the way people talk. You have syncopated rhythms of speech. How do you do that?

Paley: I don't know. I just listen to people. If you pay attention you get some things right. I also rewrite a lot. I don't get it the first time. It can take me a helluva long time to get even the simplest dialogue right. Just an exchange between two people in four lines can really drive me crazy before I get it right.

Wachtel: A lot of people say they write to create order out of chaos, but you let a certain amount of chaos into your stories. Everything isn't tidy and ordered. Things jump from one thing to another.

Paley: That really comes from the poetry. Once you write poetry you get a certain courage about jumping and making leaps. You don't feel you have to put in five paragraphs of transition every time you go from one room to the next. I don't know if one makes order from chaos, it's such a general statement. I've said it myself, to tell you the truth. But it seems to me that that's just one way of looking at it. You might just as easily and with as friendly a tone of voice say: "I'm here to make disorder from excessive order. I'm here to bring a little bit of noise into this quiet place." Why not? Why not say that too?

Wachtel: Where do you start with a story?

Paley: It could be anything. It could be a sentence. I'm thinking of a story called "Distance," which begins: "I was the lady who appreciated youth." And I just put that sentence in. I was thinking about something. I didn't go on with it for a long time. Then I wrote another paragraph. Then I realized I was writing about this Irish woman and it was her voice I was writing in, which I didn't really know until I was well into the second page and she was the mother of one of the characters in another book. So that's how it starts. Sometimes it starts with an argument, like "The Immigrant Story." I was just having this abstract argument between two characters. One was being psychological and the other historical. I was writing that argument out for myself and I realized a few years after I wrote it out that it was the beginning of a story that I had been thinking about for a long time.

Wachtel: Do you recall what it was about women's lives that you particularly wanted to write about?

Paley: In my first book—I guess it was in my mid-thirties—I was trying to understand men's attitudes towards women, which I had begun to dislike very much, after years of liking both men and their attitudes. I had lived in army camps years earlier with my husband who was a soldier when we were kids—I mean we were in our early twenties, maybe nineteen. And I liked men pretty well in those days and I like them now, but there had begun to be something very wrong. And I had begun to be aware of it in a way that a lot of women were—suddenly feeling a discomfort—even women who were presumably happily married or who had not seemed terribly dissatisfied. I had not been very ambitious, so I can't say it was because suddenly I realized I couldn't be a lawyer or a doctor or something. It was nothing like that. I didn't want to be anything. I didn't even want to be a writer; I just wanted to write. I liked having kids, I liked all that very much. But I became very resentful of the general attitude of men towards women and maybe getting older had something to do with it.

Wachtel: Where did your feminist consciousness, or whatever you want to call it, fit into your general political awareness?

Paley: It didn't for a long time. It did to this extent: that I worked a lot with women. Women, in general, have been the main workers in local organizations, even the local organizations of great big centralized organizations. But forget that. Think of ordinary things, like getting a light at a crossing. I worked for a long time, at a time when Jane Jacobs was in New York, at keeping a road out of Washington Square Park. Lots of things like that. PTAs were almost entirely women. A kind of sisterhood was happening inside local work—a lot of which involved children, but not all. And then finally, when the Viet Nam War came, there were men working with us too. We had a local [Greenwich] Village centre, but women were still doing a tremendous amount of the work.

Wachtel: To what extent do you draw on your own life? The work *seems* autobiographical.

Paley: Basically I don't, or basically I do. My life is totally different from this woman Faith's. I lived with my children's father for twenty-two or twenty-three years, whereas she's really alone. My children are different. And so in every particular way, in every accountable way, it's not my life. But on the other hand, she could be a friend of mine. She could be some friend who hasn't been registered yet.

Wachtel: Do family or friends think they appear in your work?

Paley: Actually, much less than you'd think. I had to point out to a couple of my friends that I had really jumped off their backs. That's what you do: you get on the back of a person or a sentence and you jump. Sometimes they are very close to life. I have a couple of stories, like "Friends," which I wrote in memorial for a friend of mine who died, so that happens sometimes.

Wachtel: In that story about the death of a friend, you write that you, or the character telling the story, are "inventing for my friends and our children a report on these private deaths and the condition of our lifelong attachments." Is that your purpose as a writer?

Paley: I never really think about my purpose as a writer. If I did, my standards would be so high that I would never reach them. If you said, "What should be your purpose as a writer?" I'd think something noble and gallant and great. But as it is I write because I want to tell you something. I write because I don't understand what's going on. And I begin to barely understand my writing. In that particular story, I was trying to understand all our difficult relations, not just with the woman who died, but with the other women. And another reason you write—it's just what every writer does—you simply illuminate what's hidden so in that way you become a person who makes some justice in the world. Every writer does that who's serious, but you do that by accident.

Wachtel: You equate illuminating something with justice?

Paley: Yes, if you have lives that are hidden, where nobody wants to talk about them and you shine a light on them then the world sees that light for the first time. You see that in all new work. We began to write about women and put it in the same scale as the life of men. Black women, Native Americans, different classes. The middle class shone a light in the nineteenth century or earlier, saying: This is how we live, not just the nobles. We're this rising middle class, get a look at us, we're having a good time, we just invented capitalism.

Wachtel: Is it difficult or problematic to try to integrate politics into writing without being didactic?

Paley: No, it's not difficult in that sense. It's something that for me is maybe a little easier than for someone who doesn't do a lot of politics. I really want to write about those people who think about it and talk about it. And I really believe that more people think and talk about politics than writers let on. Writers don't let them talk about anything mostly. So it's not hard. And as for being didactic, you want it to be part of the form of the story and one of the things that the story is about. So that to leave it out would be much more noticeable than putting it in.

One of the things that you try to do when you're writing—you can't really do it—but you try to give as much primary experience as you can. That is, you want people to respond to what you're writing in a way that is as close as possible to the way you yourself responded to the event. But the only way you can do it is by not telling them how to respond, because once you do that they won't. People are very stubborn. There's no dealing with them. So what you try to do is be as primary as possible—really really do the event somehow. You might do it in a very surreal way, I'm not talking about naturalism or realism. You may go way out and yet the reader knows what you're talking about. But if you start telling people what to think they get kind of grouchy. My characters' political nature just means that they're aware that they live in the world.

Wachtel: What can a writer do, while functioning as a writer, to have some impact on the world politically?

Paley: It's kind of mysterious. I don't even dare to think in those terms because it's too great a dream to think that you could be that useful. Everybody longs for that. And yet we know that there are writers who have been able to speak for different classes or groups or colors. The success of a lot of Black women writers has been empowering to women, whether they mean to do that or not. I think partly you write to give yourself a sense of possibility. In the sense that you strengthen others, you can be useful. You give courage. It's the thing writers think about a lot. And you don't really know who's the boss of beauty.

Wachtel: Who's "the boss of beauty"?
Paley: Who's the judge? Who's the critic? Who are they to say you can

be political or you can't? Who knows in what way other work will come forward that is both didactic and beautiful? Who's in charge?

Wachtel: You have this line in a story called "Anxiety" [from *Later the Same Day*]: A woman is leaning out from her window and talking to a young father she doesn't know and she says, "Son, I must tell you that madmen intend to destroy this beautifully made planet. That the murder of our children by these men has got to become a terror and a sorrow to you, and starting now, it had better interfere with any daily pleasure." Is that you talking?

Paley: It's me talking, but you don't see me doing that . . . Think of people who are doing really outstanding political work, for example in Central America. People who really decided that they're going to put their lives into trying to prevent a war down there. Take a guy like Ben Linder who went there to build dams, and to help construct—not protest—but construct a new society. These people make up their minds to put away certain daily pleasures. I'm sure they have had a great time—in fact, Linder's a clown from before and rode a monocycle and did wonderful things with children. You can't live without joy and pleasure. But there have to be a lot of serious people around, of whom other people say: Tsk, they never think of anything else. What's wrong with them? There have to be a lot of people who never think of anything else any more.

Wachtel: Are you one of them, or have you been at different times in your life?

Paley: No, I never have been totally. During the Viet Nam War, I spent a helluva lot of time doing all kinds of work, and I do again, now and then, but I'm a writer too and I have to do that. I have strong feelings for happiness.

Wachtel: How can you maintain your optimism?

Paley: Who said I was optimistic? No, I happen to have a cheerful disposition. But I'm not optimistic. I think we just may kill ourselves ecologically before we kill ourselves with nuclear war, so that's a great piece of anxiety. But at the same time, you do see—I think some of my early political struggles had some success. The little ones, the small ones, really, that shaped the city, that helped make parts of the city decent, which most of it isn't, New York, I mean. So you have some of those successes and they shape you a little bit, they give you courage for the future. And I think the United States would be at war right now in Nicaragua if it weren't for the breadth of the anti-Central American War movement—if it wasn't for that, and if it wasn't for the fact that we worked so hard during the Viet Nam period. So in general, Americans no matter how often they vote for Reagan really don't want to go to war right now. They've lost their taste for it. I'm happy that I was a little tiny part of helping them lose their taste for war.

Wachtel: Are there other American writers you have an affinity to who are writing political fiction?

Paley: There are many different kinds of writers who are thinking about these things. There's a young woman, Irini Spanidou, who isn't writing about the U.S. at all, she's writing about Greece. She has a book called *God's Snake* and it's all about women. Then there's E.M. Broner who's a very interesting writer. Mary Gordon thinks about these things a lot. There are a lot of women writing about women, but in a very narrow kind of way, in a way that is so classbound. I really don't know how to describe it because although it does what I believe in doing, it describes the lives of women, which I'm interested in, I don't really care about that particular middle class or upper middle class of women and marriages and infidelities and stuff like that. It's a little too late for that. There's got to be more of a move. Marge Piercy has given herself the great and serious task of covering all the bases, and there are people I really love like Tillie Olsen and Kay Boyle who are still writing away there—Kay is in her eighties—fierce and amazing women.

Wachtel: Are you conscious of apportioning your time towards writing or political action or happiness?

Paley: No, I'm just pulled one way or another: writing, politics, house and family. That's all right. It's an idea of life. If you can take it, and you don't feel guilty. Feeling guilty is what's wrong. I tend to be pulled without an excess of guilt—just enough so I know something is happening to me. I'm a writer but I'm also a person in the world. I don't feel a terrible obligation to write a lot of books. When I write, I write very seriously and I mean business. I write as well and as truthfully as I possibly can and I write about the things that have created a good deal of pressure in my head.

Wachtel: Who are the people who you hope or imagine will read your books?

Paley: The whole world. I'd like everybody to read them. Sometimes I'm surprised by the people who read the books. Without the support of the women's movement the response might be different. I'm very conscious of the fact that there exists a movement, a political and women's movement that supports all women writers, no matter who that writer is, even if she says: "I hate feminism and I don't really like women too much." Even so, that woman, whether she knows it or not, is supported by the historical fact of the wave of the women's movement. So that exists for all of us women right now and we're very lucky.

Wachtel: Do you think of yourself as a realist writer?

Paley: No, I don't think about where I'm lodged in the house of literature.

Wachtel: How do you want to be remembered?

Paley: I don't know. I just don't think about that. We all throw ourselves into the hearts of our grandchildren and luck.

Grace Paley
Shirley M. Jordan / 1991

From *Broken Silences*, 159–73, Shirley M. Jordan, ed., copyright © 1993 by Rutgers, The State University. Reprinted by permission.

Grace Paley was born December 11, 1922, in New York. Though she began writing poetry at the age of five, Paley has distinguished herself as a major short-story writer. *The Little Disturbances of Man: Stories of Women and Men at Love* (1959) and *Enormous Changes at the Last Minute* (1974) are both currently in print. Paley's stories have also been published in periodicals such as *Esquire, Atlantic, The New Yorker, Genesis West,* and *Ikon,* among others.

Paley has taught creative writing at Columbia University and at Syracuse University and later became a member of the literature faculty of Sarah Lawrence. She has received several awards, including a Guggenheim fellowship, a National Council on the Arts grant, and a National Institute of the Arts and Letters Award for short-story writing.

The daughter of Russian Jewish immigrants, Paley grew up keenly aware of political causes and how they affect people's lives. She has worked on numerous projects to rectify social ills. Still much in demand on the lecture circuit, Paley lives with her husband in Vermont and New York.

Jordan: What specific conditions seems to be in place when black and white women become friends?
Paley: That's very hard. . . . Well, there has to be an awful lot of trust. It has to be able to go two ways. But I think mostly the black woman has to be able to trust the white woman. By that I mean that the white woman has to be trustworthy. I could probably think of a better answer but that's a beginning. A matter of trust that can happen with work when people trust each other—or have a common experience such as children, age. . . . And it's also a class thing too, economic class.

Jordan: I was just going to ask you if the issue of class also plays a part in the forming of these friendships. If the women do not meet in situations in which they are on the same footing socially, it's hard.
Paley: Yes. But that would be true of white women too. It would be

more difficult for a black and a white woman. But two white women could have a lot of misunderstanding or different interests too.

Jordan: That's also true. Have you noticed distinctions between how black women authors portray characters and how white women portray them?

Paley: I'm trying to think of authors. I think the last book I read was by Ellen Douglas who is a Southern white woman author writing about friendships between black and white women. You'll have to refresh my memory. Her novel is unusual and truthful. In it, the black woman who works as a maid is really portrayed with a lot more feeling than the white woman. The white woman is a decent sort of woman but there is no real understanding. I just met the author, Ellen Douglas, so I paid particular attention.

Jordan: As you were drawing the character of the black female in "Long Distance Runner" [in *Enormous Changes at the Last Minute*], what particular concerns did you have about her portrayal? How was this figure born and what do you think of her now that she is actually here?

Paley: First of all I come from the Bronx, and so I will give you an example from my background to show how I started her. I have been going back there every year to visit my father and mother's house. The neighborhood has changed since then. Now there are about four houses left on the block. My father was the neighborhood doctor. Just a couple of years ago I returned. I see this little black girl sitting on my stoop and . . . well I'm overcome with happiness. She's sitting there and a woman is looking out the window—the mother I thought (this happened after I wrote the story). I was elated, I almost ran into the house like the woman in the story yelling "Mama! Mama! Let me in!" Anyway I had been going earlier—often—and I had looked at the neighborhood and had seen what was happening—it's hard to talk about a story that pretty much said what I felt. What I tried to see and maybe know is another life. Not terribly unlike my own, which was full of mommies and daddies and so forth, but still to see another life in the same place. Place being a very important thing. The same place.

I remember what the neighborhood was like. The people who lived on my block then, now have some kind of idealized view of what our street was like. It was really not a rich people's street. It was a poor people's street—at least during the ten years of the Depression—most of my childhood and adolescence. Maybe it started out and planned and wanted to be more middle class, but in those days, my days, the street itself was often lined with evictions—people thrown out of their homes for nonpayment of rent. Those were hard times for my neighbors so that it wasn't hard for me to move into the world of the story, which ends with the narrator asking "What in the world is coming next?" I want to show that in a loving way—loving and truthful, not bullshit.

And I wanted to break certain stereotypes that the narrator has—for instance, when she says she's going to teach the kid to read, it turns out he's a great reader. You want to break this thing without a hammer but crack it anyway. That was intentional. But I also wanted to show the truth of that. I don't know if it's that story—it is—but there is one house left on this street. Nothing there but rubble and dirt and so forth. There's a big sheet hanging out the window and it says, "People still live in this God-forsaken neighborhood." That was just one house. Nothing around it but rubble and dirt and junk.

Jordan: Do you think others go back too?

Paley: Well, I think people do want to go and look at where they grew up—at least if they can. I lived there my whole life until I got married, so I lived there for nineteen years. I was on the streets a lot. Kids used to play in the streets all the time so I had a kind of identity with that kid on my old stoop. I see very little street life in the white neighborhoods in Manhattan. None practically. I mean, it's really pathetic for children. I had such a nice, rich street life. So the streets themselves are interesting and exciting to me.

Now I live downtown. I've lived for years in and around the Village. It's a very strong neighborhood, and Chelsea is a neighborhood much like it. There are some city areas that aren't neighborhoods; new people are moving in and new houses are built. A community takes time anywhere. You don't have a community the minute you move in.

Jordan: To what extent do you use historical sources when you are developing a character like Ludie or Cynthia?

Paley: I just write from my knowledge. Tough little girls and stuff like that—they are all going to have some of the same characteristics, right? "She's gonna not let the boys push her around and she's gonna . . ." I mean you go to school with these kids too. I did. My children did.

Jordan: What can black and white women teach each other about writing and about living?

Paley: Another complicated question. I know this sounds silly to say this but in general white people have a lot to learn about what it means to live in this country. . . . I'm Jewish and I've been in situations—for instance, I lived in a small town in Illinois when I was about twenty or twenty-one, when I first left home. The anti-Semitism was acute and painful to me and surprising since I had lived a ghetto life. I lived in a Jewish ghetto, and there's nothing more protected than a ghetto. And in its own way, there is probably nothing more protective for little black kids too. It's kind of nice to be in a kind of cocoon for a while, protected until you get your muscle together. But then we do have to go into the world; we must go into the world. You have got to have your strength to go into the world, and you get some of it from the people you've been living your childhood among.

I have a very brutal story in that book [*Enormous Changes at the Last Minute*] about a killing. You may have read it. This story comes from a guy who was a friend of mine. I met him just after World War II. Late forties. I worked at that time for the Southern Conference for Human Welfare in New York; it was basically just a fund-raiser for the South. There were a lot of black people around even though the group was run by these very idealistic white people who were going in and out of jail. Joe Louis was the chairman, and he would come around sometimes.

But I made friends with this guy, Bill, who was working there; he was from Eclectic, Alabama. I can't believe these names. We became very close friends. We were friends until he died a couple of years ago. He told me that story, and he didn't tell it to me once. He told it to me so many times that it was as though I knew it by heart.

A writer in general has to be a person who pays attention. I would say if you're not the kid sitting under the table who listened to grownups, you're not going to be a writer black or white. I think it's that listening. ... For white Americans, of any kind, to listen is to begin to understand the country. To listen to blacks particularly is to understand the whole country historically. Slavery was a great curse the United States greedily, foolishly accepted.

Jordan: One thing I have noticed as I've been reading novels in which black and white women appear is that we see fewer novels written by black women that have a central white female figure. Do you think this pattern will remain the same, or do you see black women starting to tell stories through the white female voice?

Paley: Well—first of all— people tell their own stories, their unknown stories, and certainly black women's stories haven't been properly told by white men or women or black men so they have had a big job on their hands. In general, I think people go through this business of writing about their own people. I mean you had this whole big wave of Jewish literature and what it was, of course, was the first time they could write about their own Jewish experiences and be generally read. I'm just going to make one Jewish comparison here. When I wrote my first stories, they were really explicitly about my own neighborhood life, which I was just trying to understand and then there were a couple of other stories. And then I didn't need to explore that life so much.

When I wrote my first stories, I was afraid I'd stop writing because I have a lazy nature. I went to the New School for Social Research thinking maybe a class would keep me writing. And I had a teacher who kept saying to me "You've got to get off this Jewish dime." So I asked, "How can I write about a middle America?" What I didn't have the brains to say then was "I'm not even interested in it yet." Black women are important and interesting to black women writers. And to be able to write truthfully from where you are toward what you don't know about yourself, toward what you're trying to find out, toward your own mysteries and be read, which is possible at this time, is a very great thing. There's no reason yet for them to write with a central white character unless they were very specifically trying to understand what that person was in relation to blacks. Otherwise, they'd be writing a kind of middle America voice, the sort you hear on the radio or used to. So unless they were after something specific. . . . But it seems like there is so much yet to tell that hasn't been told and the new ways of telling are exciting.

So many women are writing now, women of all colors. It's a wonderful time. Before this, they didn't know that they could write about themselves. I remember when I wrote my first story—about a woman's life—I thought, "Gee, this must be boring. This is so boring to everybody. But I don't care. I can't help it. I have to write it." So I think that experience of suddenly being able to talk about ourselves—not just black women, I'm talking about myself and all women—is exciting and curious. And to be read by strangers as well as friends is a great thing.

Jordan: That leads me to my next question. How do you maintain your own voice or manage to remain true to the voices of the characters without succumbing to pressures from publishers or readers to write either what they want to hear or what they consider proper to write? Has this been an issue at all?

Paley: Well as far as the pressures from readers and publishers go, the only time I responded to a publisher was when I was told to write a novel. I had written my first book of stories. And I tried to write a novel and I failed. I mean I really gave it a shot. I did two years of writing a novel. And it was no good. Since then I just do what I want to do. I don't feel that pressure at all because I don't think in terms of a career or something like that. I don't think that way, and I never expected to make a lot of money writing so I teach like all writers do. [*Laughs*]

Jordan: Did you grow up aspiring to write?

Paley: I grew up aspiring, knowing that I was going to write my whole life because there was all this childhood encouragement. Every time you wrote a sentence, somebody said, "That is very good," so then you wrote two sentences. But people should not worry about this kind of pressure, not if they really want to write. I mean if their reason to write is to speak truthfully, writers must give their characters a full life and a truthful life—that's the only job a writer has.

Jordan: Suppose you're writing something so radical that you think you can't find a publisher for it, then you still don't consider the publisher but pursuing the truthfulness of the story?

Paley: See, when I wrote my first book, I got every story back again and again and again. Every single one. I mean until suddenly the University of Illinois printed two stories and that was it for the whole book. None of the others were accepted. I could have been very discouraged, and I mean I could have succumbed if I hadn't by luck gotten a publisher. I wouldn't have stopped writing though. But you really have to stick by your vision because life isn't so long really. It's always something. It's just as hard to fit somebody's—a publisher's—idea of what writing is as it is to write your own way. They're equally hard. So you might as well be hung for who you are. [*Laughs*] 'Cause they'll get you. They get you anyway . . . so . . . I mean look at publishing today. It's in such a weird shape anyway that you have to go to small presses if you're starting out.

Jordan: As you are writing, are you ever conscious of race or ethnicity in a very overt way as you allow characters to come to life, or is it the story that is more important? Therefore, you're concentrating on the story and not so much on "This is the Jewish person who has to speak" and "This is a black person who has to speak."

Paley: No. No. Well . . . I'm thinking of what I'm writing, and I'm letting the characters work their way through to the story. When I wrote "Long Distance Runner," I just began with the narrator running. I really had no plan. I did not know where I was going and when I got to the street, I didn't know I was going upstairs. And so you just sort of open yourself up to it, and by not knowing you have more tension somehow. There is some kind of great pull like a great stretch. And you stretch toward something that you don't understand totally and that then pulls you along somehow. The stretch and the tension in it I think is the way it works. So when I get the people I have to figure out how they evolve and sometimes I do the best I can. And what I also do is I read it aloud to myself. I read it aloud so that I try to get it right. Sometimes I show it to other people. It's funny when I wrote this story with a lot of black speech. I didn't feel so comfortable about it at all, and I wouldn't have for some reason. I didn't know if I could do it.

Jordan: As the story is pulling you along, what do you do when other things also demand some of your time like picking up the kids or whatever?

Paley: Oh, you mean my life? Ah, it's very hard. Some people are very organized. I talked to Mary Gordon. She puts aside the time. She has two kids, adores them, gives them a lot. But she organizes her time well, and she gets a novel out every couple of years. She is young and in another time than I am. She is the age of my children. But as for me it was always push and pull and pull and push. And then I had two children, and then I also had jobs, and I did a lot of politics too. I mean I just did it. It was a very rich period; I don't feel bad about any of it. And I would sit and talk with my children, take them to the park; they would give me a lot. In fact, they sometimes became my subject matter. So I can't really say I shouldn't have done that because that's what was interesting to me then.

But I was lucky enough to have child care. Everybody—not just writers, to hell with writers—but all women do have to have decent child care. And I don't think I could have accomplished all that I did without having a certain amount of child care. Basically, it was a settlement house in the neighborhood, which was cheap—what I could afford which wasn't much. It's hard but you gotta stick with it. [*Pauses*] Just think of a woman who really has some rotten job who is running back and forth with the kids. I'm particularly lucky to have some wonderful thing I want to do.

Jordan: Back to the protagonist of "Long Distance Runner." She seems so much at home in the community even near the beginning when she first gets into the neighborhood and there are all these people around her. She seems alert and on guard but she never seems to me afraid for her life—at least most of the time she isn't. . . .

Paley: Yeah, when she runs up there and the kid starts yelling at her.

Jordan: I thought that that scene really moves far beyond the stereotype.

Paley: It's a little surrealistic.

Jordan: That's it! She couldn't be that naïve, and I didn't think she could be that open-minded but I suppose she could have felt at home. After all, if she has returned home, she wouldn't be as afraid anyway.

Paley: I think it's a couple of things. It was quite surrealistic. No one would stand there and say . . . On the other hand, there is a certain naïveté. Even her deciding to give the little boy a reading lesson—I mean there was a kind of good-hearted naïveté about her in a sense. But it also had a surrealistic quality. . . . I mean the whole thing is invented. It's not very likely she would say those things. None of that is likely but all of it is in the realm of the barely possible. She might have gone up there in her shorts . . .

Jordan: And maybe it's the naïveté that allows her to get even that far. If she were truly just sitting around reasoning out everything, she probably wouldn't have run that far off course.

Paley: Yes. Yes. I'm nearly seventy. I come from a less fearful time. I used to have to pick up the collection boxes for the Southern Conference about forty-five years ago. I walked up and down apartment houses in Harlem, jangling shopping bags full. I never thought about it. I was afraid of the Irish neighborhoods though when I was a kid—because of Father Coughlin.

Jordan: I'm sure you have heard the following said of your work before, but I will add my compliment as well. You capture the speech of the characters so brilliantly that the words seem naturally to flow from the characters' mouths. How did you develop your ear to capture Black English on the page without it sounding like "and now here is a black person speaking" versus "here is a person speaking in his or her own way who happens to be black?"

Paley: I don't know. It goes back to listening. I think a lot of people could do better than they do. I say the dialogue aloud to myself. I can't tell you how many times I change the words. The smallest sentence I change many times. I mean any ten-word sentence I must have changed ten times. I rarely got it right. That's the main thing. I rarely got it right the first time, and I rarely got it right the third time. But it's this business of saying things aloud again and again. You know poets read aloud, right? And fiction writers don't do that so much in working. But just to say it again and again. You will get it. You may not get it perfect but you'll get it a lot better than—say—if you write it once and you say, "Oh I can't write dialogue." If you haven't been listening to people, you'll never get any kind of sound, but if you have been listening, then I think you can get it. But as I said I really have more self-consciousness right now.

Jordan: It didn't seem self-conscious in the story at all.

Paley: But that was because I rewrote it after it was in my head a long time. I wrote it, and then I made certain changes. I got it right, I think. It didn't begin with me being self-conscious. I began with the idea that I could do it, and then I only had to make the effort to and do it. I don't remember where, but I feel like I went off someplace. But that story, "Lavinia," was very much like my grandmother's story, and I wanted, in my mind, to bring people closer together. I wanted to show the same kind of story really in one case in the older immigrant woman and in this case, the working black woman. Married, didn't want children, wanted to make something of herself and had children. And then wanted her daughter to make something of herself. And it's not that the daughter went bad. I don't want her to become the bad person. What she did was live with a guy, just begin to have a lot of children. It didn't seem like she was going to do something with herself—from the old woman's view.

Jordan: When we look at the protagonist leaving the neighborhood, Ludie tells her that it's time for her to go suggesting that she understands the protagonist perhaps in ways that she does not know she really understands. How does Ludie intuitively seem to know when it is time to leave? She's accepted this stranger into her home as if that were the natural thing to do, and then she seems to know exactly when she ought to leave. Is that just her instincts at work?

Paley: I think also it's the surrealistic part of it. I wanted her to leave. [*Laughs*] She'd been a guest an awful long time, and nothing is more annoying than people telling people how to raise their children. Like telling them to go downstairs. Tell them to do this; they need more air. They would get really pissed at that.

Jordan: The protagonist is renewed by her journey back. At the end of the story, we see her at home. In particular, what has she learned from her journey back to the neighborhood—to her roots?

Paley: Well, she says that at the end, she's learned "what in the world is coming next."

Jordan: Do you think our stereotypes of interracial relationships and of sexuality keep us apart as women rather than becoming closer?

Paley: Yes.

Jordan: From the perspective of both races?

Paley: Yes, but I really think from the point of view of black women. . . . First as real people and as valuable people I can see their suspicion is historically so reasonable, but on the other hand, what it means is that white people, white women who are really interested have to prove themselves, and when people start to prove themselves, they become somewhat false. I mean not a bad false. I don't mean anything like untrue or anything like that. I mean they become unnatural and then a certain falsity sets into the relationship. And that has to happen, and that happens a lot. I think it can't help but happen. It's not anyone's fault. Our terrible history—oppression and hatred.

Jordan: It's probably one of the hardest hurdles to cross in learning to trust.

Paley: Yeah. It's a hard thing for people to act naturally together.

Jordan: Once you start to make the effort to do so then that's when the falsity sets in.

Paley: Yes, so people have to sort of recognize that falsity not as an evil thing sometimes but as an unnatural effort. Not meaning ill. And that goes both ways too. Listen, this business of suspicion between people who have hurt each other in one way or another.... What bothers me about say my own family or a lot of Jewish people I know who are really open-minded.... People think that the persecution of Jewish people started with the Holocaust. The Holocaust is *the* moment like the bringing over of slaves in our recent history. If Jews just thought about the way they've been treated in a daily way not just forty years ago but about a thousand years ago, they could identify better. Put away the most recent experience and think of what their ordinary life—just their daily life was like—not just the genocidal moment, but everything, then they would really understand better the daily life others live. And that's one of the things they don't do. So one of the arguments I have, like the idea that their neighborhoods were so great, is that they were just like any good people. I remember my mother going to Orchard Beach and saying, "Look what a mess! Our people were here." But when I tell that to my sister, she says, "No. No. We were never like that. We were never like that." [*Laughs*] Mama said that. She said that: "Our people were here. It's dirty. Let's go to another beach." [*Laughs again*]

Jordan: That makes me think about blacks and how we remember slavery. I think sometimes people my age and older become frustrated with black teenagers who—not that they don't want to remember slavery—don't make it the pinnacle of all black experience. We think that they don't fully understand and that often frustrates us.

Paley: Well, I think a lot of the kids think things are bad enough. "What are you going back there for? Why do you keep talking about that when here I am on this block, you know?" So going back has many possibilities.

Jordan: What are some of the uses of memory or history you see at work in your fiction?

Paley: Well for me, I like to go back into my parents' life, and I have a number of stories like that—stories from my father and history. There's a story called "A Conversation with My Father," which to me is historical. It is seen by a lot of people as a psychological father/daughter thing, but to me it is clearly a historical statement. More than that the father comes from a place where change is not possible. That's one thing. He has that rigidity and also he comes from a world where he says she'll never change, it's like that. It's more historical than psychological, and I'm more interested in the historical than I am in the psychological.

Jordan: When you look at young children and teenagers who do not know their own family histories and do not have or know the words to recount their experiences or what they see, what kinds of things do you think ought to be done to help them gain control over their own voices?

Paley: Well, I just think, first of all, we tell them stories from history, not just the stories that happen to Grandma and Grandpa, but also tales of the past. From my own experience, I am not religious at all but I really enjoyed stories from the Bible when I was a kid. I felt related to them, so I told my children these stories. My son has told my granddaughter too, though he has no religious feeling. It's the way that our own old stories connect us to our past, and the stories of other people connect us to their past, so that we read not just our own stories but the stories of other people to know history, to make connections. And I really think that's very useful to children to ground them and to place them among the generations. I want to tell you a good assignment that I did with kids. Exactly related to this. I didn't know it was going to work out so well. Just before Thanksgiving I said when you get home ask the oldest person there to tell you a story he or she remembers by the oldest person he or she knew. One of the women went back through great-great grandparents to slavery. In fact that's one of the stories in "Long Distance Runner." When the little kid says, "I remember that story, 'Freedom Now,' " that's the one that student had told me. She's the one who told me that story. Her grandfather told her what his grandmother had told him. This is the story of how they ran from cabin to cabin. So you can go way way back. That was one of the best. I've done the assignment again, and you go pretty far back.

Jordan: Did you want to make any comments about "Lavinia" at all?

Paley: The story came from that common experience that seems to me to be a class experience, a common women's experience. Someone said to me, "Well, why didn't you just tell your grandmother's story instead of doing this?" And I guess I was just extremely interested, and it would have been boring to do it in my grandmother's voice at that particular time because what I was after was trying to understand what it would have been like for someone else. And I had been talking to this old black woman, Mrs. Pinchner, who had told me the same story anyway—exactly the same story. And it just seemed that I wanted to tell her story. In that whole period of my life I felt as a white woman that I wanted to understand more and also try to make some kind of contribution in a sense. Somehow I should understand and help other people to understand to see certain commonalities. And also the whole female subject, the whole business of these two women saying, "We wanted to be teachers. We didn't want to have all those children," interested me.

Jordan: In growing up in the Bronx, what made you open to wanting to understand all cultures?

Paley: Well, first of all, my parents were socialists who came from Russia. They'd been in prison in Russia when they were eighteen, nineteen years old so they were very young when they emigrated. And when they came here they didn't do a lot of politics. They had to work too hard. All my aunts worked in the garment district to make my father a doctor. They were all about twenty years old. Think of all these young people coming over, and they worked very hard so he could become a doctor, and he became one. He was always a neighborhood doctor. And the office was in the house so there were always people coming and going. And there was always sickness, and there was always a lot of feeling for other people's suffering. My father, unlike some doctors, had a lot of feeling, identification with pain. In fact, so much so that by the time he was sixty he just had to stop. He couldn't handle it anymore.

So I think it began with that, and then we read the papers at breakfast and all these things were happening in America. People were being actually lynched. And the Armenians got into my head too. All those worries—the pogroms my parents went through—uncles killed or deported from this country in the repressions that followed the First World War and the Russian Revolution.

And then I had a very small but strong experience. Children in the street used to play among many other games—

>   eenie meenie minie mo
>   catch a nigger by the toe . . .

My sister gave me such a crack across the face. When I remind her of this now, she asks wondering, proudly I think, "Where did I get such an idea?" She said to me that day, "Never let me hear you talk like that ever again." I mean that was a traumatic smack. So that's an early remembered corroboration from the family. As you go on, you realize that you've said a bad thing, which will mean a sad painful thing to someone else and that leads to other ways of thinking. It moves from person to the community to the world. It's not so good if it stays in the area of personal kindness—in fact it could be dangerous if there's no wider political understanding. Anyway—with experience of other people's suffering, my sister's smack remained a lasting education. And we did have black women and occasionally men working in the household and office a lot of the time, and they totally engaged me as often happens. But because of my family's old politics, they had gotten a lot less radical actually, these conversations were socializing and useful—and also established remembrances of personal love.

Grace Paley
Mickey Pearlman / 1992

From *Listen to Their Voices: Twenty Interviews with Women Who Write* (New York: Norton, 1993), 23–35. Reprinted by permission of W. W. Norton & Company, Inc.

If you are going to a tiny wooded village in Vermont called Thetford Hill to interview Grace Paley, you might consider stashing away a small supply of Valium in your suitcase. You'll need it if you choose to ride in a car with the unique and beloved New York writer who "lived in the Bronx for twenty years and then on 11th Street [in Greenwich Village] for forty years." Suffice it to say that Paley, who loves children—hers and everybody else's—frequently looks out the side window at them while she is driving, not always in her lane. When you discover that a large truck is coming directly at you—since you are driving in his lane—you might try to energize whatever navigational capabilities you still possess for the rest of the trip. (Try to forget about the part where she stops the car in the middle of the highway to talk to her stepdaughter's husband, who is from Somalia. Since he is carrying his newborn baby, he quite intelligently declines a lift.)

There's also the problem of Paley's schedule. While you are sitting in the Hanover Inn near Dartmouth College, ready to order lunch (with your tape recorder neatly set up and ready to go), she will suddenly remember that she is the guest of honor at another lunch, taking place at this exact moment, in another village, fifteen rollicking miles away. Thanks to the hostess's good nature, you both end up eating there. That's *after* you've driven up and down several roads, through the woods, looking for the house: "I'll recognize it; don't worry!" Of course there's always the possibility that you're already running late on your schedule because Paley has promised to write a piece for "the Quakers," and since it's now several weeks overdue, you've been looking for a fax machine in White River Junction, Vermont, the nearest technological metropolis. When Paley borrows your telephone calling card (since she forgot hers), to call "the Quakers" in Pennsylvania for their fax number, she somehow calls Utah instead. Since she's already two hours late for your interview, this will hardly matter.

All of this, of course, is what might be called classic Grace Paley. The consummate peace activist, with her curly white hair flying, has probably lost track of how many times she was arrested in the sixties during protests against American involvement in Vietnam, at marches against the use of nuclear power, and at rallies for women's rights. At sixty-nine she may be slowing down a bit, (doing "less now, because I'm really a little more tired"), although this is not noticeable to any normally active mortal. In any case, and under any circumstances, you will treasure any time that you spend with this irresistible woman.

Paley lives in a sprawling country house, with a large and comforting living room, that is surrounded by farmland that her husband Bob "gave to a young guy with very little land, who is going to use it for a few years." There are sheep, whose "major job is to make doo-doo on the grass." She says that she's "very moved by living in the country because I've been given the gift of having some kind of rural sense. I loved being the city writer, 'the New York City writer,' and I feel it, but now I have the gift of this place, of a certain amount of country life among real country people, not suburban people." Needless to say, the seemingly bucolic stillness of the Vermont landscape has not quieted Paley's activism in any noticeable way. True to her history, she's "been involved since 1977 in ecological things, one of my concerns, and I've been arrested with Bob many times at Seabrook [the nuclear facility in New Hampshire]. It's my nature to get to what is being done and to try to do it, and so I've been involved in what's going on here. I'm on the recycling committee. . . . It's the closest thing for me to being in New York. You get out, right down there near the school where they do the recycling, and the people all come, sort of like being on the street corner or something. Otherwise, you could live here for a year and not see a soul or just bump into them in the post office one at a time. So the recycling is good because they all come with their garbage and . . . tell you what's going on. . . . It's a beautiful place, like a laundromat or something."

Paley also does "a lot of work around here. I have a big garden: We grow a lot of food, and I freeze a lot. . . . I hardly ever invite anyone for dinner, . . . but anyone who is around, I'll feed. . . . I do stuff." (Earlier I've had a tour of the local health food co-op, where Paley is also a member.) At this point in the interview the phone rings and Paley returns to report that "my friend Carol [Emshwiller] just called me from Montpelier to tell me that tomorrow night at seven the Women's Center is having a public forum on the Clarence Thomas confirmation hearings and that she just renamed the Ethan Allan room, where they are going to meet, the Anita Hill room. So I'll probably go to that forum. . . . Did you read my story called 'Is Country Life Boring?' . . . There's plenty to do up here," she reports. No doubt.

Although I did not want to place Grace Paley in the position of passing judgment on her "fellow" writers, I wanted to know what she thought of the position of those who were less politically active and who often voiced during their interviews the hope that "their work would do 'it' for them," would suffice as their political involvement.

Much to my surprise, Paley the activist said, "I think it's a perfectly legitimate thing to say; I hope my work will do it for me, too. It's hard for women to talk about this because, when I'm doing a reading (and I love to have questions and answers after those, especially if I'm lucky and I can think of an answer) . . . people will sometimes say, 'Why don't you write more politics?' And I have to explain to them that writing the lives of women *is* politics. I didn't know it when I began to write; I mean I was not a feminist when I wrote my first book in 1959, but it turned out that writing about the ordinary lives of women *was* a political act, and it was a natural one for me because I was always interested in people. So when these women say, they 'hope their work will do it for them,' you know, there is no reason to think it wouldn't. Their hearts should be at rest if they are doing a lot of work. I was worried in my early days, when I wrote these stories and I didn't know if they would be made use of. I felt bad that I wasn't using my writing more politically, [although] I was writing a lot of leaflets, which is also writing, you know. Looking back, I often think that in the sixties I would have been more useful if I wrote, I don't know, manifestos, instead of hanging out on the streets so much."

While not judging other writers, Paley makes the point that she's "never been writing-ambitious the way some of the younger women are. I mean, I was always a writer, I liked being a writer, I wanted to be a writer, and when I wrote, I was a writer, and when I didn't write, I was not a writer. When I didn't write I was [a person] taking part in the political life of that period, and it was terribly exciting, you know. I was a mother and that was endlessly interesting, and it turned out to be useful to my work as well. So I see life more as a whole. The word *career* drives me crazy for some reason; I hate it in men as well as women. That word *career* is a divisive word. It's a word that divides normal life from business or professional life, whatever that is. Everybody should have work they love, that's another story, but that's different from that word *career,* which says, 'I will spend any number of hours pursuing this thing, which I may or may not be interested in even, to get somewhere, and the rest of my life is another story.' So it's a disintegrating . . . an unintegrating word. It divides a person from life, from all of life, and from their own life."

Paley says that raising children became her subject matter because "I had to get out of the house when [her two children] were little, and I spent a lot of time in the park [in New York City]. I certainly never intended for that to be what I was going to write about, because I was writing poems. I didn't know that I was coming into my community. I didn't know that I was coming into my subject matter; it was a really lucky thing for me. . . . [But] I didn't begin to write about it for several years, and had life not forced me in that direction, I don't know what would have happened. It was the luck of being pushed by circumstance into [what then became] my meat, so to speak. So I've always allowed circumstance to push me. I sometimes think it knows better what I should be doing than I do.'' And, she added, ''It's my disposition.''

In spite of her own disinclination to think about money, Paley believes that the younger women who want more power and bigger financial returns for their writing "are right. They're another generation, and . . . they should be getting what the men have been getting; there is no question about it; it's what we all have struggled for." She remembers when she "first used to send things out. Here I've said that I didn't think of myself as a feminist then, but when I sent poems out I *never* sent them out as 'Grace Paley'. I'd send them out as 'G. Paley' or 'G. G. Paley' or something like that, especially if it seemed like the poem or story had some masculine voice in it. I had brains enough to know that that would help. Well, it never helped, but I thought it did! And [now] I'm always laughing, because one of my best friends is Esther Broner, E. M. Broner, and I keep yelling at her and saying, 'Don't [send your work out as E. M. Broner] any more. Everybody knows who you are: 'It's you, Esther, it's you, Esther, it's you, Esther!'" Paley laughs. "Then they'll say, 'Oh, it's *Esther* Broner; we don't want that woman.' So I appreciate what these writers are saying, and they are right."

Paley adds, however, that "I also have a politics, more of a communitarian politics. It's not to live as a poor person—I certainly don't—but it's certainly not to need so much. So I don't think about money and power issues so much. If I'm making a living, I feel okay about it, although sometimes I feel injustices at [publishing] advances." But she feels that she's older than these other writers, and, more importantly, she both writes "in a whole different way and probably lives differently as a writer. My husband probably lives more like [the other writers]—he gets up at five in the morning and writes for two or three hours before he does anything else—and he does a lot of other things and lots of politics, and he is rather exemplary. But I can't do that. I just never got in the habit. That's really one of the problems. So I don't have an inner drive to do as well as anybody else—let's put it that way. I have a great pleasure in writing and part of that is political and part of that is I'm surprised that I've done as well as I have. I really am just surprised."

Paley acknowledges that "any writer wants [the money], but then you think of how evil the whole damn thing is, and you think of others. I mean Bob has this book that came out from Johns Hopkins University Press, and I don't believe he has $150 in his promotional budget. And I spend a lot of time with other women whose advertising budgets are so low that your tendency is to want to give them half of yours, if it exists. But I understand that problem," Paley says. "It's undignified to know that some people get so much money coming their way, and although I have fought on those issues, I never get into it on a personal basis."

Even so, "when we had this big fight at the PEN conference and tried to set up the Women's Committee, I fought those guys down to the wall, and I continue to do so, but for me that's a very political act. The fight was about this great international conference, . . . and I was in opposition to much of it, although I had the best time! You also have to have a good time at whatever you do; it's not worth struggling if you're going to be miserable. . . . You've got to fight with pleasure, if you know what I mean." And it was a pleasure, no doubt, to fight with her fellow PEN members about a poetry reading that consisted of ten men and only one woman. "I was on the PEN board, so I was really, in a sense, right in the middle of it. Those things have to be fought, wherever they are!

"But," repeated Paley, "I can't think of it personally; I just don't have the habit of thinking of it personally. And when I say the word *habit*, I really mean it; I don't mean it as a moral statement. It's not just that I've been a political person. I've been a political person who has worked with people. I've never, not from my earliest times, not been part of a group that sat and argued and fought and beat out a statement. . . . I've been part of the peace movement and gone to meetings that lasted until three in the morning. So I'm not used to thinking, 'I'm not getting this, or I'm not getting that,' especially since I feel lucky to begin with! My habit is one of turning to four or five other women and saying, 'We have to really work this out because this and this is happening.' " And she added pointedly, "In my life, I've done a lot of the things I've wanted to do outside of writing. I've had kids, and they're healthy, I married two men that I liked a lot, each one of them worth living with a long time."

When she was younger, Paley "did not live a writer's life or live among writers, hang out with them, talk about literature morning, noon, and night, all that sort of stuff. I really tried to stay away from writers for many years and was almost successful until Don Barthelme moved across the street, and we became friends, and I was sort of dragged in. I mean, I was not unfriendly to them, but there was no reason for me to hang out with them. When I was doing antiwar work and I'd go after writers for signatures, they really didn't know I was a writer anyway cause I wasn't that well known—although my first book was out. But now, of course, I know almost anybody. It's hard not to know them because I'd have to put more energy into not knowing them than it's worth."

Paley recalled with obvious sadness several friends, now deceased, who were both political people and writers. "Muriel Rukeyser was always a political person and a sad loss for some of us—for all of us, but particularly for those who knew her. She was a total poet, totally involved in literature, and she took a beating as a woman and as a poet who was not part of the elite that began to develop after the forties knocked the thirties on their head. She and somebody like Meridel Le Sueur were doubly wounded. They were wounded as women by their own political men—something like black women are—and wounded again by the literary elite, who were for the birds. But on the other hand Muriel lived very deeply in literature and with literary people. She knew them from an early age; she was close to Mexican poets, American poets, and she was political at the same time. When she got to be president of PEN she went to Korea even though she could hardly walk by then; she was very brave. [Rukeyser died of a heart attack in 1980.] So there *are* people who manage to do the whole thing." Paley talked, too, about "Kay Boyle, who from a very early age had lovers, and married, but was a writer first, second, third, sixth, and foremost. And yet on the other hand, she had six children, so you can't tell me she was a writer morning, noon, and night. . . . I just received a brand new collection of her poems, and it has her whole interesting [writer's] life in it, yet she had that whole other life too."

Since sexual harassment was very much in the news at the time of this interview, I asked Paley what she thought the writer's role was in that conflict. "The only responsibility that I can think of is that the writer has to tell the truth as she or he knows it. What a writer is, really, is someone who tells the truth in the language of the country, and sustains that language, and invigorates that language, . . . and keeps lighting up what isn't known. That's why, when new people come along, they speak a little bit differently and they enhance and make more beautiful the language. So you have black speech coming in, and our own people [the Jews] came and did something with the English language and gave it a little *schtuuup* here and there . . . and shook it up a little. Women are new people, so they come in with new subject matter," and although writers may not want to be "in charge of justice or anything like that, to some extent they are if they really are illuminating what isn't seen."

Paley, for one, is not concerned by criticism of the results of her search for illumination. Her response is, "Well, I did it the best I could. If I fucked up, someone will tell me. . . . If you screw up, someone will tell you; you don't have to worry about that! The point is never to censor yourself beforehand, but to do the most truthful thing you can. People tell me, [for instance,] 'You really should be writing about gay women because you're so close to them, and you're friends with them' and everything like that, but, on the other hand, 'You shouldn't because you're not a gay woman.' And I say, 'Well, when I'm ready to write it, I'll write it, cause it'll be my way of telling the truth.''

Paley also told me that she had talked about writing to "a bunch of black kids at James Monroe High School [in New York City]. I said, 'That's your job. You have to light up the life of your people. . . . That's what you'll do naturally, and if you don't it's because you were stopped in some way. But you'll do it, and all of us will look at it and say, 'This is new, this is what we haven't seen before. Do it in your own language and that will make the general language more beautiful and truer and it will include you in it.' So the job of a writer is to aim for the truth. First of all, if you're really interested in writing, you're not going to write about what's been written about a million times, or you're not going to do it in the same old way. You can't, cause you don't know how, number one. Number two, you're not interested. You're probably becoming a writer because you're interested in trying to understand something about the world that you don't know. And, if you're truthful and you love the language, and if you are interested in society and the people, you will probably write well."

Paley reminded me that people often ask her, " 'Are you a woman writer?' I say 'Yes; I am a woman writer.' That's what I am. I'm Jewish too, a 'Jewish woman writer,' and whatever I am, I am. I don't deny any part of it. And I'm terrifically interested in what the young Chinese are writing in this country. I loved Gish Jen's book [*Typical American*]. She made such wonderful solutions to the language. And "I'm glad [the new Chinese-American, Japanese-American, Native American, and African-American writers] are writing about their own experiences. They have to do it. I mean, all these people feel like shit, so they have to. They're the new people, shining a light on what to them is hidden from the rest of the world; the world doesn't know what this Chinese life is," for instance, so "they are telling it to us. And I don't see how it can be avoided, that's the other thing. I don't know what else they're supposed to write about if not these immigrant stories. The Native Americans have to tell their story. . . . They are not going to tell your story, they are not going to tell mine. They can't. If they are truthful, they have to tell theirs." Paley noted that "people have been telling the Italian story for them for so long, the Italians ought to be really pissed." But, she added, if the new writers become too hateful toward other segments of the population, "then I say, 'Fuck em.' When they are hateful towards other peoples, then that's another story entirely."

Since Paley's new book is about rural life reflected in poems, "mostly about flowers," I asked her if she was returning to her original role as a writer. "No, it's just lucky someone wants to print them now. I always kept writing poetry, but I never pushed the printing of my poems or did much with them. I just had them in too many places—pages here and pages there, not organized. Years before I wrote the stories I sent out a lot of poems and none were bought except for two or three when I was about twenty. For the next twelve years or so I kept writing, but I stopped sending them out. When I began to write stories and they were finally collected in a book, that became my major thing and I felt I did stories better." She never became a novelist, Paley says, "because I *think* short stories and that seems to be it." After writing poems, she was comfortable writing short stories. "I was accustomed to completion. When I wrote my first stories I naturally had to make myself finish to know that I had written a whole prose piece, for God's sake. I was accustomed to finishing, so I wrote one, I wrote another, and pretty soon I was writing them all." Paley laughed and said, "A lot of these things are not so deep!"

She admits that she finally began to understand what was wrong with the early poems. "I loved literature even though I was crazy in the street and everything else, and the poems were a little too literary. Now they aren't. And I didn't have my own voice for poems. I did in the stories, and what began to happen was that some of that ease moved into the poems. Anyway, I never would have published them if one of my students, a woman who was a poet, hadn't had a printing press. She said, 'Can I go through your drawers and your piles of stuff?' and she put the collection together and I thought she was going to make a little chapbook, but it became a large poem book. . . . [But] right now I'm dying to get back to stories. . . . I just have to get a time distance from what I'm writing about."

This partly accounts for why Grace Paley only has "three books in print. If I had ten books, if I did a book every other year, I'd make a living." But then you recall that Paley is working "with the organizers of a group called Jewish Women against the Occupation and another one called Jews for Racial and Economic Justice" because "if you go to Israel you can't help but be very interested in Jewish affairs. I go to temple, which I don't do in New York at all, . . . and I sort of keep in touch with the Jewish community here. I mean, I have poems about being Jewish; I like being Jewish. I attribute it to the fact that even though my father was insanely antireligious, my parents never disliked Jews or being Jewish. There was never that certain kind of anti-Semitism that Jews sometimes have."

Paley added that her daughter, who lives in Vermont, realizes that there's "a general anti-Semitism which exists in the country that is not vicious, but it's sort of like a low-grade cold. You know, like everybody has it and passes it on to the children. She's often subjected to unimportant anti-Semitic remarks—not all of them virulent, but all of them painful—not like a knife in the back, but more like pins in the *tuchas*. So she thinks about that."

But in no way does it stem the flow of life that surges through the world of Grace Paley. Just as we are ready for another harrowing drive to the bus station, Paley's stepdaughter, Lisa, walks in:

"Can I borrow Dad's typewriter? I have to fill out a form and I can't do it on my computer, and no one else in town seems to *have* a typewriter!"

"You can use mine, darling."

"The baby took a bottle today with milk in it!"

"Good. So you can leave her here now."

The myriad fans of Grace Paley may have a long wait for the next book.

Grace Paley: An Interview by Joann Gardner
Joann Gardner / 1993

From *The American Poetry Review* Mar. 1994: 19-24. Reprinted by permission.

I find Grace Paley where she said I would, at the end of a dirt road behind the volunteer fire barn—a distant cry from the New York neighborhood where she grew up, but, somehow, a plausible domesticity. Grace and her husband Bob are sitting at the kitchen table after lunch. I have brought a strawberry sour cream pie from Maine. Ribbons of steam rise from the Connecticut River, as Grace and I retreat to her study to talk about her *New and Collected Poems* and the relation of politics to art.

Joann Gardner: You're basically known as a story writer. Where do the poems fit in?

Grace Paley: Well, I wrote poetry for years before I wrote stories. I began to be serious about prose in my thirties kind of suddenly out of a great need to deal with new subject matter. I couldn't do it in poems. Others have. At first there seemed to be two different languages. That's not true any more. Anyway I don't think I could have written those stories without the years of reading and writing poems. Still this business of being a writer—in a *Paris Review* interview I was asked, "Did you know you were going to be a writer?" I didn't know I was going to BE anything. I knew I was going to write. I think of it more as a verb than a noun.

JG: And when you travel to Europe and you fill out the Immigration card, what do you put in the OCCUPATION space?

Paley: I've been putting "Writer," but you'd be surprised how recent that is. I usually put "Teacher," because I haven't made my living really as a writer. Sometimes if I've been doing an unusual amount of sweeping, I write "housewife"—out of sheer belligerence.

JG: It seems to me that the best writers are reluctant to use the word. What is it W. H. Auden used to put down—Medieval Historian?—just to get them off his back?

You said at Aspen[1] that you've always been political. Does that come before the writing, or does that come with the writing. . .?

Paley: I think it comes along with it. My family was political. It was just their way of thinking about the world. They talked about it as a place in which society was organized sometimes for the good of the people, more often to harm them. It seems close to the life of literature. What literature adds is word form, imagination and a lot of flying around. Literature often has a sense of humor which politics hardly ever does, and when it does, it may become literate.

JG: So, what is the difference between political activism and sitting in Vermont and writing about politics?

Paley: That's the difference. [*Laughs*] Here in our town about eight grownups and fifty summer-camp kids do a vigil every August 6 to remember Hiroshima. But there's local environmental work too, a struggle for a single-payer health insurance system. Folks in many of our towns worked publicly against the Gulf War. The problem for me is that I'm used to the city streets—looking people in the eye, not their headlights.

JG: And writing's just another way of doing it?

Paley: I have very little of what my father used to call "Sitzfleisch." He said, "You will never write because you have no Sitzfleisch." I do have a tendency to leap away from the typewriter. But it's not so much that there's a difference [between writing and activism]. They both pay attention to human life and need to talk about it, and invent the best kind of communication.

JG: You've gone to Salvador and Vietnam, and you've written about these experiences. Do you think it's necessary, if one is to be a good political writer, to become physically involved, to go to these places?

Paley: No, it's not necessary. You're lucky if you can. For me, going to the park with my children turned out to be one of the luckiest things I ever did. That daily experience among other women was the source or the drive for a lot of my stories. In general, stuff is political, even if it's a turning away. Americans often think it's not nice, not so literary, so they turn away—that's a political act.

JG: It seems to me that the writers who are the most political now are women, maybe because their lives have not been heard about very much. I mean, that idea of going to the park . . .

Paley: Well, that's why when I wrote my first book, I didn't think I was doing anything political. I just thought that I was very upset about what was happening between men and women and what was not happening to women. I was in my thirties then, and it's a time when you begin to notice. Let's put it this way: for me the natural function of literature is to illuminate what has not been seen. You pick up a rock and look underneath it, and there's a whole life there. Sometimes that rock has been there for centuries. So that's one of the political acts that writing accomplishes often without meaning to. That's why women, Blacks, Native Americans . . . exiles—That's why this is an exciting period. So much work is being done, they're lifting up these rocks, shining their poem flashlights and singing Ah! or maybe Hey-look!

JG: You wrote in the poem "Responsibility"[2] that it's the poet's duty to be a woman, and then you wrote that it's the male poet's duty to be a woman.
Paley: Yeah, that gets a lot of men mad, or at least, annoyed.

JG: What does it mean?
Paley: Well, first I said, it is the responsibility of the male poet to be a woman. So people thought that I would then say, it's the responsibility of the woman poet to be a man. No. It's not the responsibility of a black person to be a white person.

JG: Well, also, the oppressed have already learned a great deal about the oppressor, trying to survive within that dominance.
Paley: They know it. Yeah.

JG: Why does that make men angry?
Paley: People think that everything has to be equalized. Also, decent guys may feel deprived of their progressive generosity. Actually many men do understand what I'm talking about.
A bird yodels.
Go ahead.

JG: I'm interested in where the poems come from. You have these poems that—well, "Responsibility" is one of them, and "A Poem About Storytelling," and "I Gave Away That Kid . . ."
Paley: The poem "Responsibility" was actually spoken at a conference sponsored by APR a couple of years ago—at which I happened to be the only woman speaking. Actually, Carolyn Forché was supposed to be there, but she was sick.

JG: It's interesting that essays start out as poems . . . and then finish up as poems, apparently.
Paley: It's not that essays start out as poems. I'm just not too good at

written prose talks, so the poem, good or bad, is it. But I'm still not satisfied with "A Poem About Storytelling."

JG: I think the voices in that are wonderful.
Paley: You think it makes sense?

JG: Yes.
Paley: I remember Marge Piercy saying at the Aspen Conference that she had "an aesthetics of clarity." And I thought, hmm, that's not bad.

JG: It's complicated, but it's clear.
Grace Paley gets up to look out the window, worries about a telephone call, sits back down.

JG: In the beginning of the *New and Collected Poems,* you and the publisher thank Bea Gates for extracting poems from your notebook . . .
Paley: Well, Bea Gates was a graduate student at Sarah Lawrence, and, as you do with students you like, you become friends, and you know each other for life. We used to read poems in that group every Wednesday, for an hour or so: mostly Blake or Milton. I also read some poems that I had written, and Bea, who is a fine poet herself, said at some point that she had a printing press and wanted to publish some of my poems. So I said, well, I might have a few. I gave them to her, and she said, "Don't you have any more?" Finally, she was dragging me through these closets and files. That's what happened.
Laughter.

JG: Is she associated with Tilbury?
Paley: No. She sold the book to Tilbury. At Granite Press, she did some wonderful things. She published me, she published Joan Larkin.[3] She did some broadsides. And then she published a book of Central American women poets, with photographs.[4]

JG: I wondered why you would go for small presses such as Tilbury House and Granite Press, rather than try to . . .
Paley: When I started with Bea, I had never submitted my poems to Farrar Straus, or hardly anywhere except *Field* magazine. I don't think they would have gone for it. I'm sure they'd publish a prose book I might give them. But I thought Bea was doing a little chapbook or something, and by the time I realized what she had in mind, I couldn't say, "Oh, oh, I have a book; I think I'll take it to my big publisher." I've always been anxious about whether Farrar Straus was mad at me.

JG: [*Laughs.*] You'll probably find out.
Paley: Well, the people at Tilbury House are very nice, very good.

They're part of a Consortium—Greywolf Press and Feminist Press—several other small presses—not so small some of them. Coffee House published a marvelous writer—Carol Emshwiller;[5] Tilbury has just published *From the Steam Room,* a novel by my husband, Robert Nichols.

JG: Will you come out with another volume of poems?
Paley: Well, I probably will, but I probably won't for another couple of years.

JG: I remember at Aspen you read the Salvador poems, and I wanted to get my hands on them right away, but they weren't out.
Paley: Oh, yeah, right.

JG: And then I began to think that I hadn't really heard them, that they didn't exist. And then they came out in this volume.[6]
Paley: Well, they came out in something else before that. It's called *Long Walks and Intimate Talks,*[7] and includes short prose pieces that haven't been published in book form anywhere else. And it has the beautiful paintings of my friend Vera B. Williams.

JG: Did you collect them?
Paley: No, Vera and I did the book originally as a War Resisters League calendar. Then the Feminist Press took over the publication.

Grace Paley suggests that we move our conversation into the kitchen. I am given my first sample of pickled herring. She settles down to a piece of strawberry sour cream pie. The cat meows loudly. Grace Paley meows back.

JG: I wonder if you'd talk about the people in your life, how they intersect with the political in your writing. I'm thinking about the poem where you say you were born in the year the sanitary napkin was invented and that your parents arrived here in 1905.[8]
Paley: It's really about what's known and not known in the family's history. I think of my deported anarchist uncle a lot these days—the silences at home. Mystery. I mean to write more stanzas. When . . .

JG: It also shows the perspective of someone born at a certain time, how she or he will look at history either more positively or more negatively, depending on their own experience.
Paley: I don't know if that's in the poem, but it's true. I'll give you an example. I'm younger than my sister and brother by fourteen and sixteen years. They grew up into the Depression. I grew up into the Second World War. I think about war more than they do. They think back to their own youthful job worries, though by that time we were well off. I mean,

my father was the neighborhood doctor. When they were young, he was going to school (and working), my mother and aunts worked in garment shops, and my mother was a retoucher of photos—all to get him through school. So I always think they're the children of the working class; I'm the child of the middle class, though it has often looked reversed.

JG: That doesn't make you politically more optimistic than them, does it?

Paley: It does, in a sense; after all, I wasn't in Europe during the war. I was here, part of the whole country's life-and-war efforts. I lived in army camps with my young soldier husband. It was worrisome but lively. In an inhospitable time, they had to figure out and make decisions about how to make a living. Wars do help capitalism to get out of economic depressions every time. I mean, I've felt quite secure, even when my kids were little and we appeared to be having a hard time.

JG: You felt safe in the world?

Paley: I don't know exactly what you mean.

JG: Even though women don't usually feel safe, economically?

Paley: My parents were immigrants. They came with nothing and did well—not just making a living, but in doing work my father wanted to do—he supported a lot of people. My mother's life was hard. I wrote a story called "The Immigrant Story," which talks about some of this, and I said I grew up in the sunlight of upward mobility, which leached out a lot of misery. I did have a more optimistic nature because of being the youngest. My father and mother had time to pay attention to me, whereas, when Vic and Jeanne were small, they really were cared for by my grandmother, and everybody was working and, you know, it's a whole different life they led. Not unhappy but different.

JG: You would call yourself a pacifist?

Paley: Pretty much, yeah. No one is a total pacifist—. Well, wrong—there are some, and I know them.

JG: I associate *rural* with a kind of staunch conservatism, which I also associate with . . .

Paley: Well, there's a degree of conservatism, but that comes with, "What are we putting our nose out there in the world for?" It's called isolationism, which can sometimes be translated into being antiwar, and other times into piggishness.

JG: What about the difference between urban and rural in your poems? You come from New York and now you live in Vermont . . .

Paley: In *Long Walks and Intimate Talks,* I have a small essay called "Country Life, Is It Boring?" Which is a total answer to your question. *Laughter.*

JG: Okay, I'll remember that.

Paley: So, what's the question now, exactly?

JG: Well, the poems seem to be working back and forth from the urban to the rural experience, and there's that one where you say you lived in the city so that you could forget your mortality, and now that you live in the country, you remember it.[9]

Paley: Yes, I know.

JG: I grew up in the suburbs, and, coming to the city, I was constantly aware of the artificiality of the experience, if not the sense of imminent death.

Paley: You may not feel it in a tropical setting. (You are teaching in Florida, right?) It's the seasons, the whole earth slowly and beautifully goes to sleep, wakes up, and sleeps—dies again. Time is measured in the country, and time is about mortality. You can't tell time in the city for the most part. It's safer.

JG: So you're safe from all the trees and the grass and signs of Nature.

Paley: There's actually a great ginkgo tree outside my New York apartment.

JG: I remember reading about it.

Paley: No, I think I wrote about sycamores.

JG: in Barcelona.

Paley: Mottled.

JG: Yes. Really nice.

Paley: But they're amazing in Barcelona. They're huge, and, as I described it, they go into tea colors and burgundies. In New York, my street is lined with sycamores. When I moved there, there wasn't a tree on the street. You know why? They said they'd clog the sewer lines up. [*Laughs.*]

JG: Yes, except the palm trees down South do get caught in the sewer lines.

Paley: Well, the truth of the matter is, it's also true in the city. *Laughter.*

JG: Well, tell me about El Salvador. You went to El Salvador. Why? How?

Paley: I didn't. I was going to Nicaragua. We had a stop in El Salvador.

JG: It was a group?

Paley: I went with Madre, an organization originally concerned with Central America and particularly women and children. Now they're in Middle Eastern work as well. And we had to stop in El Salvador, because you couldn't go directly to Nicaragua from the United States at the time.

JG: And it turns out you wrote about El Salvador.

Paley: Well, "The Dance in Jinoteca" is Nicaragua. But El Salvador made a harsher impression on me. Naturally, in Nicaragua, we were taken on tours by organs or associations of the Sandinista government, so I didn't really have time to think: poem. I felt human organization and hope. And Nicaraguans were writing their own poems, especially women. When I think about Nicaragua now, I am deeply saddened by our country's malicious destructiveness there—endless—like Vietnam. I gave a number of talk-reports but didn't write much.

JG: It's just that it was all prepared.

Paley: Yeah. I've been on other visits of that kind. It was interesting. Many young Americans have gone there and lived and been useful. But in El Salvador it was shocking to sit with these women, to look in these albums and see the faces of dead children and realize that these are the mothers of the disappeared. They had disappeared, but they'd been found in this album. And then the woman who kept saying, my first son, my second son . . . That really happened. She did have only one son.

JG: She'd just lost it, and said . . .

Paley: She said, "Now, my second son . . ." I mean, in her mind, it went on and on. And the visit to the prison was very impressive, also. There was this little girl, without a leg, and she told me the whole story, the deliberate crippling.

JG: How did you feel about being a North American, facing that kind of suffering? Carolyn [Forché] comments on her inability to be honest in the face of . . .

Paley: Oh, I think you can be honest. That's not so hard. It seems to me there's something discouraging about it, though. Not discouraging about our struggles, but about our country in general. We keep being mean—we're still mean to Vietnam. Mean to Cuba. Mean to Haiti. That kind of meanness is more discouraging to me than almost anything. You can put it in economic terms, you can make a high-class theoretical discussion about it, but there is so much mean revenge and malice against the victories of ordinary people.

JG: Are Americans naturally mean, or are they encouraged to feel safe about their xenophobia?

Paley: Well, I almost wish the Gulf War had gone on a little longer. The first propaganda was so powerful, excessive, overbearing, but a lot of those yellow ribbons would have been frayed, removed from lapels and doorways—and not only because Americans were being killed. Bush never did get rid of the wonderful "Vietnam Syndrome." For that reason, the government knew that it had to be a short war.

JG: Well, I know about the generation that grew up in the sixties with Vietnam. There was a period of time when they all seemed to have disappeared. Now they seem, as you say, to be coming out of the woodwork. I think there was a period of tremendous discouragement.

Paley: Well, part of it was other things were happening. You take the seventies, the whole Women's Movement was cresting. It had begun to pull together in the late sixties, but it really rolled its waves out into the world at the end of the seventies. Somebody asked me once, "What about the Women's Movement? What would you say to a young person?" I said that I would sit down and compare my life, when I was twenty, with hers, and she would see that she was way ahead of me, and I would say to her, that's because we've had a movement, and you have some of the rewards. And I do too—as an old woman—I have a wider life than my mother and aunts. Maybe not deeper . . .

JG: And you don't really go back . . .

Paley: She may think life was always like that, this young woman, but it was not. Of course, that poor girl of twenty, there's a lifetime of the possibility of AIDS to live with—the constriction of sexual life. You, at least, had a couple of years without it.

JG: Yeah, that's true.
What about the correspondence you set up in these poems between Vermont and Vietnam? Is that one way of showing that the two environments are occupied by real human beings?

Paley: Well, actually, there's a poem in there called "The Bridge." That's about Puerto Rico and Vietnam. I was driving along in Puerto Rico, looking at this bridge that had disappeared. I was just going back in my mind to the bridges.

JG: In Vietnam?
Paley: Yeah.

JG: Do these places begin to resemble each other?

Paley: Well, they don't resemble each other, but you make connections in your mind. It enriches the present to introduce the past.

JG: And the numbers in the Vietnam poem, are they accurate?

Paley: They're accurate. They were written, as it says, in the House of Tradition. Every time there was another raid, they'd write it down.

JG: That's the Poetry of Witness.

Paley: That is Witness.

JG: What about role models, are there people you have looked to in your writing for inspiration?

Paley: It's really hard to say that because, first of all, I wrote for so many years all by myself, but I read poetry from Mother Goose-childhood through 1000 Best Loved Poems to the Imagists on the way to Yeats, Auden and Day Lewis. My tattered Oscar Williams 1943 anthology, with the beautiful faces of Rukeyser, Schwartz . . . Also a thousand novels, stories—later on, after I'd written my first book of stories I found Babel like a cousin. But you ask what people were my models, and I think now in my seventies of my mother and father, my streetful of talkers.

JG: I guess in the literary world there's a lot of noise made about women having very few role models. I know in Ireland, women writers don't know where to go for their examples.

Paley: Well, they should go to life, forget the fucking literary people. You have the language, especially if you're Irish. There are a powerful lot of Irish women writing. They're their own models.

JG: But not until recently were they published or recognized.

Paley: Because you don't have a literature until you have a movement. And all great movements develop a literature—often at the same time actually. But you don't even know there is a movement until, suddenly, you see Tillie Olsen has a book coming out that year, too—then those books on female sexuality and literature—Kate Millett—you know what I mean? You realize that someone else is writing. After ten years of not publishing short stories, they're publishing short stories. Something's going on. There are other women, and they're writing, and finally there's support.

JG: So you think it happens unconsciously?

Paley: It happens unconsciously. The women of Ireland have been voting and fighting on all kinds of issues. There's no question but that there would be a literature coming out of their experiences.

JG: I have two more questions. And the first one has to do with mortality: there are a number of poems in here about death—I guess Vermont makes you think of these things.
Paley: Well, I'm also getting older. It comes into your mind.

JG: The last poem takes the whole book, or that series of contemplations about morality, and turns it on its head. I wonder if you could talk about that little girl who comes to you and says, "Begin again, long ago."
Paley: Virago is publishing the British version of this book, and it's called *Begin Again,* and now [my American publisher] is sorry he didn't name it *Begin Again.* I told him, *New and Collected Poems,* that's not such a great title.

JG: But *Begin Again* is excellent. It helps you understand how poetry can put you beyond the boundaries of age.
Paley: It's exactly what happened. I sat on the bus between Greenfield and Holyoke.

JG: Do you know who the girl was?
Paley: Yeah. Me.

JG: So, it was a young you?
Paley: It was me.

JG: Is it literary reincarnation, is that what it's about?
Paley: I don't know.

JG: I guess what I'm trying to say is . . . You're talking about a serious subject, but you don't get morose about it. Jane Cooper calls it "wit." Is that how you protect yourself, by making a joke about it?
Paley: Well, I guess it would be called Jewish wit. Every oppressed group has a kind of humor. It's a self-mockery in which you really think you're pretty good. [*Laughs.*]

JG: Yes, that's it.
Paley: Well, humor is about disparity, between what the world thinks of you and what you think of yourself.

JG: There's the poem about the transvestites who dress up as pregnant mothers in order to get a discount at a restaurant; that's the one Jane Cooper talks about. You say something like "I am especially open to sadness and hilarity."[10]
Paley: I said that about my father's death.

JG: Yes, that's right. Which puts an edge on it. If you move too quickly in these poems, you get cut.

I'm going to ask you to be Cassandra. What do you think is going to happen to us politically in the future?

Paley: The great East German writer who wrote *Cassandra*, Christa Wolf—I've just written an introduction to her translated book of essays. She doesn't know what's coming next, and she's Cassandra.

JG: I asked this question to Carolyn Forché, and she thought that America was disintegrating fast, that the only thing we had to keep us together was language.

Paley: You know that poem by Auden? "[Time] worships language, and forgives everyone by whom it lives."

JG: Yeah. He also says, "Poetry makes nothing happen; it survives."

Paley: Auden said something like "God will pardon Paul Claudel—pardoned him for writing well."[11] He took that stanza out of his final collection, which is pretty annoying when you want to get the quote right.

No, we have language, but we also have many languages. One of the great movements now is the Native American movement, because it occupies a very high moral position. Not just for itself; for the earth. And it's not just the Indians who talk about it. In the Old Testament, we're reminded again and again that whatever happens lasts seven generations and to keep it in mind.

JG: Is that associated with keeping your mind on Jerusalem?

Paley: [*Laughs.*] Yeah, probably. I don't know if you know the work of Kropotkin, the Russian anarchist; it's called *Memoirs of a Revolutionist*.[12] He was probably one of the noblest souls that ever lived. He writes in his book that he'd been away in the Urals—he was a geographer—and he was discovering that the mountains really ran in a different direction than everybody had thought. When he came back, he said, "There seems to be nothing left of our movements. The only movement that seems to have any power at all is the Women's Movement. And I think maybe the reason for this is that these young women are going about teaching the serfs to read." (These are inexact quotes.) He said that it might be because they were thinking not only of themselves, but also of how to share the earth with others. It was very thrilling to me to think about; it brings us back to the seventies and what was happening then.—Was everything falling apart? No, no. There was the Women's Movement growing.

JG: Which seems to be coming together again now.

Paley: Oh, yes. Again and again.

JG: I know I said only two questions, but this is the last one . . .
Paley: Go ahead.

JG: I'm quoting Adrienne Rich: "What I love most in Grace Paley's poetry is her unquenchable sense that the artist's life is not somewhere at the margins of community, that a dialogue is necessary between the poet and her people. The North American enterprise has injured this dialogue. Paley's exuberant, heartbreaking, committed poems call it back to health."[13]
Paley: I was thrilled by that. I didn't know what to say.

JG: When you read it did you say, "Yeah, that's what I'm doing"?
Paley: No, I said, "Gee, I hope that's what I'm doing." I wouldn't say that; that takes too much nerve.

JG: It's good commentary.
Paley: On my wall, I have different sentences, poem-pieces of hers. Take one down and there's another that speaks directly to you.

JG: Compare it with what Gerald Stern said. He talks about aesthetics, but she fits it all in politically . . .
Paley: Well, actually, I'm glad he said that and I thank him for it whenever I read it—you know, I'm like any writer—poet—I want the aesthetics, the beauty thing. That's the beginning—the face of the most difficult truth.

Notes

1. Aspen Writers' Conference, 1989, featuring Grace Paley, Sharon Olds, Marge Piercy, and Carolyn Forché, among others.
2. This and other poems discussed in this interview are all printed in *New and Collected Poems* (Tilbury Press, 1992).
3. *A Long Sound: A Book of Poems* (Granite Press, 1986).
4. Zoe Anglesey, ed., *IXOK AMAR. GO, Central American Women's Poetry for Peace* (Granite Press, 1987).
5. Carol Emshwiller, *Verging on the Pertinent* (Coffee House Press, 1989). Robert Nichols, *In the Air* (Johns Hopkins University Press, 1991).
6. "In San Salvador (I)" and "In San Salvador (II)," pp. 109 and 110 in *New and Collected Poems.*
7. Feminist Press, 1991.
8. "Song Stanzas of Private Luck," *New and Collected Poems,* 81–83.
9. "Fear," p. 59.
10. "On Mother's Day," *New and Collected Poems,* 29: "I am especially open

to sadness and hilarity / since my father died as a child / one week ago in this his ninetieth year."

11. "In Memory of W.B. Yeats": "Time that with this strange excuse / Pardoned Kipling and his views, / And will pardon Paul Claudel, / Pardons him for writing well."

12. Prince Peter Alekseyevich Kropotkin (1842–1921), *Memoirs of a Revolutionist*, 1899.

13. This statement and one by Gerald Stern are printed on the back cover of *New and Collected Poems*.

Grace Paley
Birgit Fromkorth and
Susanne Opfermann / 1995

From *American Contradictions: Interviews with Nine American Writers,* Eds. Wolfgang Binder and Helmbrecht Breinig (Hanover: UP of New England, 1995), 78–100. Reprinted by permission of the publisher.

Grace Paley, born in 1922, is originally from New York City, which is also the scene of most of her short stories. Although her oeuvre is small, she is considered one of the outstanding representatives of Jewish literature in America as well as one of the best short story writers since the Second World War. After studying in New York, she has also taught at different New York universities.

Her first collection of short stories, *The Little Disturbances of Man: Stories of Men and Women in Love,* was published in 1959. Two further volumes of short stories followed: *Enormous Changes at the Last Minute* in 1974 and *Later the Same Day* in 1985. In 1985, a volume of her poetry was published, *Leaning Forward: Poems. Long Walks and Intimate Talks,* a small volume of stories and poems, came out in 1991. *New and Collected Poems* was published in 1992; and in 1994 *The Collected Stories.*

Grace Paley has been honored with a series of prestigious prizes and scholarships. The stories of this masterful stylist often deal with personal relationships, particularly among the multiethnic population of New York City. They show Grace Paley as an energetic feminist and a prominent advocate of the American peace movement and of environmental protection, who has also commented on issues of political ethics in several publications.

SO: You said somewhere that the three important things in your life are writing, politics, and your family. Let's start with your family. Could you tell us about your parents?

GP: Well, my parents were Russian Jews. They were Socialists, and they were radical youngsters when they were kids. At one point or another my father has even written about some arrests, but the main one was when he was sent to, say, Arkhangelsk, and he and my mother were exiled. Then the czar had a son. When he had a son, he freed all prisoners who were less than twenty-one years old. My parents immediately, with my grandmother and aunts, came to the United States. They had already gone through a pogrom around that time that had killed my uncle, my grandmother's seventeen-year-old son, so they came very eagerly, anxiously, and finally patriotically to the United States.

SO: Who introduced you to literature? Did everybody in your family share in the story-telling? Would you say your father was the person who introduced you to literature?

GP: Oh, I wouldn't say he introduced me. I mean I wouldn't use that expression. I would just say there was a lot of stuff in the house [*laughs*], that's all. It was assumed that a kid would read. Because my parents read and didn't make an issue of it. There were always a lot of books around. My father learned English very quickly and read immediately. Dickens, I think, in the first year. He also learned Italian the first year he came to the United States because he worked for an Italian photographer. The women in the family all went to work in the shops, the garment industry, and put my father through school, so he became a doctor.

BF: Was the world of learning or literature associated more with your father or with your mother?

GP: Oh, it was associated with my father mostly in that sense. My grandmother did try to teach me Russian poems, so there must have been something there—I never got exactly what it was. But I would say my father read more, talked more. My mother read a lot, too; my aunts as well but not so deeply. In some ways, if you want to put it that way, some of their lives were sacrificed to the education of my father; and as I've said before, it paid off. He did well; he took care of the family. But I think my mother was always sad that she hadn't gone to school. They had a lot of music in the house, too. And my mother liked music; my father did. So we had very early lots of records, classical music, so we lived naturally in that environment.

SO: You said again and again that you were interested in the lives of women and children, and you focus on them in your stories; although when you began writing, this was considered a boring topic. Did you share this view?

GP: I did. I put off writing about it because I thought, who's going to read this stuff, you know. You realize it was after the Second World War and a lot of the literature was heavily masculine, and you can see why. So coming into that world, into literature in a different way, was sort of embarrassing to me actually. I thought, Jesus, these guys are doing such important things. But I was unequivocally interested and pressed and bugged by the lives around me. It got to me. And so I just said one day, "Well, I'm going to do it. That's all. That's what I'm going to write." So I wrote, but I never thought anything would come of it.

BF: Well, usually when you love literature you read all the great works and you're male-identified.

GP: That's true. Exactly!

BF: So when did you start developing a female-centered perspective?

GP: Well, if I hadn't been so interested, I wouldn't have kept writing. I probably would have been more male-identified. But it was writing in itself, and I'm thinking as I wrote, you know, that really made me a much more female-centered person. People say, "Well, were you a feminist?" Well, I was writing those things in the mid-fifties. I was aware of a lot of things. I mean it's not as if I was so naïve. I was not naïve. I already knew that I couldn't stand Henry Miller, for instance. Goodness, I already knew that there was a literature that was not about me, sexually. And I knew that certain literatures didn't free me. I mean I knew without knowing. I couldn't have written an article about it. And I wouldn't have written an article about it, but, you know, you should know there was a book that came out in 1948. It was by a woman named Ruth Hershberger, who was a poet also. She wrote a book called *Adam's Rib*. I bet you could dig it up someplace. It actually talked about what was coming in the sixties and seventies. All the truth that was written later on vaginal politics and female sexual oppression. She really got it down there. So you get hints before your knowledge really comes together like that.

BF: But especially in the fifties there was all this pressure on women to be feminine, the feminine mystique and everything. Now that was just before your first book of stories appeared. Did they praise you for the wrong thing, like writing on the feminine side of life? That could have happened.

GP: That could have happened except that was one of the things that was already bothering me, that I was already thinking about. Also, the women lead unconventional lives. At that point of my life I was already very distressed about relations between men and women, and it's not that I ever was a careerist; that is, I didn't think to myself, oh, because you're a woman, you're not going to do this and that, because I never really wanted to do anything. [*Laughs.*] I wanted to keep writing. I happened to like doing those things that are in the book, like going to the park. I happen to like those things. I never did any of that out of some literary intention or anything. I did it out of sheer pleasure and duty. I believed the children should have air every afternoon. Things like that, you know. Rigorously I felt about that, but I never was pushed in that—not feminist but feminineness—way. It had no effect on me at all, partly because my parents were very angry with me that I wasn't interested in doing anything professional. They were angry that I didn't finish school, which I didn't. They didn't like any of this stuff that I was about, and they wanted me to get a trade, to get a profession, to make something of myself. And get married also, but they didn't want me especially to go back to the kitchen or anything like that. They wanted me to be able to earn a living. Also they—mother, aunts—had a kind of Socialist puritanism: no makeup; be yourself with soap and water. I was a little like that.

BF: Were you teaching at that time?
GP: No. I didn't have any trade. I was a typist. I worked in offices.

SO: You have this focus on women in your work, but the mother-daughter relationship really doesn't figure all that much. To many other women writers it is of the utmost importance. Why is it not for you?

GP: Well, first of all, my mother died when I was about twenty-one or twenty-two, and I was really brought up in a more extended kind of family than is customary in the States. In my house lived my father, my mother, my grandmother, and when I was very young, two aunts, and finally one aunt. So I had all these women taking care of me. So I never had that terrific focus, you know, that a lot of people do have. My grandmother took care of me, my aunt took care of me. My sister is fourteen years older than me, and I think actually she sort of stole me from my mother. I'm not exactly sure; but from the minute I was born, I was in her charge and not because my mother handed me over. But I also had terrible quarrels with my mother when I was in my teens, my adolescence, which were just being resolved really. None of them were because there was anything wrong with her. She was really a remarkable and kind, really a good person, and admired. But she was very puritanical, and this is very hard on teenagers. [*Laughs.*]

BF: Are you saying that this focus on the mother-daughter relationship as it often happens is the result of the nuclear family?
GP: Yes, I think part of it is that. Also, for many women, compassion for the oppressed mother; for others, anger because that oppression was handed on. The mother also enforced foot-binding, clitoridectomies, and obedience to husband. The nuclear family does have something to do with it. All of those intense focuses are like that. So I think this was sort

of broadened out for me. Somehow or other if I felt mad at my mother, I went to my grandmother; if I felt mad at my aunt, I went to my mother.

BF: And you also had more than one role model in a way?

GP: Yes. My sister to this day is a very powerful person in my life—she's eighty-three now—so much so that people laugh at me. They say that when I talk to my sister I use an entirely different voice [*laughs*], especially my husband laughs. So there is that kind of thing. But there is also the fact that I haven't dealt with a great deal of that. It's no question about it.

BF: Do you like to be identified as an ethnic writer? A woman writer, a regional writer? Any of these categories?

GP: I don't care. I'm perfectly happy to be called a woman writer. I've done this argument in another panel in California two weeks ago with a young woman who said she did not want to be a woman writer. She would be marginalized, trivialized, and so forth. My only answer was "They'll marginalize you and trivialize you no matter what you call yourself." It's not because you say you're a woman writer. It's because they say, "What is this? A woman wrote it?"

BF: You said somewhere the difference between male and female writing is in content, not in style.

GP: Well, some of it is in style. I mean some writing seems to be, you know, like harder, and some seems softer. I know a lot of people feel that there's a great difference, but I can't. I don't know. Maybe in other languages it's true.

BF: But just think, for instance, about your own work and Christa Wolf's *Cassandra*. I don't know anything comparable in male literature.

GP: That's true. But I think a lot of it is subject. Joyce was a great model to me because I think of him as a much more female writer. I think if you move away from Stephen Dedalus to Leopold Bloom, you see that, you feel that in him. What he was to his wife is another story, but we can't talk about that. [*Laughter.*] I mean he liked her, and that's good enough I suppose. It's a start. But I do think that a lot of it is subject matter. Somebody could sit down and prove to me that I was wrong. I'm wide open on that. I'm not opinionated. But I'm not able to totally see it. I see it in relationships. I see it at meetings. I see it in all of that, and so it should probably be reflected in the work. But I can't swear to it, that's all.

BF: But don't you have the feeling that there is maybe an international community of women writers who are concerned about the same kinds of things and have tried to develop a form to suit these concerns?

GP: Listen, I not only think there's an international community of women writers, I'm working on it. You really should know about what we are trying to develop right now: from PEN, the PEN organization, where we had our own personal struggle in our own country to create a women's committee, for lots of reasons, including the fact that most of the panels, discussions, and so forth would be almost entirely men. Something even worse than last night. There would be only one woman among a dozen men. So there's that. And then my friend Meredith Tax, who's extremely energetic and bossy and driving, after she got on the board of PEN, got to go to international meetings, which I just didn't want to go to anymore. But anyway she extracted from international PEN, which is run by mostly an old-guy-bloc from France, an international women's committee. I see those things very practically, very pragmatically.

SO: Are you a Jewish writer?
GP: Yes.

SO: Do you consider your writing Jewish-American literature?
GP: Not exactly. But the particular sound of the language as I and others like me speak it, and the disharmony of our experiences, and the strong baseline on which we depend—from before Chaucer, including the King James Version of the Bible, Whitman, Dickinson, Rukeyser, Auden, Thoreau, Cather, Joyce (not to mention the Russians in translation, et cetera)—make American literature, to which the strong Hispanic rhythms are being added.

SO: Do you, then, see yourself primarily as an American writer or rather as part of an international writer's community?
GP: Well, I think as a child of immigrants in a sense, of European immigrants. I am by birth, language, literary tradition an American writer. As a very strong feminist, which I wasn't when I began writing my first book but became, I know there is an international women's community, and I hope to be a part of that. And I think we have obligations to develop, maybe just translate and publish, those voices in other countries. I mean to help free those female voices. Just as you said, I mean, tell stories. Oh, by the way, another example of women's writing would be Elsa Morante in the book *History*. That's another great book that really no man could write.

BF: I agree. Your stories often celebrate communities of women and children. There's hardly ever hate, jealousy, spite, isolation between women and among women which makes communities of women unbearable for many women. Is that just not your experience, or are you aware of that?

GP: No. I'm aware of two things. First of all, they do get mad at each other. I mean I have this story "Friends," in which an old friendship ends, and other stories where friendships end for all kinds of reasons. I don't think hatred sets in, but the friendships do end. But I remember talking to Russian women and all they could tell me about was that women would never get together, they would scratch each other's eyes out. But I think that's not true. I think there's no more anger or competition among women than there is among men. Now that may just be where I live and in my life. But the men seem in some ways a hell of a lot more competitive with each other. They kill each other—economically or actually. They do it a different way; women would be more personal.

BF: I agree. But in my village the women usually gossip about each other. There's not much help they give each other. And their loyalty is to their husbands in the first place. And in your stories the women get together and they help each other and . . .

GP: Well, first of all, one of the stories really began by my writing about women without husbands. I think that has something to do with it. I mean you hit on something that I didn't think of quite that way. I worked with an awful lot of gay women, too, you know, who also aren't that nice to each other. Most of those women, especially in the early stories, are pretty much alone. Or they are mad at men, and they are bound by common bad experiences with men. They have been insulted in one way or another.

SO: Where do you situate yourself in the contemporary literary scene?

GP: It would be up to critics to say that. You know there are a lot of writers who think about that and speak about that. I don't even know what the contemporary literary scene is, exactly.

SO: Are you writing for a specific audience?

GP: I don't consciously do that. No, I don't. Well, I think that so much of writing comes from a primary longing to tell, not a story but to tell. I want to tell you this, you know? In my book of poems I think I have a poem about how it begins as a child. You come home and say, "Listen Ma, I want to tell you this," you know. And that's a primary thing—'I want to tell you this." I know it is first the mother and then whoever else is home. Then it's your best friend—"I want to tell you this." And then as time goes on, you don't think who you want to tell, but you do think this is the way it is and I have to put it down. So your who-you-want-to-tell is broadening. But it doesn't mean that you are going to change your work for that unknown out there.

BF: Do you know who your readers are?

GP: I think that any woman who doesn't know that she is supported by the women's movement in any country is fooling herself. Because it doesn't matter whether she is a feminist or not. People will read her and be angry at her, or they will read her and be glad. But women will read her, I know they will. But I know men read me a lot too because I get, in a funny way, more letters from men than women.

BF: Do you read reviews of your work?

GP: Reviews? Sometimes.

BF: Are you influenced by them in any way? I mean do you get annoyed at them?

GP: Sometimes I get annoyed, yes. I remember my second book, which really wasn't even all that political. But they said everything was too political. I wrote a letter back to the *Times*, just simply making a point that in any other country in the world you would be laughed at if you weren't political. And all this stuff was coming up from South America at the time, you know. Yet they would tell me: not here, not in this country; there is no such thing as political writing in the U.S. There should not be. Whereas you are reading madly stuff from Middle Europe and South America.

BF: Marge Piercy said at one point that the reviews in the *New York Times* can make a book or break it in a way. Do you agree?

GP: Absolutely. It's worse for the theater because so much money is put into the theater, and a play costs hundreds of thousands of dollars, and many people's careers can just be ended by one son of a bitch. The *Times* is very influential, but other things are too.

SO: Is it difficult to support yourself by writing?

GP: Oh, I can't.

SO: If you are not dependent on writing as a means of support, of course, it's easier. You are under less pressure to produce. It does make a difference for your art, doesn't it?

GP: Well, it means that I write when I really have to, pretty much. But once you start writing, you keep writing. You don't end it. It is true that if I have a deadline—like I had to finish some of those poems at a certain point—I did really not do a thing but stay in my room and work. But my husband is a writer, and he has a lot of trouble being published and is not depending on it at the same time for a living, but he still works like hell. So what I mean is, when you're a writer, you're a writer.

SO: But still, I think of women writers in the nineteenth century, when it was even worse than it is today . . .

GP: They wrote because it was one of the few means for them to make a living, as when I was a typist and made no living at all. And then when my book came out, I began to teach. I made a modest living there. My books have been in print really since 1959, and I'm very fortunate. I won't say a bad word about whether I am making money or not [*laughs*] because I consider it that I am just so fortunate. I mean that's a large payment to me at this time of my life. So on this book [*Long Walks and Intimate Talks*] I won't make a penny. [Since this interview I did make some happy royalties.]

SO: Something that I noticed in your stories is that your female characters all seem to enjoy sexuality and don't seem to have any problems with their sex life. For many women this is still a very painful, if not the most painful area. Why do you portray sex as unproblematic?

GP: Well, partly I think that when I began writing about this I guess I was in my mid-thirties, and I found sex pretty unproblematic. That's plain and simple. [*Laughter.*] And so did most of my friends. A number of the women who became gay later on became so partly because they had been gay to begin with or because of particular sexual experiences. People get divorced and fall for some other guy or some other woman, I mean as far as I can see. I am just thinking of Andrea Dworkin. I have really known Andrea since she was very young. I have known her since she was about eighteen years old. I used to love her very much. She was very dear to me. I mean when she writes about sexual life, it's horrible. And she did have some horrible experiences, you know, but I am not writing about her. That's all I can say. For me I really want to celebrate sexuality.

SO: Because that's the way you feel about it?

GP: And because I want to celebrate it. Because I think it's one of the greatest things invented [*laughs*], and it may be a pure invention that it is so great. I could be wrong, and Andrea could be right. But I think it should be. One of the things that bothers me with a lot of my sisters in movements that I have worked with is that their anger with men really has turned them not against men, which is all right as far as I am concerned, but against sex in general, so that even their lesbian experiences don't strike me as so hot as far as that's concerned.

BF: I think that everybody would want to celebrate sexuality. I think that wasn't our point. It's just that it isn't that easy for most women. And I don't mean in the way Andrea Dworkin writes about it. I mean it's just not that easy to go to a bar, as in one of your stories, and pick up any man there, buy him a drink or two, and have a good time with him.

GP: As far as I can see, she doesn't do too much of that, going to bars. But whether it's good sex or not I didn't deal with. [*Laughter.*] I think I wasn't even talking so much about sex as relationships with guys that were extremely difficult. Well, I don't know. It's really what you read, not what I say.

BF: Let's talk about your new book, *Long Walks and Intimate Talks*. It strikes us as quite different from *Later the Same Day*.

GP: Oh, it is different. It's an altogether different thing. It's made up of things that were like articles that I wrote. Most of them were not written for this book.

BF: It's more overtly political than the rest of your work.

GP: Yes, very specifically so. This book was originally a calendar for the War Resisters League.

SO: The entire book?

GP: No, not the entire book. There's more in this, but all the things about El Salvador; those long poems were written specifically for that calendar. And the little essays or whatever you want to call them, pieces—some of them were written for different journals like *Mother Jones* or *Seven Days* or something like that.

BF: If you put together another collection of stories, would your stories be less political than the ones in there?

GP: Well, I would probably use some of those in there. I would use "Midrash on Happiness" and I would use "Three Days and a Question." I consider those stories. But I think they are the only ones I consider really full stories. So I would use those two stories in a collection of stories.

SO: Are you working on a book of stories at the moment?

GP: Yes. I'm writing some stories. I have another half or dozen or so of which I probably like about three. And I have another collection of prose pieces also.

SO: Do you feel that your writing has changed over the years?

GP: Not when I write stories. I don't feel I have in those two little stories or in *Later the Same Day*. I don't know. Again, you know, I'm not the judge of that. It's like you're getting older, right? Until you look in the mirror you think you're you. [*Laughs.*] It turns out you're not you anymore. But then you go away from the mirror and you're you.

SO: Is your poetry more personal as compared to your fiction?

GP: Well, my poems are more personal, a lot. But at one time I wrote only extremely personal poems, and now I think some of the poems in there represent political feelings, but even so they are personal.

BF: You published a book of poetry in 1992, *New and Collected Poems*. For a while you didn't want to publish your poetry because you thought it was too literary in a sense.

GP: Well, it was.

BF: What has changed?

GP: Well, just as I learned how to write stories from poetry—I've used the expression before—I went to school to poetry to learn how to write, to learn how to move language around, give it some zip. [*Laughs.*] But from writing stories I learned also how to bring that other language into poetry—that language of family and street, that more human, daily language.

BF: What about a novel now?

GP: I don't know. It's probably too late. When I listen to these guys reading their novels [*laughter*], I get sort of, you know, I get interested. I just think, well, I'm going to write a novel. It would be different than those—proving what you said. [*Laughter.*]

BF: Do you keep a diary?

GP: Not really. I keep pieces of paper.

BF: Could you imagine yourself writing your autobiography?

GP: No, I really couldn't. No. I have a couple of books written about me where I talk a lot and they ask me a lot of questions. And then they have gone ahead and looked stuff up. I can't see me writing an autobiography. I mean it seems so stupid. [*Laughter.*] You have to feel like you are telling the world something. I feel I'm doing it when I write the way I write.

BF: Did you read Simone de Beauvoir's autobiography? Were you interested in that? I mean a lot of women read her; even if they haven't read any other women's literature, they read Simone de Beauvoir's.

GP: Yes, I read it, but again it was a whole other life. Part of my life or what I've been interested in is staying this close to the people, if I can put it that way, to ordinary life, to daily life in some way. So she really did not have that much to tell me except that I was interested in her. I was interested, but I saw here is this woman who really wanted the absolute opposite of ordinary life, whereas that's the opposite of me.

BF: Well, she is in a way the archetype of the female intellectual who lived it all—the big culture, the big politics.

GP: She lived all that under some guy's thumb. [*Laughs.*] Under a generous thumb. [*Both laugh.*]

SO: Could you describe your relationship to language?

GP: Well, I partly did by saying I really went to poetry to learn, to learn how to write. I like language. I have written a lot of poems about language here and there. I just think about language a lot.

SO: Do you feel that you shape language, or do you feel that you are shaped by language?

GP: Oh, I think both things happen. What I want to say is how interesting it is to be brought up with a couple of languages around you. There is something about getting these two tunes, three tunes, in your ear. And English is very receptive to this. I mean English really warmly receives all these other languages. At least it does in the United States at the present time. So I feel that my language was shaped by the fact that in my house normally Russian was spoken. English was spoken. You never knew when people were going into one language or another. And Yiddish less so because only my grandmother spoke that. So these languages kind of speak to one another. They address one another in the nicest ways, and I think that's one of the things that happened. One of the best books that I have read in a long time is by a woman named Irini Spanidou, and it is called *God's Snake*. She's Greek. I just mean that she had that Greek and English coming together, and it gave it a new tune somehow.

BF: Do you think there is a trace of Russian in your stories?

GP: I can't call it a trace of Russian. I would just say that it was in my ear. There are inflections that are either Yiddish or Russian or something like that that are probably there and that people recognize. Probably better than I recognize because I'm used to it being me talking.

BF: Did you ever consider language to be male? Like you couldn't work in it because it belonged to men?

GP: What? Language?

SO: Some feminist theorists have this idea that language is male.

GP: My mother and my sister talked to me a great deal. I know that theory. I think too much is taken away from us by those theories, by many of those theories. It's as though we are nothing; we are just putty in the hands of fate. Because women have struggled in different ways and do talk to their babies. I mean who the hell talks to those goddamn babies but mamas. Pap comes home once in a while and says a few . . . My father was a very busy man. He worked very hard, in a poor neighborhood. He was marvelous and all that, but he didn't . . . When I got up in the morning and ran into my grandmother's room, she talked to me. When I was a baby, it was my sister and my mother who talked to me. I don't see it really. I would say that men take female language (I'm just making this up right now; I've never said this before); I would say that it's very probable that little boys who are very tender—and I have a son and a daughter; little boys are the tenderest things in the world—that little boys as they grow older grow out of their female language and go into the male world, where adult men have re-created female language. I like that. That's a good theory. [*Laughter.*] That's as good as the other one, isn't it? Where men take that language really and turn it into a means to make war and do other bad things. [*Laughter.*]

SO: In your most recent collection, *Long Walks and Intimate Talks*, you have a poem entitled "It Is the Responsibility." In this poem to be a woman seems like a moral, political objective. Actually, there is a line that reads "It is the responsibility of the male poet to be a woman." Could you elaborate on that?

GP: Well, what happened was when I was writing the poem, I wrote "It is the responsibility of the male poet to be a woman." I think I wrote that line first. And I sort of knew that everybody would think that the next line would be "It is the responsibility of the female poet to be a man." So I just couldn't do it because I didn't think it was true. [*Laughter.*] So I guess I just wrote it because I thought it was true. I thought that, for all the reasons we have talked about so far, a man poet ought to be able to be a female poet; I mean he's got to think like a woman. And really it would do him a lot of good. On the other hand there's no reason for women to change. Oh, people get very mad at me for that. That poem has created more anger at me than almost anything else I have ever written.

SO: Really?

GP: Oh yes. It's so funny.

SO: Do you perceive women as more peaceful than men?

GP: I think by history, by culture, not by birth, you know. We have a one-year-old grandgirl who is quite nutty and wild and bopping people on the head and everything. No, I wouldn't say that I think that women are more peaceful, but I will say that I think that men are quite crazy at this present time. And I don't mean my own man or my son or lots of people that I know, but I mean the amount of blood, rage in the world, which is not women doing it at all. I mean more women are being killed. Women and children. You read the papers—more women and children have been killed in Yugoslavia and all through there. And dying in Somalia. It's a male madness that's been let loose in this world right now, as far as I can see. And where it comes from I don't know. I don't think women are more peaceful; I just think men are more warlike. It seems that way if you just listen to the radio. It's not a theory. It's what we actually see and read.

One of the things that always bothers me is when women in political movements that I've been involved in, like Central America and Palestine or something like that, when the women say, "I wish I had another two sons to give. I'm the mother of heroes." That infuriates me when women do that, and I think that I always want to say to them, "You go be a hero and a martyr if you're so hot for it, but don't be giving away your boys' lives." But I notice that they aren't going around being heroes and martyrs. They say, "Son, you go be a hero." So it's a hard question to answer because deeply I don't want to believe that men are more warlike. But I think that just pragmatically, from reading the paper every day, I'd say so far.

BF: But whenever a war is going on, there are women supporting the war effort at home.

GP: Of course there are, and one hates that. And yet for the First World War women from all countries tried to get together to stop it. There were women in Yugoslavia. I had lists of their names—of women and also a list of writers and intellectuals who just all begged them to stop. There were plenty of men who begged them to stop, that's true, who were horrified by it all. But something goes wild. I used to make jokes of it. I used to say well, that's because they don't know what to do in the afternoon after work. I don't think, for instance—you know we have this thing about being drafted into the army and stuff like that—I don't think women should be drafted into the army. I think men should not. So my feeling is that in certain areas they should be equal with us, not we with them.

SO: What does feminism mean to you?

GP: It means a couple of things. First it means you begin to understand you have a lot in common with other women. It's like a class thing. This class of women is a group of people that you have a good deal of life in common with. And it begins at that point. And then you begin to think about how the world is organized and what your position in it is, socially, and you understand what a patriarchal society you are living in, and it's not yours basically.

BF: Were you active in a women's liberation group from the beginning?

GP: Well, somewhat. You see I was in the peace movement. Probably because of the Vietnam War. And unlike many young women I was already working with a lot of women in it and also with several very unusual men, older mostly. A lot of the young women in the peace movement were really just pushed around by SDS (the student organization). That is, Meredith Tax or Marge Piercy were pushed around by these guys, these young fellows in these student movements, who were really not shallow because they were very smart, but callow and full of male beans and ambition and so forth. And accustomed to or forced to play a certain role. I think the women's movement has done a lot for men, a tremendous lot for them. For men who paid attention it has taken some of the burden of machoism off their backs, which is a terrible burden to bear. If you think about it, it's horrible. It's horrible to have to be that kind of person in order to be a person.

BF: A lot of men don't seem to recognize that because there is this backlash now. Marilyn French was here with her book *The War against Women*. It's like a lot of men say, "Women are responsible for everything that's wrong in my life."

GP: Yes, but they were saying that before. I talked to her about it. I like her very much.

SO: What about that backlash? I mean Robert Bly's book and people like that. Is it just something that is puffed up by the press?

GP: A lot of it is puffed up, but a lot of it is true. You can't expect men not to respond to a lot of criticism. All of those guys from the West talk about Toni Morrison. I can't tell you how it affects me. I am so upset with them. Jesus Christ, you know. Anyway, the men are a class that privileges have been taken away from, and they don't understand that. They think it's ordinary life that's been stolen, and it's like they have lived in this room and you have said, "We'd like to have one third of the room," and they go out of their minds naturally because they have been lying all over the place. [*Laughter.*]

SO: It's been like this all the time.

GP: Yes, it's natural, but we fight back. When she says there is a backlash, that doesn't mean that the women aren't there to fight that backlash. The press doesn't say it so much, but there was a meeting with Anita Hill in New York, and they had room for about eight hundred people. And there were thousands of women who just came to that one half-day conference to hear her. And then I've been going to meetings with a group called Action Committee. They meet every single Tuesday. This is just an ordinary meeting of an organization, and between two hundred and four hundred people meet every single Tuesday. [These meetings and actions have continued since we spoke.] So there's a backlash to the backlash if I can put it that way. It encourages me very much. That's true where I live in New England as well, where the women's movement was kind of pleased with itself and dormant for a while and has suddenly got mad, and women have begun to get together again.

BF: You have got a little piece in here. One of your conversation pieces where the narrator talks to her mother-in-law on her deathbed about women's lib. She comes down the next morning and says, "Those young women—what wonderful lives they're going to have." Would you agree?

GP: Yes, I do. I think it's much better for you guys than it was for me. I mean it was much better for my daughter except for AIDS, which wrecks everything. That business of AIDS does terrible things. It prevents people from naturally loving one another, and it makes people who have ceased to love one another stick together. Both terrible things.

SO: Are your children feminists?

GP: My daughter is. My son is a little backlashed [*laughter*] but not much. Not too much.

SO: Apart from being a feminist you characterize yourself in this book as a cooperative anarchist. I like the term very much. And a combative pacifist. Which of these things is most likely to get you into trouble?

GP: As a combative pacifist I have gotten into more trouble than as a cooperative anarchist.

SO: What are the current projects politically that you are involved in?

GP: I have been very involved in a lot of Jewish stuff too, and that's very interesting because again it is mostly women. It is the women in Israel called Women in Black, who have been fighting, who have been vigiling week after week after week. And we have our own Women in Black in New York and even in Vermont and in California; only we don't wear black, that's the only thing. But we really vigil for that. Now that's part of bringing together the peace movement and the women's movement because it's mostly women who are doing it. One of the really interesting things is that, for instance, in contacts with Palestinian women we have heard them say now that they won't allow to happen to them what happened to the Algerian women—after the revolution everything was turned back. Who knows? But those are the international contacts where people help each other out to understand things. I have been involved in that as a writer and as a woman and things like that pretty much. I have moved up to the country, so my life is a little peculiar.

BF: What is your relation to Israel?

GP: I'm not a Zionist and I never was. But I don't want them destroyed. I really don't. I do think there should be two states there. I think they should behave decently. They shouldn't act like such pigs. I'm very happy about the elections, though God knows what they'll finally mean.

BF: I was surprised.

GP: I was surprised. I think they were surprised too. I think people are tired of those rotten settlements. Those people are awful. And do you want to know something? They're mostly Americans. If not mostly at least in a large percentage.

BF: How did you feel about coming to Germany?

GP: I've come a number of times and probably the first time was strange. I wanted to look into every face and see some truth. What happened was that Germans often began the conversation, and in the end I wondered how I would bear such a burden. At the same time I come from a racist country full of denial of its history and live among Christians who suffer some mild form of antisemitism at least and a more virulent form of race hatred. I am interested in history and how the generations make it, then tell it. I was glad to see hundreds of Germans come out in protest of the foreign bashing. If five thousand had come into the streets after Kristallnacht, the world's history since would have been different.

SO: Let us return to women's experiences. You said somewhere that women who don't have children are missing out on a fantastic experience.

GP: I didn't say it like that.

SO: You said, "I think it's a shame that it has become almost a fashion not to have children." Do you still think it's necessary to have a child of one's own?

GP: Oh no, no. I never thought that. My sister has no children. But I do think relation to children is important. And I don't think people have to have children. My daughter has no children. I wanted to. It was easy for me because there was no political opposition to it. [*Laughter.*]

SO: On the contrary!

GP: On the contrary, right! So I didn't put it off. I do think a relation to children is a wonderful thing. I think a relation to old people . . . I think that you can't live a single-generation life. I mean you can, but, one, you don't learn enough from it, and two, it's more boring. You can get into fights with the generation that's ahead of you, and your children you certainly get into fights with. So you get into struggles with them. They are illuminating always. And you see what's ahead of you and you see what's in back of you. I think you have a sense of time. To me children are extremely interesting, but that's me personally, and it's not what I think other people must feel.

SO: It should be an option for women to decide that they don't want to have children.

GP: Well, I would fight to the death for the right not to have children. I mean as far as the whole abortion thing is concerned, that's one of my major concerns.

SO: So you have been active on abortion?

GP: Oh yes, I have. That's a very big struggle in the United States. God knows what's going to happen. I mean we're really dealing with maniacs. There is this other little piece in there [*Long Walks*] about what it was like for us when there was no abortion allowed. It was just simply sheer oppression.

BF: Do you think that Pro-Lifers have a chance in the States?

GP: They're very strong, but they've been beaten back in every town. I mean women have really been there and not allowed them. But they are part of the whole fundamentalist movement that is crawling across the whole world, and we have to stop them.

SO: You're right. It's the same in Germany too.

GP: Oh, I bet.

SO: In your writing children always are a sort of promise, the hope for the future, new beginnings.

GP: I don't think you begin again. Sometimes when you are with children, you feel old. You feel worse than anything.

BF: Well, we wanted to ask you how you feel about turning seventy this year? What does old age mean to you?

GP: Well, if you have the book, it has a couple of hard poems in there. Golda Meir was asked that question: "We hear you don't mind getting older?" And she said, "That's true, but I never said it was a pleasure." I can't think of a better answer in this sense. I mean you get older and your time gets shorter on this earth; and if you happen to like this earth, you really get a little gloomy about having to leave it. There are a lot of things one is curious about—like what will come next in the world's life—and very angry that you won't know. And you feel that if you turn your back by dying, it'll get very bad behind your back, or something like that. The whole world will blow up, and you'll never know that's what happened. You couldn't stop it. If you'd only been there, you would have stopped it. No, I think if you're healthy . . . I'm pretty healthy. My husband is pretty healthy. We really like each other a lot, and our kids are in fairly good shape. But if you get old in another way, it's very bad. If you don't have money, it's terrible. Not that we have a lot, but I don't have to worry really, and I'm still working.

BF: So you don't worry too much?

GP: You do; you can't help it. You know, not really worry. You wake up early afraid sometimes, but you do sometimes when you're thirty-three and a half [*laughs*], and you don't know what's coming, right?

Index

Abortion/pro-choice, 70, 266
Abstractions/generalizations, 33
Abzug, Bella, 97
Affirmative action, 151
Alienation, 121, 181–82
Ambition, 111, 228–29
America (United States)/Americans, 46, 151, 160, 191, 236, 265
American Jewish Committee, 158
Anger, 95–96, 261
"Angry Arts," 152
Anne (character), 184
Anti-nuclear energy, 46, 68–69, 129, 227
Anti-Semitism, 154–55, 157–58, 216, 234, 265. *See also* Racism
Anti-war movement/militarism, 48, 80, 95–96, 121, 122, 136, 152, 210–11
"Anxiety," 210
Arms race, 46, 48, 191
Arrests/jailings, 19, 65, 96, 226–27
Asher, Aaron, 111
Auden, W. H., 105, 106, 142, 201, 206, 235, 246
Austen, Jane, 116
Autobiographical elements in stories, 40, 52, 64–65, 79–80, 179–80, 181, 201–02, 208, 217
Autobiography, 259–60

Babel, Isaac, 74, 115, 132, 142, 160
Bambara, Toni Cade, 93
Banks, Mirra, 84
Barth, John, 51, 54
Barthelme, Donald, 50, 51, 53, 54, 64, 74, 112, 113, 132, 230–31
Beats, 90, 186
Beauvoir, Simone de, 259–60
Bellow, Saul, 134, 198
Blacks, 36, 148, 151, 155, 209, 213–14, 222, 237
Black studies, 187
Blake, William, 238
Bly, Robert, 263
Boyle, Kay, 211, 231
"Bridge, The," 243
Broner, Esther M., 92, 114, 211, 229; *Her Mothers*, 92; *Weave of Women*, 92, 114

Brontë sisters, 92
Bronx, 10, 57–58, 63, 64, 73, 132, 160, 192, 214–15, 224
"Burdened Man, The," 48, 51
Burgess, Anthony, 131
Burroughs, William, 90
Bush, George, 243

Careerism, 217, 228, 251
Carter (character), 10
Carter, Jimmy, 69
Cassie (character), 171
Catholicism, 92, 157–58
Central America, 137, 210, 242
Change (social, individual's influence on), 59, 88–89, 128–29, 135, 209–10
Characterization, 30, 43, 79, 85, 108, 214, 218–19
Chekhov, Anton, 60, 73, 102, 132, 184
Children, 40–41, 58–59, 70, 79–80, 82, 101–02, 110–11, 119, 128, 191, 223, 224–25, 250, 265–66; "humanizing the male child," 147
Chile, 46–47, 150–51
China, 46–47, 150–51
Chopin, Kate, 42, 116
City College (New York), 112, 143–44, 149
Clifford (character), 45
Compton-Burnett, Ivy, 75
"Contest, The," 7, 10, 44–45, 76, 107, 118, 205
"Conversation with My Father, A," 5, 52, 60, 62, 86–87, 102, 173, 180, 183, 184, 223
Cooper, Jane, 245
Coover, Robert, 51, 54
Continuity (between stories), 173–74
"Country Life, Is It Boring?" 241
Cynthia (character), 215

Daly, Mary, 83, 112
"Dance in Jinoteca, The," 242
Death/dying, 52–53, 60–61, 63, 79, 99, 204, 245
"Debts," 59, 170, 173
Deming, Barbara, 96–97
Depression (era), 88–89, 178, 214, 239

269

Dickens, Charles, 92, 250
Didacticism in writing, 9, 209, 210
Didion, Joan, 91, 115
"Distance," 207
Doolittle, Hilda (H.D.), 105
Douglas, Ellen, 214
"Dreamer in a Dead Language," 84, 134, 168
Dreams/dreaming, 76–77, 123
Dworkin, Andrea, 257–58

Education, 44, 66, 104–05, 132, 152
El Salvador, 236, 242
Eliot, George, 116
Eliot, T. S., *The Waste Land*, 17
Emshwiller, Carol, 227, 239
"Enormous Changes at the Last Minute," 83, 168
Ephron, Nora, 138
Ethnic studies, 187
Ethnicity/ethnic writers, 11, 218, 232–33, 254; marginalization, 253
Europe/Europeans, 46, 104, 145
"Expensive Moment, The," 134
Experimentation in writing, 11, 12

Faith (character), 5, 9, 21, 50, 58, 59, 62, 63, 78–79, 130, 134, 149, 171–72, 174, 179–80, 184, 185, 201–02, 208
Faith (moral value), 59
"Faith in a Tree," 58, 134
"Faith in the Afternoon," 6, 51, 84, 93, 134
Farrell, James T., *Studs Lonigan*, 92
Faulkner, William, 10
"Fear," 241, 247n9
Female-centered perspective (in writing), 251, 253
Feminism/feminist criticism, 47, 75, 91, 121, 144, 151, 189, 207–08, 251–52, 263
Feminist theory on language, 261
Fiction vs. nonfiction, 34
Figes, Eva, *Light*, 199; *The Seven Ages*, 199
Film adaptation of stories, 84, 168–69
Film as medium, 84–85
"Floating Truth, The," 11, 12, 42
Forché, Carolyn, 237, 242, 246
French, Marilyn, *The Women's Room*, 91, 114, 116; *The War Against Women*, 263
"Friends," 31, 41, 52, 61–62, 80, 81, 99, 128, 130, 147, 166, 183–84, 190, 197, 198, 208, 255
Friends/friendships, 63, 82–83, 99, 100–01, 112, 171, 179, 189–90, 213–14; and conflict/competition, 255
Frost, Robert, 68

Gaskell, Elizabeth, 92, 116; *North and South*, 92
Gates, Bea, 238
Generation gap/conflict/attitudes, 51, 60–61, 87, 266
Giddings, Paula, *When and Where I Enter*, 158
Gilman, Charlotte Perkins, 116
Ginny (character), 9, 41, 45, 49, 51, 149, 185
Gold, Herbert, 64
Goldschmidt, Jeannie, 96
"Goodbye and Good Luck," 7, 10, 76, 79, 109, 118, 133, 190, 195, 205
Goodman, Paul, 115, 135–36
Gordon, Mary, 83, 92, 211, 219
Grace, 5, 37, 86
Greenwich Village Peace Center, 65, 208
Guilt, 45, 211
Gulf War, 236, 243

Hannah, Barry, 144
Hanover, NH, 56–57
Hawkes, John, 15, 53
H.D. *See* Doolittle, Hilda
Herbert, George, 165
Hershberger, Ruth, *Adam's Rib*, 251
Hill, Anita, 227, 264
History, 69, 110, 127, 136–37, 152, 188, 199, 223
Hitler, Adolph, 46
Holocaust, 193, 196, 197, 222
Humor/jokes/joking, 24, 34, 53, 61, 95, 122, 166, 174, 196; Jewish humor/wit, 174–75, 245
Hunter College English, 42

"I Gave Away That Kid," 237
Idealism, 65
Ideas/subjects for writing, 17–18, 28–29, 30, 31, 36, 40, 44, 48, 63, 71, 75, 99–100, 102, 109, 110, 120, 122, 170–71, 183–84, 187, 206, 223, 231–32, 250–51
"Immigrant Story, The," 6, 12, 31, 37, 81, 86, 141, 207, 240
"In San Salvador (I)" and "In San Salvador (II)," 239, 247n6
"In This Country, But in Another Language, My Aunt Refuses to Marry the Men Everyone Wants Her To," 170
"In Time Which Made a Monkey of Us All," 13, 41
Individualism (egocentrism), 126, 129, 151, 165

Index

"Interest in Life, An," 112, 120, 149, 150, 168, 186
Irony, 44
"Irrevocable Diameter, An," 45
Isherwood, Christopher, 106
Israel, 156–57, 234, 264–65

Jack (character), 130, 185
Jacobs, Jane, 207
Jeffers, Robinson, 105
Jen, Gish, *Typical American*, 232
Jewish Women Against the Occupation, 234
Jews/Jewishness, 102, 134, 145, 149, 154–62, 196–98, 222, 234, 254. *See also* Jewish humor; Anti-Semitism
Jews for Racial and Economic Justice, 234
Jong, Erica, 91; *Fear of Flying*, 115–16
Josephine (character), 7
Joyce, James/Joycean, 49, 71, 74, 102–03; *Dubliners*, 184
Judaism, 153–54; and feminism, 197–98. *See also* Religion

Kingston, Maxine Hong, *The Woman Warrior*, 34–35, 78
Korean War, 150
Kropotkin, Peter A., *Memoirs of a Revolutionist*, 246
Ku Klux Klan, 96
Kundera, Milan, 144–45; *The Unbearable Lightness of Being*, 145; *The Book of Laughter and Forgetting*, 145

Language, 8, 17, 23, 32, 36, 41–42, 54, 74, 87, 160, 163–64, 182–83, 206, 220, 231, 246, 260–61. *See also* Voice
Larkin, Joan, 238
Lavinia (character), 128
"Lavinia: An Old Story," 128, 182, 221, 224
Lee, Arnold (character), 58
Lesbianism, 83, 171, 232, 255, 257–58
Lessing, Doris, 92
Le Sueur, Meridel, 112, 231
Lewis, C. Day, 244
Linder, Ben, 210
"Listening," 134, 136, 171, 185
Listening/hearing, 35, 37, 72, 76, 107, 132, 163–66, 171, 216, 220–21. *See also* Voice
"Little Girl, The," 10–11, 59, 61
"Livid and Pallid," 44
"Living," 11–12, 129
"Long Distance Runner, The," 13, 21–22, 50, 59–60, 63, 124–25, 134, 214, 219–20, 223

Louis, Joe, 216
"Love," 64
Love, 59, 62, 83
Luddy, Mrs. (character), 59–60
Ludie (character), 215, 221

McCormick, Ken, 38, 133
McGuane, Tom, 39
Macho/machoism, 200, 263
MacNiece, Louis, 106
Madre, 242
Malamud, Bernard, 134
Male backlash, 263–64
"Male madness," 262
Marginality (women and Jews), 174–75, 253
Marriage, 44, 83, 194–95, 211
Marx, Karl, 132
Maupassant, Guy de, 49, 60
Meir, Golda, 267
Memory, 93, 223
Men, 5, 16, 43–44, 45, 48, 97–98, 108–09, 130, 138, 149–50, 198–99, 207, 263
"Midrash on Happiness," 258
Millay, Edna St. Vincent, 105
Miller, Henry, 90, 251
Millett, Kate, 244
Milton, John, 238
Miró, Joan, 27
Mood, 22, 33–34
Morality (in literature), 190
Morante, Elsa, *History*, 93, 254
Moravia, Alberto, 93
Morrison, Toni, 93, 263
Mussolini, Benito, 139

Native Americans, 209, 237, 246
Neighborhood organizations (political activities), 65, 152, 227
New Jewish Agenda, 161
New School for Social Research, 106, 217
New York, 8–9, 10, 20–21, 132, 134, 152
New York Feminist Writers' Guild, 78
Nicaragua, 150–51, 156–57, 191, 210, 242
Nichols, Robert (Bob), 40, 65, 113, 124, 134, 229; *From the Steam Room*, 239
"Northeast Playground," 65–66

Oates, Joyce Carol, 91–92, 115, 131
Old Testament, 74, 246
Olsen, Tillie, 14, 39, 54, 64, 74, 89–90, 91, 112–14, 171, 187, 211, 244
"On Mother's Day," 245, 247n10
"One Day in China," 9
O'Neill, Tip, 96

Oppositions (theme), 63
Oppression, 44, 198, 222, 237, 252
Oral tradition, 94
Ordinary lives (in stories), 9, 10, 16, 28, 49, 50, 81–82, 120, 136, 147, 191, 222, 260
"Other Mothers," 100

Paley, Grace, on childhood/upbringing, 177–78, 192–93, 218, 224, 240, 240–41; "combative pacifist," 264; "cooperative anarchist," 264; on family/family history, 40, 44, 52, 73, 80, 100–01, 103, 104, 110–11, 127–28, 132, 145, 153, 160–61, 194, 224–25, 239, 249–50; on family relations, 102–04, 154, 192–94, 252; on her father, 34, 44, 52, 73, 102–03, 127, 153–54, 180, 194, 224; on growing older, 266–67; on influences for her writing, 8, 23, 34–35, 37, 71, 74–75, 105, 115, 125, 142, 160, 169, 179, 184, 206, 218, 229, 244; on influences (personal), 54, 74, 155; on learning to write stories, 76, 107, 143, 206; on literary life, 112–13, 121, 206, 230–31; on her mother, 44, 52, 73, 100–01, 103, 127–28, 153–54, 193–94, 252; on novel writing, 9, 41, 50, 78, 124, 133, 142, 148, 233, 259; as pacifist, 65, 240; on political activism, 20, 65, 69, 95–96, 97, 104–05, 110–11, 121, 128–29, 133, 134, 136–37, 150–51, 159–60, 188–89, 229–30; on politics and relation to writing/literature, 8–9, 15–16, 30, 81, 115, 121, 129–30, 135–36, 146–47, 150, 188, 209, 228, 236, 258; on purposes as a writer, 181, 208–09, 218, 228–29, 231–32, 237; on reading in public, 165–68, 200; on relationship to other writers, 54, 77–78, 89–93, 211, 251; on response to criticism, 256; on street life (New York), 51, 70, 71, 73–74, 215; as teacher/writer, 3, 108, 143, 164–65, 189–90, 223; on work habits, 16, 38, 124, 131–32, 141, 229, 256–57; on writing and time conflicts, 4, 18–19, 38–39, 68, 69–70, 90, 109–11, 118–19, 122–23, 130, 131, 172, 200, 211, 219; on writing truth/"lies," 6, 24, 43–44, 218, 231; writer's writer, 64
Paley, Jess, 42, 66, 75, 109–10, 111, 132, 134, 161, 205
Patriarchy ("masculine society"), 138, 188, 263
P.E.N., 53, 78, 112, 186, 230–31, 254
Pessimism, 191
Piercy, Marge, 54, 136, 211, 238, 256, 263; *The High Cost of Living*, 115

Plath, Sylvia, 70
Plot, 48–49, 61, 86–87
"Poem About Storytelling, A," 238
"Poet's responsibility," 237, 261
Poetry/poets, 4, 7, 40, 75–76, 105, 106–07, 117–18, 127, 132, 140–41, 142, 148, 164, 167, 169, 201, 205, 206, 235; orality of, 166; recent directions, changes, 233, 259; "poetry of witness," 244. *See also* Storytellers
"Politics," 50
Politics and religion, 157–58
Porter, Katherine Anne, 64
Powers, James F., 92
Proust, Marcel, 71, 90
Psychology, 12, 110
Publishing, 38, 77, 117, 217–18, 229, 238, 239

Race, cross-racial identity, 214–15, 221
Racism, 158, 224–25, 265
Raftery, John (character), 185
Raftery, Mrs. (character), 9, 36, 41, 51, 185–86
Reader response, 31–32, 112, 190, 209, 256
Reagan, Ronald, 46, 69, 211
Relationships, 76, 99; male-female, 43–45, 82, 109–10, 119–20, 138, 149–50, 188, 198–200, 207, 237, 251, 258, 262; and loyalty, 255; mother-daughter, 80, 252; father-daughter, 223; falsity in, 222. *See also* Friends/friendships
Religion, 37, 150, 151, 153–54, 157–58, 162, 196, 223, 234
"Responsibility," 237, 261
Rich, Adrienne, 70, 247
Richard (character), 58, 59, 171, 173
Rosie (character), 41, 49
Rossetti, Christina, 105
Roth, Philip, 64, 132, 134
Rothenberg, Jerome, *Technicians of the Sacred*, 166
Rukeyser, Muriel, 192, 231
Russia, 47, 54, 160, 194
Russian writers, 23
"Ruthy and Edie," 129, 169

"Samuel," 61, 182
Samuel (character), 58–59
Sand, George, 116
Sarah Lawrence College, 71, 108, 143–44, 145, 238
Sayles, John, 133
Schwartz, Delmore, 244

Index

SDS (Students for a Democractic Society), 128, 263
Seabrook nuclear plant, 65, 69, 227
Selena (character), 62, 99, 184
Self-love/egotism/vanity, 33, 43
Sex/sexuality, 83–84, 103, 145, 221, 243, 244, 251, 257–58, 264; and AIDS, 243, 264; language for, in fiction, 83–84
Shakespeare, William, 116
Short story (genre, structure, form), 11, 22–23, 50–51, 85–86, 118, 139–40, 141, 143, 201; as revelation, 31; comic elements, 59, 66; illuminating/memorializing lives, 85, 91, 170, 181–82, 190, 208, 237; well-made story, 49, 139, 147–48
Sitzfleisch, 126, 236
Slavery, 216, 222, 223
Socialism, 64, 104, 154, 192–93
Socialist puritanism, 52, 252
"Somewhere Else," 63, 65, 136, 152, 173
"Song Stanzas of Private Luck," 239, 247n8
Sontag, Susan, 16, 64, 92
Southern Conference for Human Welfare, 216, 220
Spanidou, Irini, *God's Snake*, 211, 260
Spender, Stephen, 106
Stead, Christina, 78
Stein, Gertrude, 49, 71, 74, 105; *Three Lives*, 71
Stern, Gerald, 247
"Story Hearer, The," 185
Story-tellers/storytelling, 28, 35, 36–37, 72–73, 78, 86, 160, 169, 175, 185, 255–56
Stream-of-consciousness, 12
Style, 63, 64, 198, 200, 206, 253
Suicide, 42
Sukenick, Ronald, 6
Surrealism, 21, 41, 50, 220–21
Symbolism, 49–50

Tax, Meredith, 254, 263
Teitelbaum, Eddie (character), 12
Television, 42, 50–51
Thomas, Clarence, 227
"Three Days and a Question," 258
Time/timelessness, 50–51, 87–88, 93–94, 110, 241
Tolstoy, Leo, *Anna Karenina*, 42
Tonto (character), 62, 202
Totality (effect), 64, 68
Tragedy, 45, 60, 181
Transitions (style), 50, 184, 206
Trumpeter, Amy, 96–97

Urban/rural environments, 8, 57–58, 152, 202, 227; impact on writing, 203, 233, 240–41; alienation in city life, 181–82
"Used-Boy Raisers, The," 134, 180, 197, 198

"Verbalosity," 37
Vermont, 8, 20–21, 65, 134, 152, 202–03
Victims/victimization, 4, 45, 149
Vietnam/Vietnamese, 4, 47, 147, 150, 156, 242–43; "Vietnam Syndrome," 243
Vietnam War, 59, 126, 127, 152, 208, 210
Virginia (character), 149, 150
Voice/voices, 76, 91, 106–07, 118, 131, 134, 135, 163–64, 175, 183, 198, 200–01, 205–06, 217, 223

Walker, Alice, 93
"Wants," 13, 50, 173
War Resisters League, 15, 19, 20, 47, 136; *Calendar*, 239, 258
Williams, Oscar, 244
Williams, Vera, 96, 156, 239
Williams, William Carlos, 17
Wolf, Christa, 144, 246, 253; *Cassandra*, 144; *Quest for Christa T.*, 144; *Patterns of Childhood*, 144
"Woman, Young and Old, A," 7
Women and Jewish tradition, 158–59, 196–97
Women and motherhood (social role), 67, 70, 82, 89, 90, 119, 128, 219, 265
Women (collectively), 80, 97–98, 122, 193, 198, 205, 244, 254–55; as international community, 254
Women in Black, 264
Women writers, 89–93, 105, 113–16, 186–87, 209, 211, 214, 217, 228–29; and role models, 70, 244, 253–54
Women rewriting history, 199, 217
Women's equity with men, 43, 188
Women's lives (as topic), 16, 149–50, 170–71, 179, 198, 205, 228, 255
Women's movement, 75, 100, 112, 136, 161–62, 186, 188, 200, 211–12, 236–37, 243, 246, 263–64; women's backlash to patriarchy, 263–64
Women's Pentagon Action, 95–96, 122, 136, 152, 159, 171
Women's studies, 186–87
Woolf, Virginia, 71, 92, 105; *Mrs. Dalloway*, 92
World Peace Conference (Moscow), 47, 65

World War II, 149, 150, 161, 178, 239–40, 250
Writer's block, 39
Writing process/techniques, 4, 5–6, 16, 22, 23–24, 26–27, 29, 30, 31, 32, 38, 48–49, 50–51, 60–61, 71, 86, 99, 107–08, 118–19, 123–24, 130–31, 141, 143, 163–64, 173–74, 183–84, 186, 190–91, 200, 206–07, 211, 214, 218–19

Writing programs and workshops, 3–4, 139–40, 189

Yankee nuclear plant, 20
Yeats, William Butler, 32, 184
Yiddish, 23, 36, 74, 142, 159, 260

Zagrowsky (character), 185
"Zagrowsky Tells," 130, 185
Zionism/anti-Zionism, 193, 265

www.ingramcontent.com/pod-product-compliance
Lightning Source LLC
Chambersburg PA
CBHW021835220426
43663CB00005B/254